McCARTNEY
– Songwriter

McCARTNEY – *Songwriter*

Howard Elson

W.H. ALLEN · LONDON

COMET

Typeset by Phoenix Photosetting, Chatham, Kent
Printed and bound in Great Britain by
Mackays of Chatham Ltd, Kent
for the publishers
W.H. Allen & Co Plc
44 Hill Street, London W1X 8LB

ISBN 0 86379 110 7 (Comet Books softcover)
ISBN 04910 3325 7 (W.H. Allen hardcover)

Contents

'Coming Up'

IN 1979, WHEN Paul McCartney was honoured by the *Guinness Book of Records* with the award of a Rhodium Disc for his achievements in music – in recognition of album sales in excess of 100,000,000, for singles sales in excess of 100,000,000 and 60 Gold Discs – he was formally acclaimed as the most successful songwriter of all time.

Yet what the award did not acknowledge, was that in a career spanning over a quarter of a century, McCartney's music has virtually changed the course of popular music history and given it a platform on which to build and develop into the future.

As a member of The Beatles, McCartney's songwriting partnership with John Lennon revolutionized a music industry that was going stale. They knocked down the barriers of musical snobbery and widened its horizons, and in doing so, appealed to all sections of the musical community, not only in Britain, but throughout the world. Lennon and McCartney's music brought a new awareness and acceptability right across the globe, particularly in America, a country which for too long, had dominated the world of music.

America gave the world rock 'n' roll. Lennon and McCartney made it respectable.

In seven short years, during which time social values, morals and attitudes of a generation were regularly under re-assessment and constantly changing, the music of John and Paul conquered the world and established The Beatles, as Paul Gambaccini said, as '. . . the most important and best musical entertainers of the twentieth century.' They became bigger, in terms of global popularity, than Elvis Presley.

'And they did it through their music,' says Alvin Stardust.

'Elvis didn't write songs. Very few people before Lennon and McCartney wrote and performed their own material. There were a handful – Chuck Berry, Carl Perkins and Little Richard, who could write in only one style, while Buddy Holly's potential as a performer and writer was tragically never realized. John and Paul's music, however, covered the entire musical spectrum with a multitude of styles. They were musical innovators, often outrageous, often bawdy, often sentimental . . . but at no time boring. It was quality material. No-one had ever written to such an intensity, to such consistency before them.

'Lennon and McCartney brought dignity back to pop music and gave it a new direction to follow and a new hope. It had gone nowhere, stagnating, for half-a-dozen years or more. They saved it from itself, and in doing so, they endeared themselves to millions of people, and stamped their music indelibly on to a world that would never quite be the same again.

'If any proof were needed as to the impact John and Paul's music created, *or* of its outstanding quality, suffice it to say that their songs have been sung and recorded by some of the biggest stars in international show business including Frank Sinatra, Ella Fitzgerald, Nat King Cole and Tony Bennett, while many of their songs have become "standards", which is a marvellous testimony to their sheer talent and class.'

It is interesting to note, that while Lennon and McCartney's songs were covered extensively – at the last count 'Yesterday' had been recorded by well over 1,000 different artists – since the break up, Paul McCartney's songs have been recorded almost exclusively by himself, or Wings. There have been very few cover versions of his songs, apart from the material he has specifically written for others. The same is true of John Lennon.

'Everyone knows where they were in 1963 when John F. Kennedy was assassinated,' says Alvin Stardust. 'It's one of those things in life that stays with you. Likewise, everybody has a favourite Lennon and McCartney song, which conjures up memories, whether happy, or sad, or indifferent, and if you look clearly enough, there is a John and Paul song to cover every mood, every emotion.'

One of the great strengths of Lennon and McCartney as writers, was their ability to adapt. They were forever listening to music, anticipating trends, borrowing ideas to develop for their own requirements. When The Beatles broke up in 1970, and Paul went out on his own, he used that talent to his advantage. Like a musical chameleon, he absorbed the music of generations, and breathed new life into it.

'When The Beatles first hit the scene,' says Alvin Stardust, 'it didn't matter where the formula for their musical sound came from . . . it happened! But they soon learned to develop it, to progress and to keep changing gradually, so that they stayed ahead of the field. The fact that Paul McCartney has gone on and is still a world-beater, is a sign of his talent and quality as a songwriter.

'Paul has done it all so many times. He has peaked many times . . . during the '60s, throughout the '70s, and in the '80s. When music changes dramatically, McCartney changes too, ever-adapting, ever-developing, always looking and listening. And through sheer talent, hard work and dedication to his trade, he gets better and better as a songwriter. Although music might change, the world of music still looks to McCartney to follow.'

With the break-up of The Beatles, Paul McCartney went on to achieve the impossible, to shake free from the spectre of the world's most famous group and to enjoy even greater success as a writer and performer, first with Wings and later on his own. But it was a hard, often bitter struggle for acceptance, in the face of hostile criticism from all sections of the media, particularly the rock Press, who laid the blame for the break-up of The Beatles firmly at *his* feet. They believed that whatever he did in the future, he could never match the quality he attained with John, George and Ringo.

Paul proved them all wrong, and produced some marvellous music at times. Yet in the proving, he had to mature and develop away from the rock world that had helped to create his initial success, and out into a much wider world of musical acceptance for his own survival as a songwriter.

American singing star Gene Pitney said: 'Paul needed Wings to escape the clutches of The Beatles, and to lay the ghost. He emerged from it all stronger and more successful, but he had to fight for it; had to survive creatively; had to move on into wider areas of acceptance, away from the confines of rock 'n' roll.'

Unfortunately for Paul, he has been criticised ever since.

He has been lambasted for selling out to sentiment, accused of abandoning his rock roots to become simply a ballad writer. While John Lennon was extolled as a writer of genius, Paul McCartney was presented as nothing more than a writer of love songs, slushy and soppy love songs.

Yet McCartney has always refused to be compromised as a composer: 'I'm not just rock 'n' roll. I don't live my life by that kind of limitation.' And although the criticism obviously hurts, Paul stands firmly by his principles.

'One of my problems is that I tend to associate a lot of the time with sentimental subjects, romantic subjects, because I actually believe that is a very serious subject,' he said in a radio interview. 'I believe that when you get down to it and look at what life is on earth, it is people relating to each other and being in love with each other or out of love with each other, and it's all that. Even for some kid who is in detention and totally anti-authority, love is still there . . . it might be his mum, or whatever it is, but he knows that moment.

'To me, I don't think it is something you can dismiss and say it's soppy. The older I get, the more serious I think it is.

'So I say, well alright, I can understand how a younger critic will say: "Oh, God, look at him. Here he goes again – yawn, yawn – peace, love, black and white should live together – his farm in Scotland and sheep – yawn, yawn." But I say, I'll hold to that because seriously, I can't think of anything more important. It's my way. I'm not really a political person who can figure out the nuclear issue. I'll say let's not have it . . . But I'm not political enough to make my songs give the answer to that.

'As far as I'm concerned, what I am involved in – and maybe I can talk about – is that idea of relationships . . . and maybe silly love songs aren't such a bad idea.'

Having achieved outstanding success in the past – and so much acclaim as a writer, Paul McCartney could be forgiven for sitting back and enjoying his success, without ever working again. It's not his style; he is a confirmed workaholic and drives himself unmercifully.

'When you have had success for a long time, it is very difficult to keep a hard edge to what you're doing, because the hard edge tends to come with the hunger, the novelty of the whole thing,' he said. 'After a while, it is inevitable that hard edge has to go and you look for something *less* temporary.'

Several of his contemporaries, however, have hinted that Paul might find that hard edge and a new challenge to his writing in classical music . . . and it is an area he has considered.

In a British television interview, he revealed: 'Around the time of "Eleanor Rigby", when I was twenty-five, I was looking at the age of thirty and thinking, "What am I going to do then?"

'Having just written "Eleanor" and worked with George Martin on this kind of classical-type back-up instead of electric guitars for the first time, I quite liked it . . . And I did think at the age of thirty that's what I could do, more into the serious side of music rather than just pop hits. But that never really happened, and I was still intrigued with the pop hit and three minute folk song.

'I've always had this thing of composer as well as bass player and singer, and I've always really loved it, it's always been one of my secret dreams and in a corny way, I've always liked the role of *composer*.'

In 1963, with The Beatles about to break into the international arena and crack the American market, Paul McCartney was asked by newspapermen how he saw his future. He said: 'Probably, what John and I will do, will be write songs as we have been doing as a sideline now. We'll probably develop that a little more. Who knows? At forty we might not know how.'

Since then, and now past that magic age of forty – McCartney has established himself in no uncertain terms, as one of the world's greatest contemporary composers and a major influence on music – although in modesty Paul refuses to accept the acclaim: 'I just think of myself as a hack writer. I don't feel I'm a major influence on the music scene' – and his music has brought happiness to many millions of people all over the world.

'I like the idea of being able to bring joy,' he says. 'It sounds a little smarmy, but it's really true. If you can actually enjoy doing a thing . . . not only are you enjoying it, you're going to be able to communicate that enjoyment to other people. I like creating – creating a song or a story.'

He added: 'Songwriting is my great love. I'll go on writing until I drop!'

PART ONE:

'Yesterday'

1

James McCartney

THEY HAD BEEN singing and making music of sorts in Liverpool since the first century – and probably before – when the first settlement was established on the north bank of the River Mersey, near to a muddy creek, or *lifrugpool*. And there has been music in the McCartney family for the whole of this century.

James McCartney was born on July 7th, 1902 in Fishguard Street in the district of Everton, to Joseph and Florence McCartney. The McCartney lineage was long and complicated with roots going way back to Ireland and the Isle of Man.

Although Everton was one of the poorer areas of Liverpool at that time, James McCartney was brought up in a large and loving family, having five sisters – Edith, Ann, Mill, Annie, and Jin (immortalized as Aunty Jin in nephew Paul's 1976 hit, 'Let 'Em In') – and two brothers, Jack and Joseph. Another brother, Joe, had died, and sister Alice passed away at the age of 18 months in the year before James's arrival. Nevertheless, it was a happy home.

Music played a big part in the McCartneys' upbringing, too. Father Joseph, a tobacco-cutter by occupation at Cope's in St. Vincent Street, had performed in brass bands, playing 'E-flat bass oompah' as Paul says, in Cope's Band and the Territorial Army Brass Band. He also encouraged his children to take music seriously, and to learn to play an instrument if so inclined. He had a fine singing voice, too. Young James used to sing all the time, although it isn't certain whether he sang in the choir at Steer Street School, Everton, where he was educated.

While he was still at school, however, the young lad was

given part-time employment at the local music hall, the Everton Theatre Royal, as a lampboy. Paul said: 'He actually burnt bits of lime for the limelights.' He was also hired to sell programmes before each performance. Being a shrewd young man and ever eager to earn a few extra pennies, he would collect up all the discarded programmes strewn about the floor at the end of the first show and rush home . . . 'so that Aunt Millie could iron them out in time for the second performance.' Then he would sell them all over again, but this time pocketing the money.

The following day, he would pound away on the old second-hand piano the McCartneys had been given a year or so before – which had originally been purchased at the NEMS store in North End Road, Liverpool, picking out all the tunes he had heard in the hall the night before. He had a good ear for music, despite breaking his right eardrum in a fall at the age of ten, and he taught himself to play chords.

At the age of fourteen, James McCartney left school and for six shillings a week, gained full-time employment at A. Hannay & Co., Cotton Merchants, in Chapel Street, as a sample boy. He was smart in appearance, diligent, honest and hard-working, qualities he would later instil into his own sons. Fourteen years later, James was promoted to cotton salesman at the Cotton Exchange, which for a working-class boy, was a tremendous achievement, and with a salary of £5 a week.

During the First World War, James's love of music took an upper hand, and he started a swing-cum-ragtime band with his brother Jack on trombone, and several other young musicians – most still in their teens – with intentions of playing at works dances and other local functions. They were called The Masked Melody Makers, and even in those days, they had a gimmick all of its own with each of the musicians sporting a black harlequin mask . . . until on one engagement when the temperature was really rising, and the dye in the face masks trickled slowly down The Masked Melody Makers' cheeks! After that incident, the band's name was quickly changed to Jim Mac's Band – and the stage uniform became dinner jackets with paper shirt-fronts and cuffs.

Over the next few years, Jim Mac's Band became a popular attraction on Merseyside – nothing spectacular, but they enjoyed themselves playing at dances and socials, and occasionally in cinemas. On one such engagement, the band provided incidental musical accompaniment for the screening for the silent Hollywood movie, 'The Queen Of Sheba'. The group's repertoire included many of the standards of the day, like 'Birth Of The Blues', 'Some Of These Days', 'Chicago', James's favourite song, 'Stairway To Paradise', and one of his own compositions, 'Walking In The Park With Eloise'. By this time, too, Jim McCartney was doubling on trumpet besides playing piano . . . 'until his teeth gave out,' says Paul. 'Then it was just piano!'

Paul McCartney was very proud of his father's musical achievements, although they were on a modest scale, and Jim Mac's Band left a deep and lasting impression, sowing the seeds for his own career in music much later.

In a letter to a journalist who had shown interest in the burgeoning Beatles in 1959 – although at that time they weren't too sure what to call the group – Paul wrote: 'The overall sound is rather reminiscent of the four-in-the-bar of traditional jazz. This could possibly be put down to the influence of Mr McCartney, who led one of the top local jazz bands (Jim Mac's Jazz Band) in the 1920s.'

The letter revealed another of Paul's own influences as he continued: 'The group also derive a great deal of pleasure from re-arranging old favourites ("Ain't She Sweet", "You Were Meant For Me", "Home", "Moonglow", "You Are My Sunshine" and others.)'

In 1974, Paul McCartney and Wings, along with country and western musical legends, Chet Atkins and Floyd Cramer, recorded a version of Jim Mac's 'Walking In The Park With Eloise' and released it as a single under the pseudonym of The Country Hams. That song was also one of the eight McCartney selected for his appearance on BBC Radio's long-running series, 'Desert Island Discs', in 1982.

With the outbreak of World War II, Jim McCartney's musical days of playing in public finally came to an end. There were many other changes, too. The Cotton Exchange was closed down for the duration, leaving Jim to transfer his services to Napiers, the munitions company specializing in the Sabre aircraft engine, where he worked as a lathe operator. Exempt from National Service through his hearing disability, although at 37 he was probably too old to be called up for military service, Jim's contribution to the war effort comprised nightly fire watch duty during the blitz, when the city of Liverpool was often pounded into rubble by the German Luftwaffe.

At about the same time, Jim met Mary Mohin – a nursing sister at the Walton Hospital – one night at sister Jin's house. They fell in love and on April 15th, 1941, were married at St Swithin's Roman Catholic Chapel, Gill Moss, Liverpool, and made their first home together in furnished rooms in Anfield. Jim, a committed agnostic, was approaching his 39th birthday; Mary was 31.

At the end of 1941, Mary McCartney became pregnant, and as the birth of her first child grew nearer, she gave up her work at Walton General. She returned to the hospital on Thursday, June 18th, 1942, where she gave birth to her first son, christened James Paul McCartney. Father James, who that same evening had been on fire patrol in the city, described his son as looking awful – 'He just squawked all the time.' Back home, Jim broke down and cried for the first time in many years – tears of joy after the birth of his son.

2

James Paul McCartney

LOVE WAS NEVER in short supply at the McCartneys' bungalow home in Roach Avenue on the Knowsley Estate in Liverpool, to where the family had moved following the birth of their second son, Michael, in 1944. And although the boys were brought up with a firm hand and taught to show respect, to have sound values in life and to be thrifty – in those days *that* was a necessity with money so tight – there was always lots of attention and plenty of affection from Jim and Mary. It was the one thing the boys *never* wanted for.

The family had moved several times since Paul's birth, and were destined to uproot the homestead on several future occasions, too. Whilst still working at Napiers, Jim had been given council house accommodation in Wallasey, but had moved back into Liverpool just prior to Michael's arrival on the scene. Mary, meanwhile, had returned to work as a health visitor following Paul's birth, but it was a job she didn't enjoy as much as nursing.

After the war, Jim left Napiers and joined Liverpool Corporation's Cleansing Department as an inspector. The job was poorly paid, so to supplement the family income, Mary returned to nursing and midwifery full-time. She became a domiciliary midwife, which meant free council house accommodation once more for the family, in return for her midwifery services. Her first position took the McCartneys to a flat in Sir Thomas White Gardens, before moving to the rapidly expanding suburb of Speke, initially at Western Avenue and later at Ardwick Road. The free accommodation was a godsend and one of the main advantages of Mary's job, yet the great disadvantage was that she had to be on call by the communities she served, for twenty-four hours each day. She was called out nearly every single night! Still, she soon became something of a legend to those she served . . . for her kindness and diligence, and above all, for her love.

If love was always readily available in the McCartney household, so, too, was music. Jim still pounded away on the NEMS piano, re-living memories of Jim Mac's Band and 'Stairway To Paradise'. The boys at that time, however, were decidedly uninterested. Paul and Michael had both been sent for piano lessons around the corner once a week. But it had been hard to hold their interest when other, more exciting things, like playing with their friends, were available. At family get-togethers, though, Jim would provide the accompaniment for the riotous singalongs.

Jim McCartney was a gentle man. He encouraged his sons all the time in whatever they wanted to do, and believed strongly in them. He also firmly believed in discipline – 'moderation and toleration' was a family maxim. Paul, unlike his brother, never showed emotion when he was on the wrong end of a telling off from his father. He would simply sneak into his parents' bedroom and rip the lace curtains a little at the bottom, so it didn't show and no-one would notice, and that made him feel a lot better. The two brothers were completely different personalities. Paul was quieter, diplomatic and yet mischievous; Michael was dominant, noisy and argumentative. Both were fiercely independent. The McCartney boys were both good-looking, although Paul tended towards puppy fat on occasions, chubbiness on others. Michael used to call him 'fatty'.

'Even when they said it was puppy fat, it didn't make it any easier,' said Paul.

Mary McCartney was very proud of her children. She always insisted they looked and dressed smartly, and made sure that their clothes were always cleaned and pressed, despite her own heavy work load. But her fervent wish was that her sons should discipline themselves to speak well . . . and not in the broad Liverpool brogue that infested the Speke estates. She was forever trying to correct their accents which at times made Paul and Michael over-emphasize the scouse dialect on purpose.

In 1962, when The Beatles made their first appearance on television on Granada's 'People and Places', and were interviewed for the first time, Jim McCartney was terribly upset because Paul came over talking in a broad Liverpudlian accent. But as his son explained . . . 'it was part of the image'. Mary, however, wouldn't have approved.

There were many childhood memories for Paul and Michael to share. Paul remembers the smell of washing and ironing. 'Once a week, the women would sort of get the laundry out and smell it and iron it all,' he said. 'It makes a boy feel good.' There were visions of dad taking them to the barber in Penny Lane which actually did have photographs in the window on display of the various hair-styles that were available inside – 'In Penny Lane there is a barber showing photographs of every head he's had the pleasure to know'. There were memories, too, of listening avidly to the radio in bed at night to that very special agent, Dick Barton. Jim had rigged up a special device in the boys' shared bedroom that allowed Paul and Michael to listen to the radio downstairs through ear-phones. Nearer to the city centre in Menlove Avenue, Woolton, Aunt Mimi had fixed up a similar system for her nephew John Lennon, who too, enjoyed the wonders of Dick Barton.

The radio brought another source of music to Paul McCartney. 'When I started to listen to music, the kind of music was Fred Astaire, and "The Billy Cotton Band Show"' – a popular favourite who had his own Sunday afternoon radio series – "Cole Porter's type of lyrics," he said.

'From an early age I was interested in singing tunes. I like a nice tune, "White Christmas", "Over The Rainbow", the old stuff. My dad used to play a lot, so I suppose I was quite influenced by him. "Stairway To Paradise" and "Chicago", tunes like that, the trad jazz tunes.'

There were other memories, too, of going to the pictures where Paul particularly liked the Hollywood musicals. Fred Astaire was a great favourite: his version of 'Cheek To Cheek' was one of Paul's favourite songs. So, too, was 'White Christmas' by Bing Crosby. They all left their mark.

In the mid-1970s, commenting on his early musical influences, Paul said: 'I like the Astaire films they show on television. I think, wow, great, boy can they dance. Boy, can they arrange tunes. They were only doing what we're doing now, but some of the time they were much better at it. Think of the choreographing of some of the big numbers. We all know it's the money they had, but the class is still there for someone like myself to look back on and say, "That's a great idea!"' He always wanted to be a song-and-dance man.

Although christened and brought up Catholics, both McCartney brothers were educated in Protestant schools, first at Stockton Road Primary School in Speke – where Paul emerged as an engaging, above-average pupil – and later at Joseph Williams Primary School, Gateacre, where he excelled at English and art.

At the same time as the boys were undergoing formal education, Jim McCartney decided to leave the Corporation to return to the cotton trade he knew so well. But it wasn't the industry he had left only a handful of years before. He was lucky to earn £8 a week, as the decline and fall of a once great and proud industry in the north of England, started to bite. It would never recover.

Money was still very tight in the McCartney household, yet they were happy days for Paul and Michael, who were blissfully unaware of just how difficult the times were becoming for their parents. Like all young boys, they got up to all sorts of mischief – scrumping apples, slagging off school, playing 'dare' and 'chicken' on the railway tracks.

On several occasions, however, Paul nearly didn't make it to adulthood. During one childhood prank, both he and Michael almost drowned.

Close to the McCartney home was a large lime pit to one side of a builders' work dump on the proposed site of a new playing field. When it rained, it filled up rapidly with water, making it a lethal proposition for anyone who might fall in. Jim McCartney banned the boys from going near it. But, boys being what they are, and curiosity gaining an upper hand, the McCartney brothers soon turned the lime pit into a pirate's paradise. When Paul ventured out on to the rickety plank they had placed across the pit he slipped and fell into the white liquid below. In falling, he reached out in desperation and dragged his brother down with him. Neither of the boys could swim – and the evil liquid well covered their heads. After frantic thrashing about trying to tread water for what seemed like an eternity, and going under the white water time and time again, Michael managed to grab on to a twisted tree stump or root that was protruding from the bank, while with the other hand, he grasped hold of his floundering brother's arm and held on tight. Then both boys screamed for help. Fortunately a passing neighbour heard them and came to the rescue.

Another time, the boys nearly set themselves on fire when experimenting with petrol at Aunty Jin's house in Huyton. Trying to discover if brick would burn like wood and paper, the boys laid a trail of petrol up the side wall of Jin's garage and on to the tarpaulin roof, where Michael positioned himself to inspect the handiwork. Paul put a match to the quickly evaporating liquid and in an instant, the flames had engulfed the garage and almost taken the brothers with it, particularly Michael on fire-watch on the roof. Fortunately a passing policeman came to the rescue this time.

Because of Paul's academic abilities, it came as no surprise when he sailed through the 11-Plus Examination, allowing him to transfer to Liverpool Institute, then the most respected and best known of the city's grammar schools. Once he had settled in, his reports noted that he was good at English and showed aptitude at foreign languages.

Jim and Mary were very proud of their son's achievements. Now, with a good education behind him – O-Levels, A-Levels, even University – they hoped Paul might go on to take up a position in the professional field, a teacher, or business manager, or civil servant.

'I suppose I was of average intelligence,' said Paul. 'Not bad. I went in for a few exams the other kids didn't go in for. So I must have been a bit above average, but I couldn't concentrate. On all my reports it was, "would do well if he could concentrate".'

Paul did, however, work hard during his first year at the Institute, and made several friends, notably Ivan Vaughan who would later introduce him to John Lennon. But after that first year, although a competent student, able to handle most of the work with confidence, Paul McCartney started to bluff his way through lessons. Busking. Doing . . . 'just enough' to get by. Friends also described him as 'a bit of a lad' at school, mischievous and boisterous, ready to take part in any prank, but devious enough not to be caught.

It was during his early days at the Institute, that Paul at last started to take more than a passing interest in music, especially the rock 'n' roll and pop music that had started to filter through on the radio. It soon became an obsession . . . and the bedroom earphones were well used.

At the age of twelve, he saw his first pop concert at the Liverpool Empire Theatre, starring drummer Eric Delaney And His Band. It left an indelible impression on the receptive youngster. From that moment on, he was totally committed to music at the expense of all other things, his school work included – 'We were into rock 'n' roll and couldn't take all that algebra,' said Paul.

When Paul was thirteen, the family moved once more, this time from Speke to Allerton, and another council provided property in Forthlin Road. Jim was relieved that his wife had finally agreed to give up her demanding job as a midwife; he was convinced that all the unnatural hours had been bad for her health; and he was quite contented when Mary took a job as a school nurse working in the districts of Allerton and Walton. At least she wouldn't be called out on duty at night.

The McCartney family hadn't been in Forthlin Road long when Mary started to suffer pains in her breast. In her mid-'40s and heading for the menopause, she put the pains down to the change of life and several doctors she had consulted had all agreed with her own diagnosis. The pains, however, refused to go away. They got worse!

Mary was worried now and sought the advice of a specialist. He was worried, too, and made immediate arrangements for her to be admitted into Liverpool Northern Hospital where breast cancer was diagnosed. Mary was prepared for a mastectomy operation, which couldn't be carried out when surgeons discovered the extent the cancer had spread. On October 31st, 1956, Mary McCartney died. She was forty-seven. According to Michael McCartney, in her final moments, his mother had told her own sister-in-law, Dill Mohin, 'I would have loved to have seen the boys growing up.'

It was a shattering blow to the closely-knit and loving family. Shocked by his mother's death, the first thing Paul could say on hearing the news was, 'what are we going to do without her money?'

Like his sons, Jim McCartney was shattered. But Paul and Michael were spared the funeral grief and went to stay with Aunty Jin, to stop them seeing their father's devastation at the tragedy. Mary's death affected them all deeply.

Talking about his mother's death on British television in 1984, Paul revealed: 'I was fourteen. It's a very difficult age, fourteen, because you are growing up and you're getting your act together. So it was a tough time to have something as devastating as that happen. I think I probably covered a lot of it up at the time, as you would, a fourteen year-old boy.' He added that his father was . . . 'devastated. He was left with two boys and you'd start seeing him cry . . . you'd never seen him before.'

Jim McCartney, at the age of fifty-three, was left alone, to be both father and mother to two teenage boys, and bring them up on a meagre wage packet. He coped magnificently well. It was a tough time all over again, but the family rallied round. Sisters Jin and Mill took it in turns each Monday to go to Forthlin Road and clean the house for the men, and make a full Sunday roast lunch. Neighbours helped out, too.

Although Paul admitted to covering up his true feelings towards his mother's death, it affected him badly. Each night for several months he prayed for Mary's return. And he would be inspired to write songs to his mother's memory in later life: 'When I find myself in times of trouble, mother Mary comes to me, speaking words of wisdom, let it be.'

Michael McCartney has hinted that one main result of their mother's death was that brother Paul became obsessed with music. It became a substitute almost. 'He would get lost in another world,' said Michael, 'particularly after mum died. It was useless talking to him.' Paul certainly became more engrossed in rock 'n' roll following Mary's death.

At that time, skiffle music was all the rage in Britain, after the hit parade success of Lonnie Donegan's 'Rock Island Line'. A former banjo and guitar player with the Chris Barber Band, Donegan was the recently elected leader of a new generation of British teenagers. Paul and his friends were mighty impressed.

Donegan's influence on the youth of Britain spawned hundreds of skiffle groups all over the country, all emulating their hero. Liverpool had its fair share, too. It was easy. All you needed was a guitar and three chords, a washboard and thimbles, and a string bass which could be made from an old tea chest, a broomstick and literally, a piece of string . . . and you could make music. Good music at that.

Paul remembers seeing Lonnie Donegan at the Liverpool Empire, and actually queuing up during his school lunch break at the stage door to watch him arrive at the theatre for rehearsals. Paul was becoming star struck and would regularly hang around the Empire's stage door to secure autographs. Prized possessions were the signatures of Wee Willie Harris and Eddie Calvert.

It was Lonnie Donegan, however, who inspired Paul McCartney in his quest for music. After seeing the 'king' of skiffle playing on stage, Paul, too, wanted to sing and play guitar . . . and get involved. For Jim McCartney, the committed musician of the family, it was music to his ears.

Not long before, Paul had been given a trumpet by his cousin, Ian, but although able to play passable tunes, he soon realized that he couldn't sing *and* blow at the same time. He wanted a guitar.

Jim had always encouraged his children's interest in music and so he scraped together £15 and bought his son the treasured instrument, and then sat down at the piano to teach Paul some chords. The teenager soon found he couldn't play the guitar; something was drastically wrong. But it didn't take him too long to realize that he, being left-handed, was playing the guitar 'upside down', and that the strings were positioned for a right-handed player. 'I couldn't get on with it until I thought I could change the strings round,' said Paul. 'I think I got it off Slim Whitman; he was left-handed. I've still got the guitar.'

So back to the shop he went and had the guitar re-strung in the left-handed style . . . and before long, McCartney was totally captivated by the instrument. He had a talent for picking out tunes almost by instinct. From a 'teach-yourself-to-play' manual, he learned chords. He had an insatiable appetite for learning and would play the guitar whenever and wherever he could: in bed, in the bath, on the lavatory, at the dinner table, in the garden – everywhere. He learnt every chord he could find to learn, and those he couldn't find, he made up.

By now, though, rock 'n' roll had replaced skiffle in Paul's affections. He had soon learned enough chords to handle the entire skiffle repertoire of numbers, and he needed to move on. He loved the new songs that were coming over from America. Elvis Presley knocked him out. But Gene Vincent, Chuck Berry and particularly Little Richard, were great favourites. There were several others whose music would inspire The Beatles' own material in a few years.

Whenever he could afford it, Paul would buy their records; failing that, he would listen to their music on Radio Luxembourg and transpose the chord sequences on to his own guitar. Only when he had accomplished the music, would he carefully write down, and learn, the words. If the truth be known, like any other budding rock 'n' roller, Paul McCartney would almost certainly have adopted Presley poses, or Gene Vincent, or Eddie Cochran, for the benefit of his bedroom mirror, as he strummed along to his favourite numbers . . . top lip quivering. In fact his Little Richard impression, as performed to a few select friends at the Institute, became legendary.

He was also starting to write his own songs, or at least trying to write. The most successful effort at that time was a three chord number called 'I Lost My Little Girl', based on the sequence of G, G7 and C.

'In Liverpool,' said Paul, 'you'd know about Chuck Berry and Big Bill Broonzy and the other ones, and rock 'n' roll guitarists, long before most people in America had heard of them.

'Liverpool was also called the capital of Ireland, because we had lots of Irish folk living there. And then there were the songs from the Broadway shows which the sailors wanted to hear. Put the whole lot together, and you'll find my influences.'

Paul was also very much inspired by the music of the Everly Brothers and bought every new record of theirs that was imported into the country. From Phil and Don (to whom he also paid homage on his single, 'Let 'Em In' and for whom in 1984, he penned their successful reunion single, 'On The Wings Of A Nightingale'), he discovered the romance of rock 'n' roll.

With his grammar school friend, Ian James, who could also play guitar, Paul used to emulate the Everlys. They dressed like them, wore their hair like them. They were Everly Brothers-daft and used to go around together with their guitars.

Paul admitted: 'We used to go round to the fairs, listening to the latest tunes on the Waltzer' – the fairgrounds were a hotbed for the latest American music and records. 'Occasionally we'd get really depressed, so we'd maybe go back to his house and put on an Elvis record – "Don't Be Cruel" or

"All Shook Up" – and five minutes later we'd feel good again.'

During this time, Paul also became friendly with another Institute boy with whom he travelled to school on the bus. He, too, could play the guitar and, although he was a year younger than McCartney, he struck up a great friendship with Paul. They would often play their guitars together at each other's houses, teaching one another new chords and riffs. The younger boy had a friend who lent him his Buddy Holly records which the two guitarists copied endlessly, meticulously trying to recreate every single note they heard on the record.

It would be well over a year, though, before George Harrison would join Paul in a group.

McCartney had tried on several occasions to persuade his own brother to join him in a double act where they could sing and play the songs of the Everly Brothers. Somehow, Michael wasn't interested; he was still only twelve. But it had to be said that the two boys performed a very good impromptu version of 'Bye Bye Love', which Jim McCartney liked immensely. The McCartney brothers did actually perform the song together in public in the summer of 1957 at Butlin's Holiday Camp, Filey, in Yorkshire, where their cousin-in-law, Mike Robbins, worked for the season as a Red Coat.

Following Mary's death the autumn before, Jim McCartney decided that what was needed for everyone concerned was a chance to get away from it all, to go on holiday. It had been a tough few months coping on his own, even with the help of his sisters and other relatives and friends. The boys had helped, too. Matters were made worse in July, when Michael, away from home at a scout camp near Sheffield, seriously fractured an arm after an accident with a pulley system, some rope and a sturdy oak tree. He was taken to the Sheffield Royal Hospital, where he remained for the next few weeks. So Jim figured a holiday would be the best medicine for the family.

At each Butlin's Holiday Camp throughout the British Isles, a weekly talent contest was held in conjunction with a major national Sunday newspaper, as part of a nationwide 'Search For A Star' competition. The various heat winners later went on through several more rounds to a Grand Final at the London Palladium and a £500 First Prize. With that in mind, Paul, who never went anywhere *without* his guitar, persuaded Michael – suitably carrying his left arm in a sling – to enter a heat of the show.

On a sultry morning towards the end of summer, The McCartney Brothers stepped out on to the stage of the Gaiety Theatre, at Butlin's, Filey, to make their first – and what turned out to be their *only* – public appearance together, singing 'Bye Bye Love'. When the duet was over and received cursory applause from the audience, Paul launched into his Little Richard routine with a version of 'Long Tall Sally'.

Needless to say, The McCartney Brothers failed in their bid for the big time. They didn't win their heat and would have been disqualified anyway for being under the stated minimum age of entry, of sixteen.

However, just a few weeks before, Paul had taken the first tentative steps on the road to stardom, though he didn't know it at the time, when he was taken by a friend to a church fête in Woolton, on the pretext of picking up girls. There he was to meet his destiny in the beery shape of one John Lennon.

3

John Winston Lennon

THE AFTERNOON OF Saturday, July 6th, 1957, was pleasantly warm and sunny when Paul McCartney cycled from his Allerton home to meet his school friend, Ivan Vaughan, outside St Peter's Parish Church in Woolton.

Ivan had asked Paul over on that particular afternoon on the pretext of picking up girls who he admitted were attracted to the fête in droves. But there was another, more serious reason. Ivan wanted his friend to see and listen to a skiffle group, called The Quarry Men, who were to provide some of the entertainment at the event, playing in the open air in a field next to the church itself. Vaughan was rather proud of them, and sometimes appeared with the group, sharing duties on the tea-chest bass with Nigel Whalley, although today, another Institute pupil, Len Garry, was playing the home-made instrument. Nigel had already decided to call it a day as far as being a musician was concerned and had announced to everyone that he was becoming the group's manager. After all he had the contacts.

The Quarry Men were led by guitarist John Lennon whom Ivan admired greatly. He had gained favour with Lennon on several occasions by introducing interesting boys into their circle of friends, people who shared their interests, and he had built up a reputation for himself with his cronies of only bringing 'great fellows' to meet John. He had brought Len Garry into the group, and knew from conversations they had had at school, that McCartney was interested in the idea of a skiffle group, and he seemed a thoroughly great fellow. John, he figured, would be drawn to Paul.

The skiffle group had been formed more than a year before by Lennon and Pete Shotton at Quarry Bank Grammar

School, and took their name from a line in the school song – 'Quarry Men strong before our birth'. The line-up had a habit of changing from time to time. But the general formula comprised Lennon and Eric Griffiths on guitar, Pete Shotton on washboard, Len Garry or Ivan Vaughan on tea-chest bass, Colin Hanton on drums and Rod Davis on banjo.

The week before the Woolton fête, the group had suddenly realized just how good or bad they were, when they were beaten in a talent contest at the Liverpool Empire organized by television and radio 'star maker', Carroll Levis . . . and they had failed to make his 'Discoveries' show. They were still smarting over the experience.

The Quarry Men's repertoire consisted of skiffle standards, 'Cumberland Gap', 'Railroad Bill' and the old Merseyside favourite, 'Maggie May'. When Paul first saw them, they were in the middle of the Del Vikings' 'Come Go With Me'. He was quietly impressed.

'They weren't bad,' said Paul. 'They played things like "Maggie May" but with the words a bit different.'

He added: 'It was mainly John who was the impressive one, he was the lead singer up there, and he'd taken a song, but he didn't know the words. So he was making them up, like "down, down, down to the penitentiary." He hadn't got the record yet, but he knew no-one else would know. So he made them up. I thought, wow, he's good. That's a good band there.'

After The Quarry Men had finished playing, Ivan took Paul 'backstage' across the road to the church hall, to meet the group, and in particular John Lennon.

After introductions were exchanged, Paul, although a little hesitant, showed the boys how to tune a guitar which was something neither guitarist Lennon nor Griffiths could do yet. They had to rely on one of their friends to help them whenever their guitars went out of tune. McCartney further impressed them when he showed John how to play Eddie Cochran's 'Twenty Flight Rock' and Gene Vincent's 'Be Bop A Lula', and actually wrote down all the *real* words for them.

Then, as if going for broke – and showing off – Paul lurched into his Little Richard routines, playing to his wide-eyed audience. At the height of his impersonation, he suddenly became aware of a figure breathing beer fumes down his neck. 'It was John.' This time, Paul *wasn't* impressed.

'He'd just had a few beers. He was a couple of years older than me. I was a bit innocent . . . and he was drinking a bit. I remember thinking – "Gosh, he's all a bit smelly and beery."'

When he had taught them some more chords, to another song which he had actually learned from Ian James, Paul left for home. 'I felt I'd made an impression,' he admitted.

John said: 'It was obvious that Paul knew how to play the guitar. I half thought to myself, "he's as good as me." I'd been kingpin up to then. "Now," I thought, "If I take him on, what'll happen?" But he was good, so he was worth having.'

John also remembered that Paul liked Elvis Presley – 'so I dug him.'

It wasn't John, though, who asked Paul McCartney to join The Quarry Men. That distinction went to Pete Shotton.

'A couple of weeks later I was cycling home when I met Pete,' Paul remembers. 'He said: "They'd like you to be in this group. They thought you were pretty good knowing all those words. You're in!"'

So Paul became a member of The Quarry Men and he made his début with the group, playing guitar, at the Broadway Conservative Club in Liverpool, where during one of the numbers, he was given his chance to impress, with a guitar solo. 'I had a big solo,' says Paul, 'and it came to my bit and I blew it. I couldn't play it at all, and I got terribly embarrassed. So I goofed that one terribly. So from then on I was on rhythm guitar,' he says.

After the engagement was over when the boys were packing away their sparse equipment, Paul, in an effort to redeem himself in the leader's eyes and to make amends for the missed guitar solo, played Lennon a couple of new tunes that he hadn't heard before. He was immediately taken with them, and wanted to know where McCartney had found them. They were two of Paul's own song-writing efforts, including 'I Lost My Little Girl', and he told John that he was now writing his own songs. Legend has it, that not to be outdone by his new friend's talent, Lennon started making up a song of his own, there and then, and presented it to Paul as *his* new song. In reality, John had actually started to adapt tunes of his own and was trying to write suitable lyrics. The arrival of McCartney on the scene was just the stimulus he needed to develop his own material. Although at first John Lennon had had second thoughts about inviting the younger boy to join The

Quarry Men, now he was certain he had made the correct decision. The future – and the music – was looking very bright indeed.

It was McCartney's attempts at songwriting that inspired John Lennon to write. He also recognized and respected Paul's much wider musical talents and wanted to learn from him. Yet, it was Lennon's character and personality that had a profound influence on McCartney.

Paul said: 'I went off on a completely new direction from then on. Once I got to know John, it all changed. He was good to know. Even though he was two years older than me, we thought the same sort of things.'

The two budding musicians and embryonic composers became partners, but it was a very unlikely combination, the attraction of totally opposite poles. Lennon was brash, abrasive and arrogant. He could be cruel, forceful and direct – cynical and resentful of all authority. Careless and carefree and too often matter-of-fact. A rebel drastically searching for a cause. And yet . . . he was an incredibly generous person with money. Jim McCartney didn't approve – 'He'll get you into trouble,' he told Paul after meeting John.

McCartney was the romantic, steady and unwavering. A born worrier, who always had to appear in the best possible light; like Ivan Vaughan had said, 'a great fellow'. He was softer, tactful and diplomatic, and tolerant. But he knew his own mind and even at that young age, he was totally professional and expected that same professionalism to be reciprocated by others. Circumstances at home had made Paul thrifty and very careful with his money. John's Aunt Mimi thought Paul was 'nice and polite'.

Music was the attraction that brought Lennon and McCartney together. They shared a passion for guitars, Elvis Presley and rock 'n' roll.

John Lennon was born in Oxford Street Maternity Hospital at 6.30 p.m. on the evening of October 9th, 1940 – at the height of a German Luftwaffe raid on Liverpool – to Freddy and Julia Lennon.

His parents' marriage had been a strange affair.

They had officially married on December 3rd 1938, on a whim to annoy Julia's parents, and on their wedding night, Julia returned home to sleep at her house, while the bridegroom went home to sleep at his!

Freddy Lennon was one of Liverpool's fly-by-night characters. He couldn't settle. A ship's steward by trade, he had left his wife only hours after their wedding and had gone back to sea. He returned to Liverpool briefly in 1940 and again in 1942, before he deserted his wife and young son for good. Needless to say, when John was born, Freddy was away at sea once more.

Julia's elder sister, Mimi, arrived at the hospital twenty minutes after the birth, and it was she who chose the name John. Julia selected the second name, Winston, in a moment of pure patriotism.

Within eighteen months of bringing John Winston Lennon into the world, Julia had become involved with another man whom she wanted to marry, and with whom she saw the chance of happiness and a loving relationship at last. The only problem was John.

Mimi, who was devoted to her nephew, came to the rescue. 'No-one wants another man's child,' she said, and she decided to give her sister her freedom, by agreeing to take John off her hands.

John went to live with Mimi and her husband, George, in Menlove Avenue, Woolton, where he was brought up as their own child. He called them Mimi and Uncle George.

After attending Dovedale Primary School where he first met Ivan Vaughan – another Dovedale pupil a few years younger than John was George Harrison – Lennon went to Quarry Bank Grammar School at the age of twelve. Here he found himself in the company of an old buddy, Pete Shotton, who had been an inseparable friend since the age of seven.

During his early teens, however, John struck up another friendship . . . with Julia, his mother, who had come back into his life in a big way and was now living in Allerton. They became very close, and John and his friends respected her more as a mate than a matriarch. It was Julia who was always ready to fight authority, who helped her son become a rebel. She also encouraged him to visit her home, and if that meant playing truant from school, so much the better.

By this time, Julia had two daughters of her own by the liaison with a waiter called John, with whom she was living, although she was still officially married to Freddy Lennon. John, the waiter, had a facial tic which prompted Lennon and his friends to call him 'Twitchy'. It was a cruel sign of affection.

Like many youngsters of his age, John Lennon became fascinated with rock 'n' roll. Although never greatly interested in music up until that point, rock 'n' roll seemed to hit him like a bolt from the sky. His conversion was spectacular. It started to happen in 1954 with the movie 'Blackboard Jungle' which featured the teenage anthem, 'Rock Around The Clock', and gathered momentum through Lonnie Donegan and skiffle. By the time Elvis Presley came along, Lennon was a convert. He couldn't get enough of the imported American music, and Radio Luxembourg, which featured rock 'n' roll records, became a nightly delight.

Years before, Uncle George had brought John a mouth organ which had been an early introduction to making his own music, and John could pick out tunes quite well. Now with rock 'n' roll running rampant, he wanted a guitar. He pestered both Julia and Mimi to buy one for him – and it was his aunt who relented in the end and picked up a second-hand guitar for £7. It was Julia who taught him how to play the instrument, showing him some banjo chords Freddy Lennon had once taught her. Before long, he had mastered his first song – 'That'll Be The Day'. The guitar became a source of great delight to John although Mimi told him: 'You'll never make a living with it.'

Eventually, John and his best friend, Pete Shotton, formed themselves into a group, trying to emulate the skiffle groups they heard on radio and saw occasionally on television. They called themselves The Quarry Men and dressed like Teddy Boys. When several other friends joined the line-up and they sounded good together, John thought it would be a good idea if they started making money from their enterprise and offered their service for hire. They had some business cards printed which read: Country. Western. Rock 'n' Roll. Skiffle. The Quarry Men. Open For Engagements.

When Paul McCartney joined John in The Quarry Men, his impact was felt immediately. It was at his instigation that they brought in a group uniform – shades of Jim Mac's Band – which comprised black trousers and white shirts with black bootlace ties. As lead vocalists, John and Paul were allowed to wear white jackets to complement the outfit. Paul also had a large say the the group's musical repertoire, preferring to bring in the kind of numbers that suited his voice; some rock 'n' roll, and some of the more mellow song standards he'd heard on the radio or at the cinema in Hollywood musicals. And he started to make suggestions on how the other members of the group should play their own instruments. John only encouraged him.

The group was working steadily, performing at local dances, parties and hops, and as Paul's more professional approach to work began to take a hold, the standard of engagements improved. But there were changes in the air as the band moved on and gradually evolved to Paul's specifications. Pete Shotton was the first to go, after a drunken argument with Lennon. He had been John's best friend for several years, but he could see that McCartney had now replaced him. Paul was also vying with Julia for John's attention.

Earlier in 1957, John had left Quarry Bank Grammar School after failing all his exams and, after his Aunt Mimi had persuaded him against joining the Merchant Navy and running off to sea, he enrolled at the Liverpool Art College where he commenced a full-time study course in the autumn. Paul, meanwhile, was still entrenched at the Institute, studying for O-levels. That summer, he had sat Latin and Spanish, passing only the more modern of the languages, and he was due to sit six more subjects in his fifth year at school. Then, it was hoped, he would either go into the Sixth Form or study at teachers' training college.

By a coincidence of design, the Liverpool Institute and the Liverpool Art College were built next to each other, allowing John and Paul ample opportunity to meet during the day . . . and to arrange to play truant from their respective seats of learning, in order to quench their growing thirst for musical knowledge back home.

Since joining The Quarry Men, McCartney and Lennon had spent most of their time together, totally engrossed in their music, writing new songs, learning new numbers for the group to play. On the days when they took time off, the two boys would end up back at Paul's house in Forthlin Road, where the front room would become a music studio. Paul knew they wouldn't be disturbed at home because his father was out at work. Sometimes they practised in the bathroom where the acoustics were much better and their voices picked up echo from the porcelain tiles.

'John and I used to slag off school and go to my house and just try to write songs,' said Paul. 'We'd put on a Buddy Holly record, then after we'd listened to it several times, we'd sit around with our guitars and then try to write something like it.'

Their early songs were deliberately written in the key of A, not because either John or Paul preferred to sing in that key, but simply because they believed Buddy Holly wrote his songs in A. He actually wrote a lot of them in C!

Buddy Holly was a great influence on Lennon and McCartney, although they were also impressed by other American writers such as Leiber and Stoller, Ellie Greenwich, Jeff Barry and Phil Spector, Mann and Weil, Wes Farrell and Larry Williams. John and Paul believed they were going to emerge as Britain's answer to Gerry Goffin and Carole King, and they based a lot of their early songs on the American songwriting team's material. They also liked the idea of a partnership and shook hands on an agreement that no matter who wrote the songs, either together or individually, all the material would be credited to the team of Lennon and McCartney. For a very short while it was McCartney and Lennon, though even Paul had to admit that Lennon and McCartney flowed off the tongue better – but only just. (When The Beatles made their first album, 'Please Please Me, all the self-penned songs are credited to McCartney and Lennon.)

Between 1957 and 1959, John Lennon and Paul McCartney wrote over a hundred songs between them. They spurred each other on to write as if in some demented race and that life depended on it. Paul, meticulous as ever and well organized, neatly wrote down the lyrics and chords to all of the songs in an exercise book. At the top of each new entry, he wrote: 'Another Lennon and McCartney original.' That exercise book survived into the mid-'60s when Jane Asher threw it away after a spring-cleaning session at Paul's house in London. John would remember the chords to his songs, and write down the words on any old scrap of paper, which he invariably lost.

Of those early songwriting creations, many were instrumentals, like 'Looking Glass', 'Catswalk' and 'Winston's Walk'. There were full-blooded vocals, 'Thinking Of Linking', 'Years Roll Along' and 'Keep Looking That Way', all referred to by Paul in the famous letter to the interested journalist in

1959: 'Modern music, however, is the group's delight, and as if to prove the point,' wrote Paul, 'John and Paul have written over fifty tunes, ballads and faster numbers during these last three years.'

Adolescent love was the main subject of the songs at the start, which was only to be expected as they were growing teenagers themselves. But as they went along, their music and lyrics reacted to their own personal circumstances and the changing world around them.

The Beatles only ever recorded a handful of this early music, simply because at that time, John and Paul were writing purely as a dance band, catering for one particular kind of audience – the people they were playing to on their various engagements. They had no intention of writing songs for a listening audience, because no-one ever listened! Their material was tailor-made to be danced to, or smooched along to . . . nothing more. A recording contract was way beyond their wildest dreams.

However, several songs did find their way into the studios at a later time. 'Love Me Do', which Paul called their most philosophical song, gave an insight into the extent of the Lennon–McCartney collaboration. Paul penned the verse, while John contributed the middle-eight. There was 'One After 909', revived for the 'Let It Be' album and movie in 1969, and 'I Saw Her Standing There'. Paul wrote 'When I'm 64' as a ragtime musical tribute to his father, Jim McCartney, with the flavour of the 1920s. It was the type of material he imagined Jim Mac's Band would have played in their heyday. Lennon helped out with some of the lyrics, supplying among others, 'Vera, Chuck and Dave' and 'doing the garden, digging the weeds'.

One of Paul's compositions, written in 1958, which for some unknown reason was never credited to the Lennon–McCartney partnership, was 'Hot As Sun'. He developed the number further over ten years later and it re-surfaced on his first solo album, 'McCartney'.

In those carefree days, however, the two teenagers seemed possessed by the urge to write songs. They worked at an amazing pace as if trying to outdo each other in their writing. It was like a big competition. It appeared as if they could write at any time, anywhere.

In one interview, Paul recalled that he would often have to

walk home to Forthlin Road from town, after taking girls out to the cinema when his pocket money wouldn't stretch to the bus fare home, which was all of 3d (1½p). On these walks at night to Allerton, he alleviated the boredom, and passed the time, by mentally writing songs. 'I used to walk home,' he said, 'but I never minded that. I wrote lots of songs on those walks home . . . "World Without Love" and "Love Of The Loved" .'

On other occasions he would walk over to John's house in Woolton with his guitar slung over his shoulder so that on the walk back he could write new songs. If anyone discovered him singing or playing, he clammed up and whistled sheepishly until they had passed him by.

4

George Harrison

George Harrison was never formally asked to join The Quarry Men. He had been introduced to the group by his school-friend Paul McCartney – who thought he would make an ideal addition to the line-up – towards the end of that eventful year of 1957, in the dingy cellar of an old derelict house in Liverpool's Old Roan district, that served as a club called, The Morgue.

By this time, young Harrison had become a quite competent guitarist, having learnt to play at thirteen. Now a year older, he was still a few years *younger* than the rest of the group and as such was eyed with suspicion by the boys. He idolized John, who thought he looked no more than ten years old.

George, like Paul and John, was guitar-mad and his instrumental party-piece was a bluesy-bass tune called 'Raunchy' with which he would regale his friends and play for anyone who would listen. He would dearly have loved to become a Quarry Man, but for the time being at least, he had to content himself by sitting in on guitar with various other neighbourhood groups. He built up quite a reputation for himself, and it was never doubted that he was a competent guitarist, with bags of potential. Paul was convinced.

When his guitar-playing services were not needed by other local groups, George would accompany Paul on engagements all over Liverpool, and he avidly watched his pals on stage, from the sidelines. Quite simply, he was a fan.

George did have his uses to the group. His home in Upton Green, Speke, was always made welcome to the boys by Mrs Harrison, who allowed the group to practise there at weekends . . . and she would often lay on plates of baked beans on toast whenever they were hungry. Her son became a regular Quarry Men camp follower, but it would be a good six months before he was allowed to join the group on a permanent basis.

George Harrison was born in the Liverpool district of Wavertree on February 25th, 1943, to Harold and Louise Harrison. He was the youngest member of a family of four children – three boys (Harold, Peter, George) and daughter Louise. George's father, like John Lennon's, had been a merchant seaman, but after the birth of their first son, he quit the service and joined Liverpool Corporation, first as a bus conductor and later as a driver.

From an ealry age, George was strong-minded and fiercely independent. He attended Dovedale Primary School, three years behind Lennon, and made a good impression. After passing the 11-Plus, he transferred to the Liverpool Institute, where he made a bad impression. He hated school, and much to the distress of his teachers, he became a Teddy Boy and often dressed in outrageous (for the times) outfits. Michael McCartney, who also served 'time' at the Institute, remembered George wearing a lime-green waistcoat hidden under his school blazer, and blue suede, winkle-picker shoes!

School, however, did have its compensations. Each morning, he would meet Paul McCartney at the bus stop on the corner and travel to school with him. Upstairs, they would talk passionately about music and guitars.

By now, George, too, had succumbed to the influences of Lonnie Donegan and skiffle. 'Skiffle seemed made for me,' he said. He had also put the school timetable to good use, by designing guitars during lessons. He desperately wanted a guitar of his own, and when a boy at the Institute offered to sell him one for £3, George borrowed the money from his mother to make the deal . . . and then accidentally broke the instrument. It was his brother Peter who mended it.

With great endeavour and patience, George mastered the rudiments of guitar playing, with a little help from his mother, who encouraged him enormously. But it was a painful process.

When he felt he was good enough, he formed a skiffle group of his own, with brother Peter, and three friends. They called themselves The Rebels and made their one and only public appearance at Speke British Legion for the grand sum of £2.10.0 (£2.50).

Shortly afterwards, George's mother lent him the £30 he needed to buy a brand new Futurama 3 electric guitar made by the German firm of Hofner, which had two cutaways, allowing for the higher frets to be reached with ease. When Paul McCartney saw it, he was highly impressed. George, however, had to repay his mother's generosity and took a Saturday job working as a delivery boy for a local butcher. Saturday evenings were occasionally spent in the company of The Quarry Men as they worked steadily to make their name across Liverpool.

As the fortunes of skiffle gave way to rock 'n' roll, the fortunes of The Quarry Men changed as well. Paul's influence had been well and truly felt within the group, and added to the outside pressures of schoolwork and imminent examinations, several regular members drifted away from the band. Rod Davis had thrown in the towel in an attempt to knuckle down at school and gain some kind of qualifications. Nigel Whalley and Len Garry later contracted serious illnesses – Nigel was stricken with tuberculosis, while Len caught meningitis – and Ivan Vaughan (The Ace On The Bass), had stepped aside to allow other, more talented musicians a place in the group. The Quarry Men were left with John, Paul and Eric Griffiths on guitar, and Colin Hanton on drums. Occasionally, George Harrison would busk along for the ride if John felt like letting him. Eric Griffiths on the other hand, was destined to be replaced, ousted in a bloodless coup by Lennon and McCartney, which meant that by the summer of 1958, George Harrison had become a permanent fixture in the group.

1958 proved to be another eventful year in the group's history, particularly for John Lennon. It was to throw up a great tragedy in his life, yet at the same time, bring John and Paul much closer together.

In the early evening of July 15th, John's mother, with whom he was becoming so loving, so close, was knocked down and killed by a car, just a few hundred yards from her sister's home in Menlove Avenue. Julia had spent the afternoon at Mimi's and was making her way to the bus stop, to catch the bus back home to Twitchy and the girls, when the accident happened.

Nigel Whalley was on his way to call for John and had briefly chatted with Julia only moments before, when he heard the screech of tyres. He saw Julia's body tossed in the air on impact like a broken doll, to come slamming down again. He knew she was dead before she hit the ground.

Like Paul before him when Mary had died suddenly, John Lennon showed no outward emotion at the loss of his mother. He kept it all to himself, brooding, simmering, silent. Paul could see the signs. 'That was one of the big bonds between us, John and I,' he said.

Julia's death brought him closer to Paul. They shared a common loss, and like McCartney, John would be inspired to write songs about his mother in the future: 'Half of what I say is meaningless, but I say it just to reach you, Julia.'

John and Paul's writing together intensified, following Julia's death. In John's case he needed to express his emotions somehow; songwriting was the perfect vehicle. But he became more and more bitter. Paul simply liked to write and needed no excuses. But John's added impetus stimulated him to write even more. The competition between them increased. In some strange act of fate, both Lennon and McCartney threw themselves into their music after the death of their mothers. Their tragic loss was music's gain.

That same year, another woman entered Lennon's life at Art College, and Cynthia Powell was to have a great effect on John.

1958 saw the end of the name Quarry Men. It wasn't appropriate any more. None of the boys in the band was attending Quarry Bank Grammar School.

By now the group's engagements became irregular; they played wherever they were wanted, but without Nigel Whalley to find them work, their dates included birthday parties, the odd social club and working men's club appearances. Still, they stuck with it, improving as an outfit as they went. Like George, John Lennon became the proud owner of an electric guitar, but the group had no amplification. George had to wire the guitars into the house microphone system whenever they performed, before they could play a note. It was a wonder they escaped electrocution!

The boys also entered another local contest at the Liverpool Empire to win a place on Carroll Levis's talent-spotting show once again, only this time on television. They competed along with most of the other Liverpool groups, and managed to win their way into the semi-final of the competition being held in

Manchester. For their second appearance on the show, The Quarry Men became Johnny And The Moondogs. It was a name they all liked because it had the same ring to it as Cliff Richard And The Shadows. In those early days of rock, all the groups had a leader whose name was given top-billing. Many of their contemporary groups on Merseyside had similarly styled names, including Liverpool's most successful group, Rory Storm And The Hurricanes, Lee Curtis And The All Stars, Cass And The Cassanovas and Derry And The Seniors. And, as John was the leader, he took pride of place.

Johnny And The Moondogs made their début at the Hippodrome Theatre in Manchester, on the Carroll Levis Discoveries talent show. They played competently enough, but missed out on the final judging by means of audience applause and reaction, because they had left for home before the show ended. Having no transport of their own, Johnny and the boys, had to rely on public services for their return to Liverpool. So an evening that started with so much promise, ended in tatters – and the group had to wait four more years before being 'discovered'. The wait did them good.

Not long afterwards, drummer Colin Hanton decided he had had enough and left them, which effectively meant that the group had ended as far as personal appearances were concerned. John and Paul, though, continued to write their songs together. There were the odd party bookings where the group name would be changed – one time they all arrived in multi-coloured shirts, so they called the band The Rainbows. On another occasion John and Paul went down to Reading to appear in the pub run by Mike and Bett Robbins – McCartney's cousin and former Butlin's Red Coat – where they were billed as The Nerk Twins. George Harrison, meanwhile, joined another group, The Les Stuart Quartet, with guitarist Ken Brown.

Away from the group, John Lennon had settled into Art College, where besides meeting Cynthia Powell, he had also befriended a very talented artist called Stuart Sutcliffe. At times, Lennon seemed besotted by the quietly spoken, good looking student who had a passing resemblance to James Dean. Stu's influence on Lennon was most noticeable. From being a sarcastic, apathetic student, John suddenly found a new drive and impetus to want to work and study again. He respected Stuart immensely, and spent a lot of his spare time cloistered in deep discussion with him. If there was only some way he could get Stu into the group. Lennon was working on the idea.

Paul McCartney's school-work had been drastically affected by his extra curricular activities in the music field, so much so, that out of the six O-Levels he had taken in the summer term, he managed just a single pass, in art. Instead of going straight into the Sixth Form at the start of the next autumn term as he had hoped, Paul had to stay in the Remove Form until he could sit his exams once more.

In actual fact, Paul had toyed with the idea of leaving school and getting a job. But he had few qualifications . . . and there were no jobs for aspiring rock 'n' rollers who could play the guitar. Jim McCartney was against the idea of leaving. He would have none of it. He knew that Mary's greatest wish was for their son to study hard and eventually to become a teacher. Had she lived, it is doubtful whether she would have allowed Paul to pursue his musical career with such vigour and selfishness . . . and part of the history of popular music might well have been re-written.

So, Paul McCartney stayed in the Remove, set his sights high, and at the earliest opportunity sat his O-Levels again, this time passing French, English and German, to gain access to the Sixth Form where he studied Art and English for A-Level.

In the summer holidays in 1959, a new coffee-bar-cum-club opened in the cellar of a large Victorian House in West Derby, named the Casbah. The club had been the brainchild of Mona Best, who owned the house, after her son, Pete, had cleared out the cellar in order to have a permanent meeting place for his friends. At last they had somewhere to go. Mona realized that with the right décor, and run correctly, a club had great potential. When eventually The Casbah was redecorated and refurbished along similar lines to the dozens of coffee bar clubs that were springing up all over the city, Mona decided that they needed a resident group as an added attraction to bring the punters through the door. Through a friend, she approached Ken Brown, who in turn, brought along *his* friend, George Harrison. George suggested two of his own friends, John Lennon and Paul McCartney, might also be interested in making up the numbers in the group. They were!

On opening night, over 300 turned up at the club and gave the group a rousing reception. The Quarry Men, with the addition of Ken Brown on guitar, were back in business!

The residency, however, didn't last long . . . just over two months. One evening, when Ken Brown arrived at The Casbah suffering from a heavy cold and was told not to play by Mrs Best, a row over money developed at the end of the session.

When the group had finished playing, Mona paid out the regular fee of £3 – 15 shillings each – which included 15 shillings for Ken Brown. Naturally, John, Paul and George objected to the share-out because Ken Brown hadn't been well enough to play, so why should he be paid? The incident got out of hand and Ken Brown resigned from the band, while the other three walked out. Shortly afterwards, Ken Brown approached Pete Best – who was slowly getting his own act together as a drummer – to start a group of their own. As The Blackjacks, Ken and Pete, and two others, took over the top spot at The Casbah.

5

Beatles

John Lennon got his own way once again when he invited his good friend, Stu Sutcliffe, to join the group in 1959. They had been close friends since the start of that year and Stu, like George before him, had spent a lot of his time away from his studies, following the group around, watching them play on engagements or in rehearsal. The idea of becoming a musician certainly appealed to his artistic nature.

Paul was instantly taken with Stuart's intellectual style because he had introduced himself as a student of Liverpool University and *not* just as a Sixth Former from Liverpool Institute.

Stu had been born in Edinburgh in 1940 to a Scottish mother and father, but the family had moved south to Liverpool where the young boy was brought up, at the height of the war. He had endeared himself to the other members of the group when he persuaded the Art College Committee to buy them an amplifier for use at College dances, providing, of course, that it should not be taken out of the building at any time. That part of the agreement was never kept.

Although Stu's musical ability was very limited, Lennon dearly wanted his friend to join the group. The trouble was, he had no guitar, or drums for that matter if, maybe, he wanted to become a drummer. The group certainly needed one!

But then, providently, Stuart's own artistic talent came to his rescue. When one of the paintings he had entered for the John Moores Exhibition at the Walker Art Gallery, was purchased by John Moores himself, Stu used the £60 sale fee to buy a new electric bass guitar. He was in . . . even if he couldn't play the instrument. It was left to George Harrison to teach him to play and help him out, though George admits that Stu picked up most of his musical training on the road out of necessity, playing on engagements. On stage, however, he spent most of his spare time with his back to the audience so that no-one would see that he couldn't play the guitar. He just strummed passable bass notes every so often, and pretended to play most of the time. But somehow the air of aloofness he presented on stage, through no design of his own, by ignoring the people who were watching the group, helped him create an image of mean moodiness.

'Anyone who knew would realize that Stu couldn't play bass,' said Paul. 'He just used to turn his amp down and sort of make a bass noise. He didn't know what key we were in half the time. He put a lot of bass on it and sort of bluffed and stamped a lot.'

Shortly after Stu became a member of the group, they finally decided on a permanent stage name, when he suggested they might call themselves *Beetles*. It was a variation of the theme of animal names copied from Buddy Holly And The Crickets. John wrote down BEATles, a pun on *beat* music . . . and the others agreed. John was still the leader so they called themselves Long John and the Silver Beatles, and later just The Silver Beatles.

With a new name, The Silver Beatles also picked up a new manager in the form of Welshman, Allan Williams, who owned the coffee bar club, The Jacaranda, a favourite hang-out for Liverpool musicians.

Williams started to procure the odd engagement for the group, and put them forward for an audition that London impresario, Larry Parnes – who handled such British rock 'n' roll stars as Billy Fury, Marty Wilde, Dickie Pride and Duffy Power – was holding in the city. Parnes was not impressed with the group, but did book them for a two-week tour of Scotland in May 1960, as the backing group for one of his stable of stars, Johnny Gentle. Williams, too, fixed the group up with a drummer for the tour, although at thirty-six, Tommy Moore was old enough to be their father. He worked as a Beatle for the duration of the tour – no longer.

The excitement of Scotland prompted the boys to change their own names, adopting contrived pseudonyms which in their choice says much for each one's character. Paul took the '20s sounding title Paul Ramon, very Rudolph Valentino;

George became Carl Harrison after his guitar idol Carl Perkins; Stu surfaced as Stu de Stijl, after the famous painter; Lennon adopted the name Johnny Silver. Tommy Moore stuck with his own name.

In the early days of the 1960s The Silver Beatles were still finding their feet musically. They were influenced by a number of sources and this was reflected in their repertoire, which was made up mostly of American music.

'We started off imitating Elvis, Buddy Holly, Chuck Berry, Carl Perkins, Gene Vincent, The Coasters, The Drifters – we just copied what they did,' admitted Paul.

The black American rhythm and blues groups were other prominent influences, along with Little Richard, Marvin Gaye and Larry Williams, whose music was all featured heavily in The Beatles' stage act. Later, when they were recording, they returned liberally to these sources to borrow much of their music. These influences have stayed with Paul McCartney ever since, and throughout his career he has written songs in the style of his music mentors *and* acknowledged their inspiration. He wrote 'Lady Madonna' initially for Fats Domino, paid homage to Chuck Berry on 'Get Back', while 'I'm Down' was pure Little Richard: 'it was a big finisher,' says Paul. 'A loud rocky number that was as a painter would say "after Little Richard."' On the album 'London Town', Paul's song 'Name And Address' is a tribute to Elvis Presley on which he captured perfectly the feel and very essence of the early Sun recordings.

In 1982, when he appeared on 'Desert Island Discs', McCartney recognized the debt he owed to so many American singers and writers, by including several of his own personal favourites on the programme: 'Heartbreak Hotel' (Elvis Presley), 'Sweet Little Sixteen' (Chuck Berry), 'Searchin'' (The Coasters), 'Tutti Frutti' (Little Richard), and one of the songs that started it all off, 'Be Bop A Lula' (Gene Vincent).

Paul was also very much attracted to the popular musical standards – a legacy inherited from his father – and 'Till There Was You', 'Besame Mucho', 'The Honeymoon Song', 'Red Sails In The Sunset', 'September In The Rain' were all featured in the group's stage act, and Paul experimented himself by trying to write songs in a similar style. Even at this stage of the group's development, he was looking for more permanent music than rock 'n' roll. There were also a number of humorous contributions to the act with 'Sheik Of Araby' and Fats Waller's 'Your Feet's Too Big', and even these comic renditions were helping to shape Paul's ability as a songwriter. In later years, he would write his own witty songs with great effect.

And, of course, the rapidly expanding catalogue of Lennon and McCartney originals was regularly plundered for such songs as 'Love Me Do', 'I Saw Her Standing There' and 'One After 909' for live performances.

After Scotland, The Silver Beatles returned to the usual round of Liverpool engagements, picking up work wherever they could. At one time they accompanied a stripper at a club in the city's Chinatown district. 'We all wore pink, shiney suits and played weird music. Each time she finished her act, she'd turn round and look at us straight in the eye. We were still only lads and didn't know where to put ourselves,' said Paul. The stripper had actually given them sheet music to play from, but as none of the group could read music, they played the only recognizable instrumentals they knew . . . 'The Harry Lime Theme' and 'Moonglow'.

Dances at the Grosvenor Ballroom in Wallasey were a regular employment where nearly every Saturday night hop ended in a free-for-all punch-up with the local Teddy Boy community.

On the album 'Tug Of War', McCartney returned to these musical roots to compose the song 'Ballroom Dancing' – the Grosvenor Ballroom providing the historical backdrop to the fantasy song that recaptured childhood memories. He never forgot, and used the song and its symbolism again as one of the spectacular production numbers in his movie 'Give My Regards To Broad Street', complete with fighting Teds.

Looking back on those days at the Grosvenor, Paul remembered: 'There'd be a hundred lads from one gang and a hundred lads from another on opposite sides of the ballroom. Then someone would ask a girl from the other mob to dance . . . and then the bottles would start flying.'

He also recalled that The Beatles would often enter talent contests at the Grafton Ballroom in Liverpool, while dances at Litherland Town Hall were another standard entry in the date book.

In July 1960, after one appearance at the Town Hall, the

group was attacked by a bunch of louts in the car park. Even though they could handle themselves pretty well in a fight, John Lennon had to rescue Stu from a beating after he had gone down in the scuffle and been kicked in the head. That one incident was to have tragic repercussions in Germany.

Paul McCartney left school in the summer of 1960 after sitting A-Levels – he passed Art – with the intention of training to become a teacher. George Harrison had been working as an apprentice electrician since the age of sixteen. John and Stu were still at Art College. The Beatles still had no permanent drummer.

Manager Allan Williams hadn't been idle in his quest to promote the groups he handled, including The Beatles who by now had dropped their colourful prefix.

Following a lead in Germany from the West Indian Steel Band he had recently employed at his own Jacaranda Club, Williams made a trip to Hamburg, to see if the rumours were true that English groups had become all the rage in the night-clubs of the German port. They were!

A meeting with impresario Bruno Koschmider followed and a useful contact established.

Back in Britain, Williams, sensing money in the air, met Koschmider in London and fixed up for Liverpool group, Derry And The Seniors to play in Hamburg. When they later proved a big attraction in the clubs, Williams was approached again to supply another group from Merseyside. Initially, he chose Rory Storm And The Hurricanes who unfortunately had already signed up for a summer season at a Butlin Holiday Camp. So Williams turned to The Beatles to help him out of a spot. Although he managed them, he didn't rate them much as a group!

It was all a great adventure for The Beatles; professional employment at last. But first, Paul had to persuade his father to let him make the trip overseas.

'At first he wasn't very keen,' said Paul, 'but he could see we were really excited. It was the first real employment we had . . . and the others in the group were very hot on it. They didn't have many problems with their parents on it. But my dad was good. He checked it out that we had a decent manager and stuff like that.'

It was Paul who also persuaded Pete Best, Mona's son from the Casbah, to join them as their drummer.

Following the recent break-up of The Blackjacks, Pete was no longer permanently set up in a group. He had occasionally sat in with The Beatles on odd engagements and knew the lads well. When Paul offered him £15 a week, regular work *and* a trip abroad, he jumped at the opportunity.

'Allan Williams took us to Hamburg in his van first of all, and dropped us at the club thank you very much,' said Paul. 'And it was all the night life, Reeperbahn and all the nightclubs.

'It was fascinating for us. It was looney really because we were just schoolboys.'

Later in an interview, Paul described Hamburg: 'A sort of blown up Blackpool, but with strip clubs instead of wax works; thousands of strip clubs, bars and pick up joints, not very picturesque. The first time it was pretty rough, but we all had a gear time. The pay wasn't too fab, the digs weren't much good and we had to play for a long time.'

The Beatles started the Hamburg episode of their career playing at the Indra Club – often performing on stage for six or seven hours each night. Their accommodation, as Paul hinted, comprised three small, squalid rooms in an attic, in the Bambi Filmkunsttheater cinema, which had no proper heating, light or sanitation. The boys' sleep would regularly be disturbed during the day by the noise of the film being shown to punters downstairs. They spent much of their day at the Seaman's Mission – the British Sailors Society – where their staple diet often proved to be a bowl of cornflakes and milk, or whatever else their meagre wage would run to.

They became regulars at the 'Mission', and John and Paul would be allowed to go upstairs to a room behind the bar, where on an old piano, they could write their songs together. These new songs would later be tried out on stage in front of an audience they not only had to entertain with their music, but by putting on a show for them to watch as well. 'Mak show! Mak show!' was the plaintive plea from the management. The Beatles, outrageous as ever, would 'mak show'! Lennon had a field day!

Within weeks of arriving in the German sea port, The Beatles' music was becoming finely tuned. They were getting tighter as an outfit the more they played together . . . *and* more outrageous on stage with their madcap antics in an effort to entertain. Hamburg was the making of The Beatles.

They spent two months at the Indra, competing nightly against drunks and rowdies in the audience. There was often a fight, just like they were used to in Liverpool at the Grosvenor or Grafton Ballrooms. Nothing had changed . . . only the language. But the club was finally closed down after complaints about the noise from local residents, and the boys were moved on down the road to the Kaiserkeller. Not long after playing at the larger venue, The Beatles were joined in Hamburg by their old friends from the Liverpool circuit, Rory Storm And The Hurricanes, and the two bands got on famously together, competing with each other to see which group could be the more outrageous on stage. It was always a close run thing. Drummer Ringo Starr became a great favourite with John, Paul and George. Pete tended to keep himself very much to himself.

Stu, meanwhile, had met some new friends. Former intellectual student Klaus Voorman, now a brilliant artist and designer with a passion for music, had discovered The Beatles playing at the Indra and had been captivated by them. It was he who introduced Stu to his photographer friend Astrid Kirchherr. Within weeks of their meeting, Astrid and Stu became engaged.

Astrid had a marked influence on The Beatles, and spent many long hours photographing them – capturing through her lens the group's identity, their humour, their heart. She also dabbled at designing clothes and soon started making items for Stu to wear, particularly the collarless jackets that The Beatles themselves would adopt later. But most of all, Astrid was encouraging her British lover to express himself more in his own art and design.

In the winter of 1960, The Beatles' contract with Bruno Koschmider had finally run out. The boys had made something of a name for themselves in Hamburg with their heady music and lively stage antics, and it was only a matter of time before they were offered better and more lucrative work. The offer came of an engagement at the impressive Top Ten Club, which was far superior to both the Indra and Kaiserkeller. It was in a different class to the other, seedier dives. The Beatles eagerly accepted. However, just days before they were due to open their new residency, it was discovered that George Harrison was still only seventeen and as such, under age to work in the Hamburg clubs. He had no work permit, either, or a resident's permit, and was promptly deported from the country. George travelled back to Liverpool by train, completely demoralized.

It was left to John Lennon to take over on lead guitar when the group opened their season at the Top Ten Club. It proved to be their one and only appearance there.

In the rush to vacate their rooms at the Bambi Kino, and move into the accommodation that came with the new job at the Top Ten, Paul McCartney and Pete Best accidentally started a fire in the cinema. Both boys were arrested and thrown into jail, before being sent home.

John was the next to go when his work permit was taken away – and Stu followed shortly afterwards.

The individual Beatles came back to England just before Christmas 1960 . . . penniless. The future of the group, like the British weather that winter, looked decidedly bleak. They were even too disgusted with themselves to contact each other for several days after their return. And Paul McCartney actually took a 'real' job to earn some money, working first on a delivery van, and later winding coils at Massey & Coggins, electrical engineers, for £7 a week.

It looked to be the end of The Beatles, but as McCartney was to admit later, they were driven on by a tremendous belief in themselves and undying faith in the fact that they always knew they would make it one day. As John would chant: 'Where are we going?'

'To the top, Johnny,' came the reply from the other Beatles. 'To the top.'

'And where is the top, fellows?'

'To the toppermost of the poppermost!'

On December 27th, 1960, after making their first post-Hamburg appearance in Liverpool at Mona Best's Casbah a few days before, The Beatles were booked to appear at Litherland Town Hall, on the recommendation of local disc jockey, Bob Wooler. The Beatles asked for a fee of £8 for the evening. They accepted £6! Billed as 'Direct From Hamburg' and playing *without* Stu whom they hadn't contacted since their return, The Beatles caused a riot – literally! Liverpool, brought up on a diet of rowdy beat groups, had seen nothing like this before. The girls screamed . . . and went wild!

Lennon said: 'It was the evening that we really came out of our shell and let go. We discovered we were quite famous.

This was when we began to think for the first time, we were quite good. Up to Hamburg, we thought we were OK, but not good enough.'

Gone was the casual approach to their work, a hallmark of pre-German Beatles. In its place, there was a very tight sound with a hard-driving edge, harnessed to a 'let's-all-have-some-fun-tonight' stage act, in the finest 'mak show' traditions. It was exciting. Different. There wasn't a group for miles around to compete with The Beatles. Hamburg had certainly made them.

John Lennon summed it up: 'It was Hamburg – that was where we'd really developed. To get the Germans going and leaping up and down for twelve hours at a time, we'd really have to hammer. We would never have developed so much if we'd stayed at home. We had to try anything that came into our heads in Hamburg. There was nobody to copy from.

'It was only back in Liverpool that we realized the difference.'

After the Litherland engagement, they began a long and historic association with the Cavern Club in Matthew Street, playing initially on Tuesday nights, but later making regular lunchtime appearances at the former jazz club, for £5 a time. It was Bob Wooler again, who recognized their potential and recommended them to the club management. Bob shortly became the resident Cavern disc jockey and in 1961, long before the world had discovered The Beatles, he wrote: 'They resurrected original rock 'n' roll. The Beatles exploded on a jaded scene. Here was the excitement, both physical and musical, that symbolized the rebellion of youth. Truly a phenomenon!' He predicted: 'I don't think anything like them will happen again.'

After playing a mish-mash of music from the hard rock of Chuck Berry and Little Richard, through the romance of the Everly Brothers and Buddy Holly, to Paul's songs-from-the-shows, The Beatles were still searching for an individual sound of their own, despite featuring a small selection of their own songs, courtesy of Lennon and McCartney. They were simply too apprehensive to showcase more of their own songs on stage. What if no-one liked them? They never realized that they had actually found the sound they were looking for. They thought the answer lay in importing obscure American material, and re-working it into their own style of playing, for British audiences.

'We were trying to find the next beat, the next sound,' said Paul. 'The *New Musical Express* was talking about calypso, or how latin rock was going to be the next big thing.'

Never slow to pick up on a new idea once they had found the right direction to follow, John and Paul wrote several songs in the calypso beat, or reflecting the latin feel, including 'Ask Me Why' which became another great favourite on stage. Even at this early stage in their songwriting career, John Lennon and Paul McCartney were utilizing other people's ideas for their own ends, listening, watching, developing. They picked up on everything they thought might be useful.

In April 1961, for the grand sum of £40 a week each, and with guaranteed work permits, they returned to Hamburg for a second stint at the Top Ten Club, where this time, they shared accommodation with Tony Sheridan – a singer they had often seen and heard on television's top rock 'n' roll show in Britain, 'Oh Boy!' Once again, though, the accommodation left a lot to be desired.

It was during this second visit that relationships within the group reached breaking point on occasions, and rows became the order of every day between Pete and the boys. Paul was becoming increasingly aware that Stu's musical ability, particularly at playing bass, could never match the rest of the group's talents. He was certainly holding The Beatles back, and this worried McCartney.

'One of the main problems was that Stu wasn't that good on bass,' said Paul. 'He couldn't play . . . So what you had to do if you were having a photo taken, was to tell Stu to turn away, do a mean and moody thing, looking over his shoulder, because you didn't want anyone to see what he was actually playing . . . he couldn't play it.'

He added: 'The only reason I had a little thing against Stu, was purely musical. He was a great guy . . . but it's true, I didn't understand him.'

Stu Sutcliffe was now living with Astrid and he had become almost alienated from the rest of the group. But under her influence, he blossomed as an artist. His paintings came alive again – his music was now taking a back seat. When, at his fiancée's prompting, he was offered a grant to attend Hamburg State Art College *and* a chance to study under Eduardo Paolozzi, one of his great idols, Stu decided to quit the group . . . after all, he still believed that he was only a

Beatle because of his friendship with John. He left them gradually, though, often sleeping only three hours a night in an effort to fulfil two commitments: a lengthy session, playing at the Top Ten Club at night, and an intensely creative lesson with Paolozzi during the day. He also left them a parting gift when he turned up one night at the Top Ten Club for work with a new hairstyle, having abandoned his Teddy Boy cut. Astrid had cut and combed his hair forward into a fringe in the French style above the eyes. John, Paul and George loved it, and before long, they too, would adopt the new style. Pete preferred his quiff.

With Stu's departure, John Lennon at first asked George Harrison to play bass guitar. When he refused, Lennon turned to Paul McCartney, who borrowed Sutcliffe's Hofner President guitar until he could afford to buy a bass of his own. Paul's own guitar had blown up, meanwhile, and he had resorted to playing piano on stage.

'Then Stu left the group and lent me his bass, and I played bass for a few weeks,' said Paul. 'I used to play it upside down. And he used to have piano strings on it, because you couldn't get bass strings. They were a bit rare . . . and they cost a lot, too. So he would cut these big lengths of piano strings from the piano and wind them on the guitar.

'I'm in Hamburg,' he continued, 'and I have a little bit of money together and I finally saved enough to buy myself a Hofner Violin bass. It was my bass then.'

To augment his money he earned with The Beatles, Paul would often sit in with various other groups, *playing drums* – and once doubled up performing for a week with Tony Sheridan's group as drummer.

It was Sheridan who suggested that The Beatles make their first record in Germany. Tony had been signed to Polydor Records by producer/composer Bert Kaempfert, and when he needed musicians to back him on the recording, The Beatles were approached to play on the session for £25 a man.

Besides providing an instrumental backing and vocal back-up for the English singer, The Beatles also recorded several songs on their own during that brief sojourn in the studio, including versions of 'Ain't She Sweet', 'My Bonnie Lies Over The Ocean', 'When The Saints Go Marching In' and a haunting George Harrison–John Lennon instrumental called 'Cry For A Shadow', which had been pulled together by accident when someone asked George to play The Shadows' great hit, 'Apache'. He couldn't quite remember how the number went, but thought he was near enough. 'Cry For A Shadow' in its rough form came out instead. They liked it, wrote it down . . . changed it around a little, and kept it.

But when John and Paul played some of their own original songs to Bert Kaempfert, the German composer wasn't interested in them – they didn't sound like the hits of the day. He turned them down.

That summer, The Beatles returned to Liverpool. They came back home with an even harder edge to their music if that was possible; they came home with a new bass guitarist and some brand new professional recordings. But they came home *without* Stu, who had decided to remain in Hamburg, to study . . . and to marry Astrid. Prior to leaving, however, Stu had been asked by the boys to write and send a letter to Allan Williams, dispensing with his services as The Beatles' manager. As *he* was staying in Germany, at least Stu wouldn't have to face the Welshman back home in Liverpool.

6

Brian Epstein

BRIAN EPSTEIN SAW The Beatles for the first time on the afternoon of Thursday, November 9th, 1961, performing one of their action-packed, 'mak show' sessions, at the Cavern.

They had been home from Germany for four months and had slipped easily back into the routine of the Liverpool ballroom and club circuit. But by now, they had gained a certain notoriety, and emerged from out of the shadows of Derry And The Seniors and Rory Storm And The Hurricanes, to become Merseyside's most popular – and most exciting beat group. They were playing three and sometimes four times a week at the Matthew Street club, lunch times and evenings. It was dark, hot and sweaty – just like The Beatles' music.

Brian's interest in the group had been aroused a fortnight earlier. On the afternoon of Saturday, October 28th, one of his regular customers – 18-year-old Raymond Jones, whom Brian knew to be a great Carl Perkins fan – called into NEMS, the Epstein family-run music store in the city's Whitechapel district, and asked for the record, 'My Bonnie' by The Beatles. He said something about Germany.

Epstein prided himself in having Liverpool's largest record shop with a reputation second to none. If a record existed, he would either have a copy in stock, or could certainly get one within a few days. Indeed, the advertisements he ran in the local music paper, *Mersey Beat*, described the store as having 'the finest record selection in the north'. Epstein also had a filing system for cataloguing records and new releases that he believed to be foolproof. On this occasion, Raymond Jones had just cracked the code!

Brian Epstein made it a 'rigid rule' never to turn away any

customer. So he wrote a note to himself to aid memory – *'My Bonnie'. The Beatles. Check on Monday.* Before the day was out, however, he had had two more requests for the same record, this time from girls. He was now intrigued. 'I was sure there was something very significant in three queries for one unknown disc' . . . and he started making enquiries amongst his friends and acquaintances. He discovered, to his surprise, that The Beatles were in fact a local group and regularly played sessions at the nearby Cavern Club. It fired his imagination; he didn't know why; he just felt an excitement. After making arrangements through a mutual friend with the Cavern management, he decided to visit the club and see for himself what all the fuss was about. He wasn't disappointed. He arrived resplendent in a suit and tie, looking his usual dapper self, but this time completely out of place amongst the leather jackets and jeans. He carried a briefcase, too. Still, it was dark in there.

When The Beatles came on stage, he was spellbound, fascinated. 'They were not very tidy and not very clean,' he said later, remembering first impressions. 'I had never seen anything like The Beatles on stage. They smoked and they played and they ate and talked and pretended to hit each other. They turned their backs on the audience and shouted at them and laughed at private jokes.

'But they gave a captivating and honest show, and they had very considerable magnetism.'

After that first session, DJ Bob Wooler announced from the stage that Mr Brian Epstein from NEMS was in the audience and would they give him a round of applause? He became embarrassed.

When Brian finally met The Beatles backstage, he was greeted by George Harrison: 'And what brings Mr Epstein here?' So Brian told them he was interested in their new record and asked to hear it. It broke the ice.

Before he left the club, after staying to see The Beatles' second afternoon set, Brian arranged a meeting for the boys to come to see him at his Whitechapel office. A time of 4.30 had been agreed, on the afternoon of Wednesday, December 3rd.

'When I met them I was struck by their personal charm. It was there that really it all started,' said Brian.

Yet as he made his way back to the North End Music Store, he didn't really know why he had made the appointment. He shivered at the prospect. All he did know was that The Beatles excited and aroused him. Their music was certainly different to a man with a preference for Sibelius. But . . . he was captivated by them.

Brian Samuel Epstein had been born in a private nursing home in Rodney Street, Liverpool – comparable to London's Harley Street – on September 19th, 1934.

His father, Harry, was the son of Isaac Epstein, a Polish/Jewish immigrant who had opened a furniture business in Walton Road, on which the family fortune had been made over the ensuing years. Harry had later taken over the running of the business – I. Epstein And Sons – and through hard work, dedication and a certain flair (all family traits), he had established a successful venture. In the 1930s, the family increased its holdings by taking over NEMS.

Brian's mother, Malka (Hebrew for Queenie) Hyam had been born into a wealthy Jewish family in Sheffield, running another highly successful furniture business.

In 1940, the Epsteins were evacuated from Liverpool at the height of war, to Southport, where Brian attended Southport College. Three years later, the family returned to their Queen's Drive home and their eldest son was sent for private education at the Liverpool College from where, at the age of ten, he was expelled for drawing obscene pictures during the maths lessons.

At fourteen, after public schools in Tunbridge Wells and Dorset, he was accepted at Wrekin College in Shropshire, where he excelled at art and drama. Two years later, however, he left school without a single qualification – even having failed to sit the school exam – but with aspirations to become a dress designer. Instead, he was ushered quietly into the family business as a salesman on a salary of £5 a week. Against all the odds, he proved quite adept at selling, and his genial personality brought him favour with the customers.

In 1952, Brian was summoned for National Service, with the prospect of spending the next two years in uniform. He chose the Royal Air Force; he was recruited into the Army. He wanted to train as an officer; he was enlisted as a private and put in the Royal Army Service Corps as a clerk. He hated it. After twelve months, he was discharged on medical grounds after being found guilty of impersonating an officer. It was something he did rather well – he got away with it often enough.

On his discharge papers it was written: 'A conscientious and hard working clerk who uses his initiative and can, in every respect, be depended upon to see a job through satisfactorily without supervision. Of smart appearance and sober habits at all times, he is utterly trustworthy.'

Back in Liverpool, he returned to the bosom of the family firm again, but he couldn't settle even though he found great delight in using his talents to re-organize and run the record department at the NEMS store, where he could indulge his love of classical music.

By now, Brian's other great passion in life was for the theatre which he visited avidly. He also turned his hand at acting with a local amateur drama group, and it was through this love of the stage – and the persuasion of some friends – that he decided to apply to, and audition for, the Royal Academy Of Dramatic Art in London. Somehow, he got in. His family weren't impressed.

For Brian, however, acting proved to be merely an infatuation that didn't last long. Within eighteen months, he had returned home to the family business once more, though this time to run a new branch of the Epstein empire in Great Charlotte Street, which singer Anne Shelton opened in 1958. The Epsteins had retained the name NEMS, and although selling electrical goods, the shop had a large record department. A year later, the business expanded with the opening of another NEMS store in Whitechapel, which had an extensive record department for both classical and popular music, spread over two floors. It was Brian's brainchild and he ran the department with great love, great enthusiasm and efficiency, introducing several of his own innovations for its smooth running, including a comprehensive index and filing system. He also inaugurated the store's own chart, or 'best-selling records list' as he called it.

By the start of the 1960s, Brian Epstein had a well-organized and successful lifestyle. He was rich, eligible and emerging as a celebrity in his own right on Merseyside. He was just about the best record retailer in Liverpool. But Brian was bored with his life; he needed that stimulus of a new challenge. A Teddy Boy from Huyton called Raymond Jones would soon provide it.

Brian Epstein ordered 200 copies of 'My Bonnie' by The Beatles, once he had tracked down the record company and distributor. He sold over 100 copies in a few days and the single went on to be a moderate local success.

Epstein, however, had made several subsequent visits to see The Beatles at the Cavern prior to the appointment at NEMS, and had also spent long hours researching their background, talking to people who knew them. He became obsessed with them.

On the day in question, The Beatles arrived at NEMS for the meeting with Brian at 4.30 p.m., minus Paul McCartney, but with Bob Wooler whom John had brought along as their advisor.

Brian was annoyed that Paul was late and summoned George Harrison to find out what had happened to him, only to be told by the guitarist that McCartney had just got up and was having a bath. Epstein, who hated to be kept waiting, exploded: 'This is disgraceful! He's very late!'

'Yes,' said George, 'but very *clean*.'

The Beatles were very impressed with Brian Epstein, though. John thought he looked efficient, very business-like and rich, *and* he drove an expensive car.

'He had a Zephyr Zodiac,' said Paul. 'So we were impressed. You didn't see many of them, let alone get a ride in one. He was a very nice fellow – a little mixed up, but he had a big heart. A great fellow.'

When Paul eventually arrived, they all chipped in with their dreams and ideals for The Beatles' future, and Epstein realized they had no management. A further meeting was arranged the following week, at which Brian told them that they desperately needed a manager and he was offering his services. He outlined what he believed he could do for them in terms of projection and promotion and, after satisfying Paul that it would make no difference to the group's music, and what they wrote and played, he was given the go-ahead by the group to draw up a formal management contract. They agreed to pay him 25 per cent of all earnings.

Lennon simply said: 'Right then, Brian, manage us.'

Four days later, a rough agreement was written out and signed by the five parties, yet it wasn't until mid-January 1962 that an official management contract between Epstein and The Beatles was drawn up, which John, Paul, George and Pete signed. Brian never put his signature to the agreement. 'I had given my word about what I intended to do and that was good enough. I abided by the terms and no-one ever worried about me not signing it,' he said. The contract was never legally valid. When George and Paul signed the agreement, they were under the age of twenty-one and still considered minors.

Throughout the remaining weeks of 1961, Epstein worked hard on The Beatles, combining his activities as group manager with his work at NEMS. He had formed a new and separate company to manage the group which he called NEMS Enterprises. NEMS had been a lucky name for the family in the past and he saw no reason why it shouldn't remain lucky for him in the future.

At that time, group management was only a part-time occupation, yet Brian used his position as one of the biggest record retailers in the north of England to his advantage in the advancement of The Beatles' career. Through his numerous contacts, he arranged for a recording test with Decca Records. A and R man Mike Smith had been coaxed up to Liverpool to see The Beatles performing at the Cavern and had shown great interest in them, enough to organize an audition in the London studios for January 1st.

Prior to that audition, Epstein's influence had been felt in The Beatles' camp. Far from changing their music, as Paul had feared, Brian encouraged the group to work out a set programme for their appearances – featuring a well-balanced act – and to stick to it. He made the group cut out the ad-libbing, the joking and the high-jinx on stage. He took over the bookings of the group from Pete Best, and insisted, from the moment he became their manager, that The Beatles would never work for less than £15 a night.

Brian organized them completely. 'Brian put all our instructions down neatly on paper and it made it all seem real,' said John. 'We were in a daydream till he came along. We'd no idea what we were doing, or where we'd agree to be. Seeing our marching orders on paper made it all official.'

Epstein also made the group abandon their leather jackets, jeans and cowboy boots that had become their stage outfit and image, in favour of something cleaner, and tidier.

'He wanted us to get suits on,' said Paul. 'We all had the leather gear. But he thought breaking into the big time required a suit.' Lennon was horrified.

In Paul, Brian found an ally within the group. Always the

showman, and having learned from his father that presentation and smartness were essential on stage in the days of Jim Mac's Band, McCartney convinced the rest of the group that suits were vital for the future career of The Beatles, and after all, hadn't they agreed that Brian should manage them? They had to trust him and his decisions. Then, as if to convince himself, Paul insisted that the new suits be tailored with velvet collars. 'Ours are different to anybody else's,' he said. 'Ours have *velvet* collars.' Opposition from the rest of the group caved in.

Paul McCartney secretly admired Brian Epstein. In the early days he copied the style of dress Brian favoured and became the bridge between the manager and the group. Paul was always the first Beatle Brian phoned when he had news to relay to the boys, or when he needed help.

They only ever had one argument. One night Brian and the boys arrived in Allerton to pick Paul up, and found him still in the bath. He politely told them to wait for him, he'd only be a few minutes. They drove off to the engagement without him.

'So I said, "If they can't be arsed waiting for me, I can't be arsed waiting for them." So I sat down and watched television.'

Brian was mad with Paul's attitude, but it was McCartney's gentle way of rebelling against the system.

'I'd always been the keeny, the one who was always eager, chatting up managements and making announcements. Perhaps I was big-headed at first, or perhaps I was better at doing it than the others. Anyway, it always seemed to be *me*. But I realized I was being more false by not making the effort.'

On New Year's Day 1962, The Beatles arrived at the Decca studio in London for an audition with Mike Smith. They were very excited . . . but also very nervous.

Epstein had told them that the only way he believed they would impress the recording chiefs, would be by playing many of the standards they featured in their stage act. Brian figured that by showing their versatility in their imaginative arrangements, Decca would be sufficiently impressed to offer them a contract. He advised them to keep their original Lennon and McCartney material to a minimum. Thus only John's 'Hello Little Girl', and Paul's 'Love Of The Loved' and 'Like Dreamers Do' made that 15-song session, along with such material as 'Besame Mucho', 'September In The Rain', 'Till

There Was You', 'Money', 'The Sheik Of Araby' and 'Memphis'. The result of the audition wasn't as good as they expected. All the boys were apprehensive. At one point, Paul's voice cracked up through sheer panic.

Still, Mike Smith seemed pleased, and confident Beatles returned to Liverpool hoping they had done enough to secure a coveted record-deal.

Back home, a few days later, they learned they had been voted Liverpool's most popular group in the *Mersey Beat* music paper's poll – ahead of such stalwarts as Gerry And The Pacemakers, The Remo Four and Rory Storm And The Hurricanes. It didn't matter that they had each sent in dozens of votes for themselves. What did matter was that their success was down in print for everyone to see.

But in London, however, Dick Rowe – Decca's Head of A and R – was making a decision that would haunt him for years to come.

Faced with the choice between two groups for one recording contract – Brian Poole And The Tremeloes and The Beatles – Dick Rowe chose the Dagenham-based outfit. He then told Brian Epstein, as if justifying his decision to turn down The Beatles, that guitar groups were on the way out, and intimated that the Liverpool group had no future whatsoever in the music industry. 'We don't like your boys,' he said. 'The boys won't go, Mr Epstein. We know these things. You have a good business in Liverpool. Stick to that.'

Brian's reply was to tell the Decca executive that The Beatles would one day be bigger than Elvis Presley. Dick Rowe laughed; he'd heard it all before.

But such was Epstein's belief in The Beatles, or in his own ability as a manager, that he spent the next few months hawking the demo tapes around the other various record companies. They were rejected at Pye, at Philips, at EMI, at HMV, and at Columbia, besides a handful of smaller companies and independents.

Meanwhile, The Beatles had been working extensively on the home front. In March they had auditioned for the first time for BBC Radio in Manchester. They were well received and easily passed their audition, but Peter Pilbeam, who had the distinction of being the first BBC producer to book the group for a radio show, wrote on their audition report: 'An unusual group, not as rocky as most, more country and western with a tendency to play music.' Against the two vocalists he added: 'John Lennon – yes; Paul McCartney – no!'

Their engagements at the Cavern had been supplemented with the usual round of ballroom and club appearances, as well as several concerts Brian Epstein had personally presented. He billed his protégés as '*Mersey Beat* Poll Winners. Polydor Recording Artists. Prior To European Tour'. The European Tour in question was the group's third excursion to Hamburg and a six-weeks' season at the Star Club on the Reeperbahn. It proved to be an unhappy reunion for Germany and The Beatles. Prior to flying out to Hamburg, courtesy of Brian Epstein who thought it was good for their image, news reached them in a telegram from Astrid, that Stu Sutcliffe was dead. He had died of a brain haemorrhage as a result of being kicked in the head, following an incident at Litherland Town Hall back in the summer of 1960. The Beatles were devastated!

The German engagement, however, went ahead as planned and, left to his own devices, while the group was out of his way, Epstein decided to have a final assault on trying to secure a record contract for them. He returned to London, making immediately for the HMV record store in Oxford Street, where for £1 he knew he could have the demo tapes transferred to an acetate disc, which was far more convenient when it came to playing it to busy A and R men. The engineer who cut the disc was impressed with what he heard and recommended Brian to a publisher friend, who in turn made an appointment for him to meet George Martin, head of A and R at Parlophone Records, a subsidiary of EMI, which had already turned the group down. Parlophone and Martin were noted more for their comedy records, having had success with Charlie Drake and Peter Sellers in the past, and Flanders and Swann. A year earlier, they had enjoyed a Number One hit with 'You're Driving Me Crazy' by the Temperance Seven.

'Brian Epstein walked into my office one day and said he'd got a group he wanted me to hear,' said George Martin. 'Their music wasn't frightfully original – there were no great songs there – it's just that the sounds were interesting. I arranged a test with them at Abbey Road . . . which meant I was going to spend a couple of hours with them finding out what they could do.' He was very taken with Paul's voice, even on the demo disc. 'He had the most commercial voice of the lot.'

Epstein had his foot in the door and cabled the group in Hamburg: 'Congratulations, boys. EMI requests recording session. Please rehearse new material.' The news fired John and Paul to start writing together again with even greater fervour.

The Beatles came back to Liverpool at the beginning of June. On June 6th, they were in Abbey Road Studios in London auditioning for Martin. During that session, George Martin made them run through a lot of their stage material. 'I got them to sing lots of different things to find out which voice was good,' he says. 'I was thinking that on balance I should have Paul as leader. Then I realized that if I did, I'd be changing the whole nature of the group. Then it suddenly hit me right between the eyes. Why the hell should I find a solo singer, why not just have the lot of them as they were!'

After the audition, George Martin took Brian Epstein to one side and told him that if Parlophone did decide to go ahead and record The Beatles, he would have to bring in a session drummer for the recording. He had already decided that Pete Best was totally unsuitable for recording with the group.

'He couldn't play drums too well,' said Martin. 'He couldn't keep time too well. The band weren't tight – they needed that binding force a drummer should give them.'

George Martin had no way of knowing that Paul McCartney and George Harrison had already decided that Pete Best should go . . . but it wasn't because of his inability as a musician, far from it. Pete was becoming far too popular with the girl fans, and Paul and George didn't like it. Pete had become the focal point of the group, simply because he was the best looking of the four. He was also a loner, who didn't fit in with the others. George Martin's comments to Brian Epstein made it easier to dispense with Pete's services . . . and they knew exactly whom they wanted as a replacement.

When George Martin contacted Brian Epstein at the end of July to confirm that the group had a deal, and that Parlophone would offer a contract for a one year period, with options, and that they undertook to record four titles in that year at a royalty of one penny per double-sided record, Pete Best was never told. It was left to the manager to break the news to him that he was no longer needed in The Beatles, and to tell him that their old friend from Hamburg, Ringo Starr, was the new drummer.

Brian put the blame on George Martin.

There was outcry in Liverpool amongst Beatles fans when the news of Pete's dismissal got out on the street, following an exclusive article in *Mersey Beat*, on August 23rd. A day later, the group had other things to attend to – John Lennon and Cynthia Powell were married by special licence at Mount Pleasant Register Office in Liverpool. Brian Epstein was best man; Paul McCartney was a witness . . . and all three Beatles wore their stage suits for the ceremony.

The Best incident left a nasty taste. When the group next appeared at the Cavern with Ringo on drums, they were attacked by their own placard-waving fans. George Harrison was punched in the face and played the ensuing set with a black eye.

Three weeks later, on September 12th, 1962, The Beatles recorded two Lennon and McCartney original songs as their first record release on the Parlophone label. The A-side, 'Love Me Do' – written all those years ago when John and Paul first started composing their own material – took seventeen takes before The Beatles got it right. 'P.S. I Love You' made up the B-side, a song written in the style of one of the boys' favourite American girl groups, The Shirelles, with a hint of that latin beat they had read about in the music papers as being the next 'new' sound . . . Already, John and Paul were developing an uncanny knack of being able to reproduce the styles of other writers in their own composing – and they could do it to order.

Two versions of 'Love Me Do' were recorded each with a different drummer. Ringo played on one version, which subsequently became The Beatles' first single release, while session drummer Alan White played on the other, which was later used on the group's 'Please Please Me' album. On 'P.S. I Love You', Ringo played maracas.

The single was released on October 5th. By the end of the month, it was in the British chart, peaking at 17. The Beatles were on their way to 'the toppermost of the poppermost'.

7

Ringo Starr

George Martin took a great gamble when he decided to go with 'Love Me Do' as The Beatles' first single. He knew John and Paul were keen only to record their own material, and he played his own instincts by going along with them. It was against all the conventions of the music industry: it was unheard of for an unknown group to insist on recording their own songs. It would have been far easier to find a suitable song from one of the numerous music publishing companies that abounded in London at that time.

'"Love Me Do" was the best song,' said George Martin. 'I was very conscious that it wasn't the big hit I was hoping for.'

But for the group's second single release, Martin played safe and presented The Beatles with a ready-made song, 'How Do You Do It'. John and Paul didn't like it very much and told George Martin in no uncertain terms.

'When you can write material as good as this, I'll record it. Right now, we're going to record this!' he said.

Suitably chastised, the boys went into the studio, played the song in a totally lacklustre style. Their performance was lifeless. Dead. George Martin knew what was wrong and relented. He asked them what new material they had; they played him 'Please Please Me', a song they had originally written in the style of Roy Orbison's rock bolero, but had recently refurbished it and speeded it up.

'As soon as I finished the record, I knew it was a Number One,' said George Martin. 'It had great atmosphere to it.'

The atmosphere was captured in one single take, even though Paul and John forgot the words at various times during the chorus.

'How Do You Do It', the song Martin originally wanted the

boys to record, had been discovered by an old friend of the producer's, music publisher Dick James. It was through George Martin's recommendation that James became John Lennon and Paul McCartney's music publisher in November 1962. James agreed to form a new company – Northern Songs – to handle Lennon and McCartney exclusively. He would take 50 per cent of all publishing royalties, with John and Paul sharing 40 per cent, and Epstein receiving 10 per cent. The first song the company published under the agreement was The Beatles' third single release, 'From Me To You'.

'Please Please Me' was released in January 1963 and for once, George Martin was proved wrong. The record stormed into the chart and just failed to reach the top spot, peaking at two. But it was enough to post warning that The Beatles were very much in business.

An album, simply called 'Please Please Me' after the single, followed. It was recorded in February and took under thirteen hours to get down. The LP featured material from the group's state act, including four more John and Paul originals as well as their two hit singles and the B-sides, 'P.S. I Love You' and 'Ask Me Why'. There was also a gentle ballad for Paul to sing, 'A Taste Of Honey', It would be the first of many. The album reached Number One in April and stayed there for a massive thirty consecutive weeks!

By now, Ringo Starr had settled well into The Beatles' routine.

He had been born Richard Starkey on July 7th, 1940 to Richard and Elsie Starkey, in the Liverpool district of Dingle.

When he was three, his father walked out on the family, leaving young Ritchie to be brought up by his mother and grandmother. Three years later, during his first year at St Silas Junior School, he was rushed to hospital suffering from a burst appendix which developed into peritonitis. He was in a coma for ten weeks and stayed in hospital for over a year.

At the age of eleven, Ringo attended Dingle Vale Secondary School where he was good at drama, poor at music . . . and most other things. But he wasn't there long. Within two years – shortly after his mother had got married again, to Londoner Harry Graves – a bad cold turned to pleurisy, and he was taken into hospital once more and later transferred to Heswell Children's Hospital where he spent the next two years. He never returned to school.

His first job was with British Railways as a messenger boy. It lasted six weeks. Then came a stint as a barman on the Mersey ferries, before he became an apprentice joiner at a local engineering firm. When the skiffle craze hit Britain, the apprentices formed themselves into a group with Ritchie as the drummer. He'd actually played a bit, too, in hospital. Harry Graves bought him his first second-hand kit for £10 in London, and carried it back to Liverpool on the train. Later, in the Eddie Clayton Skiffle Group, the youngster bought a brand new set of drums for £100, and later still, he turned professional with The Ravin' Texans who went on to become Rory Storm And The Hurricanes. The boys in the group nicknamed the drummer 'Rings' because of his liking for rings – his fingers were covered in them. 'Ringo' sounded more cowboy-like, more country and western. He took the surname 'Starr' so that the group could announce his formidable drum solo on stage as 'Starr Time'.

In 1961, Ringo met The Beatles in Hamburg and often shared a meal or two with them at the Seaman's Mission. He sat in on drums with them, too, when they recorded a song in a make-your-own-record booth on Hamburg station!

When he was offered a permanent berth in The Beatles at £25 a week, John Lennon phoned Ringo and told him to comb his hair forward and shave off his beard. 'But you can keep the sidies,' he said.

With the initial success of 'Love Me Do', The Beatles set out on an inevitable round of touring to satisfy a demand they were slowly beginning to create around the country. Their first tour was with Helen Shapiro at a fee of £80 a week, just prior to 'Please Please Me' breaking in the singles chart. They travelled everywhere by coach, and it gave John and Paul an ideal opportunity to spend the many long hours they had together on the road in transit from one theatre to the next, huddled together writing new songs. In this way, during a period from 1963 to 1964, Lennon and McCartney wrote more directly together on tour than at any time during their career.

'They started out by writing songs together,' said George Martin. 'But it didn't last long. They generally wrote their own songs and then played one to the other. The other might suggest a change in the middle, but that was the extent of their collaboration. It was very much a competition between them, and a healthy one, too.'

On that first major tour, however, they wrote 'Misery' together, originally for Helen Shapiro. When her management turned it down, Kenny Lynch (also appearing on the tour) stepped in and recorded it himself. It wasn't a hit. On the road between York and Shrewsbury, John and Paul were inspired to write another song after reading the letters column in the *New Musical Express,* which went under the heading: From You To Us. Lennon and McCartney called their song 'From Me To You' and it became their third Parlophone single release in April . . . and their first official Number One! The B-side of the song, 'Thank You Girl', was also written on that tour and had been earmarked as the follow-up to 'Please Please Me' instead.

Together, in a coach touring Yorkshire, they penned 'She Loves You' which became The Beatles most successful single of all time, and topped the chart in September after first entering the Hit Parade the week before at Number Two. On release, 'She Loves You' had advance sales of over 500,000!

Of 'She Loves You', Wilfred Mellors, musicologist of York University wrote: 'It is quintessential. It exists in the moment, without before or after. For although its key signature is the E-flat beloved of Tin Pan Alley, the opening phrase is pentatonic, or perhaps Aeolian C which veers toward E-flat. The timeless present affirming modality is instinctive: The Beatles are through their music, as if new born. It is this pristine quality that helps us to understand the potency of their appeal.'

It was one of the last songs they consciously sat down together to write as a joint effort.

Throughout 1963, The Beatles completed tours supporting American stars Chris Montez and Tommy Roe in March, and Roy Orbison in May. But by the end of the year, they were headlining their own package. *And* causing riots wherever they appeared. Beatlemania had arrived. It would be a long time going.

1963 was the year The Beatles finally broke through to outstanding success in Britain. Their records sold like wildfire, and at the end of that year, their fifth single release – 'I Want To Hold Your Hand' – went straight into the charts at Number One, knocking 'She Loves You' down to Two.

The song had been written by John and Paul in the basement of the London home of McCartney's girlfriend, Jane

Asher, whom he met in May. The young English actress would become one of the biggest single influences in Paul McCartney's life over the next few years, inspiring him directly to write some of his most memorable songs.

When The Beatles had became successful in 1963, Paul was still living at home at Forthlin Road, Allerton, with his father and brother. When the fans discovered the address, it became impossible to stay there any more, so Paul spent much of his time at Jane Asher's home in Wimpole Street, London, where he had his own room. He later bought his father a detached house in the Cheshire countryside at Heswell, which they called 'Rembrandt'.

Although they had enjoyed tremendous chart success, appeared regularly on the TV pop shows, and were mobbed wherever they went, it wasn't until October 1963 that The Beatles won national acclaim in Britain, right across the board. It happened on October 13th, to be precise, when they topped the bill for the first time on the country's top-rating TV show, 'Sunday Night At The London Palladium'. In the same way the American public had melted after Elvis Presley's performance on 'The Ed Sullivan Show' some seven years before, the British public took The Beatles to its heart following that one TV appearance. The next morning they were headline news, and household names.

The boys were back on stage at the Palladium within three weeks, to appear in front of the Queen, in the Royal Variety Show, during which Lennon made the immortal comment when introducing 'Twist And Shout' on stage: 'Will the people in the cheaper seats clap your hands. And the rest of you, if you'd just rattle your jewellery.'

At the end of the year, in the *New Musical Express* Readers' poll, The Beatles had been voted World's Top Group. Their fan club numbered 80,000 members, and their second album – 'With The Beatles', featuring seven Lennon and McCartney songs . . . one by George Harrison . . . and Paul McCartney singing 'Till There Was You' – was released to an advance order of over 300,000. It topped the album chart for twenty-one weeks from December 1963 to May 1964.

One of the songs on that album was the McCartney classic, 'All My Loving', which he wrote while shaving one morning. 'I wrote that one like a bit of poetry,' he admitted. 'And then I put a song to it later.' It was as simple as that. Arranger Milton

Okun described the song thus: 'The melody of "All My Loving" has the elegance of a 16th century court song.'

Paul McCartney and his partner John Lennon were emerging as a conveyor belt production line for songs. Their music had elevated The Beatles beyond their wildest dreams, and now their contemporaries were clamouring for new and original Lennon and McCartney material to record. The almost magical name of Lennon and McCartney could in itself virtually be guaranteed to help a song gain a place in the British charts.

During 1963, much of their material was covered by other artists: Billy J. Kramer scored with Paul's 'I'll Keep You Satisfied' and 'I'll Be On My Way', and John's 'Do You Want To Know A Secret' and 'Bad To Me'; The Fourmost charted with Lennon's 'Hello Little Girl' and 'I'm In Love'; Paul wrote 'Tip Of My Tongue' for Brian Epstein's protégé Tommy Quickly; while Cilla Black took McCartney's 'Love Of The Loved' – written on a long walk home to Allerton when he'd run out of bus fare – into the charts.

Their music was beginning to inspire a generation in Britain and it would soon cross the Atlantic.

Commenting on their work together, William Mann of *The Times* called John and Paul, 'the outstanding English composers of 1963', and added: 'Lennon and McCartney have brought a distinctive and exhilarating flavour into the genre of music that was in danger of ceasing to be music at all. The autocratic, but not by any means ungrammatical attitude to tonality; the exhilarating and often quasi instrumental vocal duetting; the melismas with altered vowels ("I saw her yesterday-ee-ay") which have not quite become mannered; the translation of African Blues and American western idioms into tough, sensitive Merseyside – these are some of the qualities which make one wonder with interest what Lennon and McCartney will do next.'

If any proof were needed that The Beatles had been accepted by the establishment, this was it. Later, *The Sunday Times* called John and Paul . . . 'the greatest composers since Beethoven'.

The Beatles could do no wrong. Everyone loved the Mop Tops, the Fab Four.

Of all the early film taken of the group during those days, Paul McCartney is the one who looks as if he is thoroughly enjoying every moment of it all, and everything that comes his way. He sparkles. The three others seem a little bemused.

8

Beatles Over The World

From 1963 to 1970, The Beatles – and the music of John Lennon and Paul McCartney – dominated the world. Brian Epstein *had* been right – The Beatles became bigger than Elvis Presley.

In that time, they enjoyed seventeen Number 1 singles in Britain and eleven Number 1 albums! In America, they scored with twenty Number 1 singles and fourteen Number 1 albums – and they brought many outstanding innovations to their music, and to recording techniques which others would take up and exploit further into the future. The Beatles were the pioneers of pop . . . the rest, camp-followers.

It had started in 1964, after tremendous success in Britain, when 'I Want To Hold Your Hand' topped the US Hit Parade, and broke down a barrier so often elusive to British rock and pop acts. An appearance on the most popular television show in the world, 'The Ed Sullivan Show', followed and together with a series of sell-out concert engagements in New York and Washington, non-stop coverage on radio, television and in the newspapers, America laid down its arms and surrendered in record-breaking time. The Beatles conquered the States in a few months. Britain had taken years. As a measure of their success across the Atlantic, on March 13th, 1964, they held the first four positions in the Cashbox Top 100 – 'She Loves You' at (1); 'I Want To Hold Your Hand' (2); 'Please Please Me' (3); and 'Twist And Shout' (4). The rest of the world would be easy by comparison. Thirteen days later, they topped even that when in Australia, they captured the top six chart places – 'I Saw Her Standing There' (1); 'Love Me Do' (2); 'Roll Over Beethoven' (3); 'All My Loving' (4); 'She Loves You' (5); and 'I Want To Hold Your Hand' (6).

Back home in Britain, they started work on their début movie, 'A Hard Day's Night', prior to massive tours of Australasia in the spring – on which Ringo Starr was replaced by session drummer Jimmy Nicol for the first few dates, after collapsing with tonsillitis – Europe; their first major tour of America; and an extensive British tour in the winter.

Amongst it all, 'A Hard Day's Night' was given a Royal première in July, while the soundtrack album from the film – which was made up entirely of Lennon and McCartney material for the first time ever on an LP – spent twenty-one weeks at the top of the album chart. At the end of that year, The Beatles' single, 'I Feel Fine', became their sixth consecutive Number 1 in Britain, while their Christmas album, 'Beatles For Sale' was a chart-topper on and off for eleven weeks.

'Beatles For Sale' was an unusual album. It featured music from The Beatles' rock 'n' rolling roots . . . by Chuck Berry, Carl Perkins, Buddy Holly and Little Richard, together with eight original Lennon and McCartney tracks. The songs written by Lennon alone were very much influenced by Bob Dylan.

During the next six years, The Beatles took everything in their stride, without even stopping to enjoy it. Touring. Filming. Recording. They were depicted by the world's Press as the happy-go-lucky *good* guys of pop music, played against The Rolling Stones' image which stood for everything *bad*. The Beatles' music was optimistic and full of hope, The Stones' was pessimistic and dreary . . . it didn't matter how the true story went.

The Beatles' major project of 1965 saw them filming their second movie, which was originally called 'Eight Arms To Hold You' until someone came up with 'Help'. Again, in the summer, the film was given Royal patronage at the première, just weeks after John Lennon, Paul McCartney, George Harrison and Ringo Starr had been awarded the MBE in the Queen's Birthday Honours List . . . which prompted several former recipients to return their insignia.

The release of the 'Help' soundtrack album – which Paul acknowledged as once again being very much influenced by Bob Dylan – highlighted a McCartney song that was to make history; that was to become the most recorded song of all time, with over 1,000 different versions in existence at the last count. The song featured Paul McCartney alone on the recording, singing to a solitary guitar accompaniment, augmented by a string quartet. It certainly *wasn't* rock 'n' roll. But 'Yesterday' is still the most memorable of all Paul McCartney's songs and one of his own personal favourites. 'I really reckon "Yesterday" is one of my best. It was one of the most instinctive songs I've written . . . it is the one I reckon that is the most complete thing I've ever written.' He wrote it so easily, however, that he was convinced he had heard the tune somewhere before.

'I woke up one morning and there was a piano to the left of where I was sleeping,' he said. 'I just knew this tune in my mind and I sort of got to the piano and found the chords to this tune I was doing. It was so simple, so complete . . . that I couldn't believe I'd written it. I literally went around for about two or three weeks to all my friends saying, "Listen here, what's this? Tell me what this song is." And they would say, "It's quite nice, but I haven't heard it before." After two or three weeks, I convinced myself that I had written it.'

Before he finally wrote the lyrics, he called the song 'Scrambled Eggs'. When he revived 'Yesterday' for his 1984 movie, 'Give My Regards To Broad Street', Paul wrote of the song in the accompanying book: 'I didn't have any words for it and about two weeks later I went on holiday. I remember being in a car on one of those long journeys from the airport and I was beginning to think of the words, but they came slowly.

'I remember thinking consciously that people liked sad songs. I had just begun to realize that. Being about twenty-two, it was a bit of a revelation to me – people *do* like sad songs and smoochiness – and I thought it would be nice if I could get one sort of saddish.

'When I came to record it, we couldn't think what the group could do. So John said, "Well, just sing it yourself with the guitar, it sounds great the way you sing it."'

George Martin suggested putting strings on the record – but Paul was against the idea, fearing 'Yesterday' would be given a Norrie Paramour or Mantovani treatment.

'So I told Paul that I didn't really mean strings like they were on Gerry And The Pacemakers' "You'll Never Walk Alone",' said George Martin. 'And Paul confirmed that he wanted something different. I suggested a small amount of strings, perhaps a classical string quartet and he liked the idea because he was living with Jane Asher at the time and hers was a very classical family. So that's the way it happened and he worked with me on the score – we actually sat down at the piano and said: "We'll put a cello on this note . . ."'

As George Martin had hinted, Jane Asher was having a very big influence on Paul McCartney. He smartened himself up considerably, and started changing his attitudes to life. They were seen together at concerts and first nights in the West End. Always one for musical experimentation, McCartney began to take a more serious interest in classical music. He was once quoted as saying: 'I was always frightened of classical music. And I never wanted to listen to it because it was Beethoven or Tchaikovsky . . . and Schoenberg. A cab driver the other day had some sheet music of a Mozart thing on his front seat. And I said, "What's that?" And he said, "Oh, that's high-class stuff, you won't like that. Highbrow!" And that's the way I always used to think of it. I used to think, "Well, that's all very clever all that stuff." But it isn't, you know, it's exactly what's going on in pop at the moment. Pop music is the classical music of now.'

In 1982 on his appearance on BBC's 'Desert Island Discs', Paul chose 'Courtly Dances' from 'Gloriana' by Benjamin Britten and played by Julian Bream Consort, as one of his eight selections, to represent his love of classical music, on the programme.

Back in the mid-'60s, however, he told the London *Evening Standard*: 'I'm trying to cram everything in, all the things that I've missed. People are saying things and painting things and writing things and composing things that are great and I must know what people are doing.'

Paul learned to play the recorder – taught by Jane's mother – and set about learning how to read and write music. Until then, he had no need to learn such things; there were others far more competent than he who could help him out. But somehow, he never quite mastered the technique himself. He still can't write or read music to this day.

Early in 1965, he bought a large house in the St John's Wood area of North London for £40,000, close to the Abbey Road recording studios, and Jane Asher moved in with him. A year later, he bought a farm in Scotland, saying that it had always been his ambition to own a farm in Scotland. When marriage was hinted at by the newspapers, McCartney denied it all and quashed all subsequent rumours. They were just good friends.

Paul's relationship with Jane Asher lasted for five years – they even got engaged, telling both sets of parents at Christmas 1967. But by the summer of the following year, the romance had cooled . . . and they parted. By then, Paul had already met Linda Eastman, who was destined to become Mrs Paul McCartney. They were married in March 1969.

Yet during those five years, Jane Asher inspired Paul to write some magnificent music. Many of his love songs were dedicated to her. 'And I Love Her' – which retained that elusive latin beat Paul was so fond of; 'I Will'; 'Here There And Everywhere'. There were others . . . He wrote 'For No One' when they were on holiday together in Switzerland; he wrote, 'I'm Looking Through You' after a tiff with Jane when she left him and went off to Bristol.

It was through the young actress that Paul McCartney became musically involved with her brother, Peter Asher and his singing partner Gordon Waller. The two ex-public schoolboys worked together as a double act called Peter And Gordon. Paul wrote several songs for the duo, including the chart-topping 'World Without Love', a song that had been plucked out of the McCartney archives. It had been written several years before on one of those famous night-time walks back home to Allerton. He also penned 'Nobody I Know' for them and 'Woman', which he wrote under the pen-name of Bernard Webb, 'a student from Paris.' He wanted to see if the subsequent record release would stand up on its own merits without having the name 'McCartney' to help it. It did.

In the summer of 1965, The Beatles undertook their second American tour, which opened at Shea Stadium in New York to a record-making audience of 56,000, while in the winter they completed a further tour of Britain. But the touring was starting to take its toll as the four Beatles began to drift apart from each other. They suddenly realized that they all had their own individual lives to lead. The following year, it would start to turn sour.

The Beatles opened 1966 with a new album at the top of the chart, 'Rubber Soul', a title coined by Paul to send up the fact that the British record market was at that time dominated by soul music. The album contained another McCartney masterpiece, written this time with just a little help from John Lennon, 'Michelle'. It was composed for the daughter of an

American millionaire, and became the second most recorded of all Beatles songs. The same year, The Overlanders took their own cover version of 'Michelle' to the top of the British chart.

It was a unique song, containing a line of French lyrics.

'I just fancied writing some French words,' Paul confided in Paul Gambaccini. 'I had a friend whose wife taught French . . . and I just asked her . . . what we could figure out that was French. We got words that go together well. It was mainly because I always used to think the song always sounded like a French thing. And I can't speak French, really, so we sorted out some actual words.'

John Lennon explained to David Sheff how his contribution to the song came about: 'Paul and I were staying somewhere, and he walked in and hummed the first few bars with the words. And he says, "Where do I go from here?" I'd been listening to blues singer Nina Simone, who did something like "I Love You" in one of her songs and that made me think of the middle eight – "I love you, I love you, I love you".'

'Rubber Soul' showed The Beatles in a different light. They were drawing away from their 'live' audiences, if that was possible, developing as recording artists, while John and Paul were maturing as songwriters.

Things started to go wrong in June for the group who everyone believed could do no wrong. Whilst undertaking selected engagements in Asia, the group accidentally snubbed the President of the Philippines' wife following a misunderstanding, and they were jeered, jostled and abused all the way to Manila Airport on their way out of the country.

From the safety of London, McCartney said: 'I wouldn't want my worst enemy to go to Manila.'

Worse was to come. In an interview with the London *Evening Standard* some months before, John Lennon had been quoted as saying: 'We are more popular than Jesus now. I don't know which will go first – rock 'n' roll or Christianity. Jesus was all right, but his disciples were thick and ordinary.'

That statement reverberated through America. The Beatles were condemned – their records were banned by radio stations across the States. In the deep South, Beatles records, photographs and memorabilia were publicly burnt.

Prior to the group's American tour in August, John made a public apology, saying he had been misquoted and misunderstood. The tour went ahead as planned. But . . . it wasn't the same any more.

On August 29th, 1966 at Candlestick Park in San Francisco, The Beatles gave their last live public performance together. There would be no more concerts; no turning back. John, Paul, George and Ringo had had enough; they had grown tired of touring. In truth, they had outgrown it all. What had once been exciting, an adventure together when they first started out on the road, had now become a monster they would live without. They didn't like being manipulated by promoters, or attacked by the media. And they hated the macabre rituals that accompanied most performances. Back in their dressing rooms, wheelchair patients, cripples and blind people were pushed in to see them, in the hope that a single touch from a Beatle hand might cure them, might make them walk again . . . or see.

Touring had become a nightmare. With no effort to secure an audience for themselves, their music suffered badly; their playing at times was appalling. They couldn't hear themselves singing or playing on stage anyway above the incessant high-pitched screaming. So why bother any more?

There were other reasons, too. Paul said: 'Why we didn't play live any more was that we wanted to record. That had become the big, big thing.'

What had actually happened was that The Beatles had moved on to another musical dimension. The music they were writing, creating in the studio, was impossible to recreate on stage 'live'. They wanted to give their audience the best, a legacy from Epstein, not poor imitations of the real thing, and the best could only be obtained in the studio. Already they had hinted at things to come with the release of the majestic album, 'Revolver', which ran the gamut of musical progression. The album gave a whole new edge and sophistication to The Beatles' writing, particularly McCartney's, whose versatility as a composer came to the fore on the album through the enigmatic 'Eleanor Rigby', the optimistic 'Good Day Sunshine', the soul-influenced 'Got To Get You Into My Life', the tenderness of 'For No One' and 'Here There And Everywhere' and the fantasy sing-along of 'Yellow Submarine'. 'Revolver' was Paul McCartney's *tour de force* as a writer.

It was after this album had been acclaimed by everyone as a

masterpiece, that Paul McCartney and John Lennon began to be compared with the great English romantic poets of Wordsworth and Blake.

'Revolver' was brilliant. The best, however, was on its way . . .

9

Billy Shears

'It was Paul's idea of making "Sergeant Pepper's Lonely Hearts Club Band" a bit of a link," said George Martin.

The inspiration for the album, admitted Paul, came from The Beach Boys' LP, 'Pet Sounds' . . . 'The musical invention on that is just amazing. When I heard it,' he said, 'I thought what the hell are we going to do? My ideas took off from that standard.'

'Sergeant Pepper' was originally intended to be a theme album about the group's childhood in Liverpool. Paul had contributed 'Penny Lane', a light and breezy celebration of his childhood memories; fond recollections of the barber, the banker, the fireman and the pretty nurse. It painted a vivid picture of a fantasy world and was very Lowry-esque in content. It was an optimistic song, based on reality . . . and like most of McCartney's material, full of hope. John Lennon's contribution was the haunting, eerie and strange, 'Strawberry Fields Forever' with its pessimistic approach to life. The bitterness and aggression of Lennon was again finding expression through his songs. It proved a perfect foil to McCartney's opus. But then . . . they ran out of ideas.

It was Paul who later came up with the idea of writing a fantasy song about a brass band, and as it developed, he suggested the group make the album as if *they* were the brass band, and they were totally divorced from the music and The Beatles. Billy Shears and Sergeant Pepper's Lonely Hearts Club Band became The Beatles' alter ego.

'I was just thinking of nice words, like Sergeant Pepper and Lonely Hearts Club, and they came together for no reason,' said Paul explaining how he wrote the title track. 'But after you have written that down you start to think, "There's this

Sergeant Pepper who has taught the band to play and got them going so that at least they find one number. They're a bit of a brass band in a way, but also a rock band in a way, because they've got the San Francisco thing".'

John Lennon told *Playboy*: 'It was Paul's idea and I remember he worked on it a lot and suddenly called me to go into the studio and said it was time to write some songs. Under the pressure of only ten days, I managed to come up with "Lucy In The Sky With Diamonds" and "A Day In The Life".'

By now, all four Beatles were experimenting with drugs and LSD. They had been involved with taking drugs since the Hamburg days when preladin would keep them awake for their manic six and seven hour sets. But later they moved on, through an assortment of substances, hallucinatory drugs, hashish, and pills, to LSD. It 'widened' their minds as they admitted, and helped them write some stunning music, which manifested itself in 'Sergeant Pepper'. It is pure speculation, however, to assume that without LSD, 'Pepper' would never have been created.

In February, with the group firmly entrenched in the studio recording – 'We were into that total psychedelic thing where we got into the studio and made it a magic world,' admitted Paul. 'We were making our own little Pepperland in the studio,' – 'Penny Lane' and 'Strawberry Fields Forever' were released as a double A-sided single. It was The Beatles' fourteenth Parlophone single, and the first one *not* to make it to the top of the chart in Britain since 'Please Please Me'. It was kept from the top spot ironically, by Engelbert Humperdinck's 'Please Release Me', although it did go to Number 1 in the USA. The critics said The Beatles were slipping; could this be the end?

Not long afterwards, they had their answer.

'Sergeant Pepper' took 700 hours of studio time to make. It cost £25,000 and was recorded only on a 4-track system! When it was finally released, the *New York Times* said it had the power to *destroy* rock 'n' roll. John Lennon warned Paul that the album might not sell. It became a musical masterpiece, universally acclaimed for its magnificence and invention.

'"Sergeant Pepper" was the watershed which changed the recording art form from something that merely made amusing sounds, into something that will stand the test of time as a valid art form: sculpture in music if you like,' said George Martin.

Critic Kenneth Tynan added: '"Sergeant Pepper" – a decisive moment in the history of Western Civilization.'

Professor Langton Winner of the Massachusetts Institute of Technology echoed: 'The closest Western Civilization has come to unity since the Congress of Vienna in 1815, was the week the "Sergeant Pepper" album was released. For a brief while, the irreparably fragmented consciousness of the West was unified, at least in the minds of the young.'

Amazingly, there are no love songs on 'Sergeant Pepper'. Yet the songs in themselves are superb.

Of the dozen track package, McCartney wrote five – 'Sergeant Pepper's Lonely Hearts Club Band', 'Lovely Rita', 'Fixing A Hole', 'Getting Better' and 'When I'm 64' – written long before he ever dreamed of making it to the toppermost, when *he* was 16. Paul collaborated with John Lennon on 'With A Little Help From My Friends', 'She's Leaving Home' and the masterful, 'A Day In The Life'.

At the time of 'Pepper', Lennon and McCartney had got back into old habits, they were writing together once more, collaborating, sparking off ideas in each other. It was good to see.

John said: 'Paul and I were definitely working together, especially on "A Day In The Life". That was real . . . the way we wrote a lot of the time: you'd write a good bit, the part that was easy, like "I read the news today" . . . then you got stuck or whenever it got hard, instead of carrying on, you just drop it. Then we would meet each other and I would sing half and he would be inspired to write the next bit or vice versa. He was a bit shy about it, because I think he thought it's already a good song. Sometimes we wouldn't let each other interfere with a song either, because you tend to be a bit lax with someone else's stuff, you experiment a bit.'

On 'A Day In The Life', the composers were inspired by a newspaper story from the *Daily Mail*, in which John's friend, Tara Browne, the Guinness heir, had been killed in a car crash: 'He blew his mind out in a car . . .' Paul wrote the phrase that pulled the song completely together: 'I'd love to turn you on . . .' and contributed the entire middle section, which was in truth, a totally separate song.

'It was another song altogether,' said Paul. 'It just happened to fit. It was just me remembering what it was like to run up the road to catch the bus to school, having a smoke and going into class. We decided, bugger this, we're going to write a turn-on song. It was a reflection of my schooldays. I would have a Woodbine and somebody would speak and I would go into a dream. This is the only one on the album which was written as a deliberate provocation. A stick-that-in-your-pipe . . . but what we want is to turn you on to the truth rather than pot.'

The song was subsequently banned by the BBC for its connections with drugs.

'Sergeant Pepper' re-established The Beatles – if they ever needed re-establishing – as the world's foremost pop group. And in June, they were chosen to represent BBC Television's contribution to a live, round-the-world, TV special, as part of the Canadian Expo '67 celebrations. John and Paul wrote 'All You Need Is Love' specially for the show. A worldwide television audience of 400,000,000 saw them recording the song in the studios, with a little help from some of their friends from the rock and pop world, including Mick Jagger, Keith Moon, Marianne Faithfull, Keith Richard, and Paul's brother, Michael. The song once again put them back at Number 1 in the charts, but with that exposure, it couldn't fail!

That summer of all-you-need-is-love-and-happiness saw Paul and the rest of the group in Bangor, North Wales, studying meditation under Maharishi Mahesh Yogi, to whom George Harrison had introduced them. They were desperately looking for themselves, trying to find the hidden meaning of life. They had tried drugs . . . and that had failed! It was here they were told of Brian Epstein's death from a supposed overdose of sleeping pills and alcohol. Not for the first time in their career, The Beatles were devastated.

Paul said: 'No-one could possibly replace Brian.' He added that The Beatles would not appoint another manager.

Brian's death effectively meant the end of The Beatles. Although his influence on the group had long since passed, Epstein was the man who literally kept them together – and kept them from destroying themselves. They respected him immensely because he allowed them to indulge themselves in their music, while he got on with the business, though at times, some of his dealings on the group's behalf left a lot to be desired. He actually lost more money than he made, through naive business transactions. Prior to Epstein's death, however, Paul McCartney even suggested bringing in a business associate to help Brian and the group over the financial transactions. The name mooted was Allen Klein! Paul had been impressed with how the American business manager had handled The Rolling Stones' monetary affairs. He was sure he could do the same for The Beatles.

John Lennon was to say later: 'After Brian died, we collapsed. Paul took over and supposedly led us. But what is leading us when we went round in circles? We broke up then. That was the disintegration.'

The first post-Epstein enterprise The Beatles undertook, was a fantasy film – 'Magical Mystery Tour' – which flopped badly, and the group came in for some bitter and twisted criticism when the movie was shown on BBC Television on Boxing Day 1967. Because of the adverse reaction from the critics and the public alike, the film was never released in America.

Paul, who directed the film said: 'We goofed really.' The film was one of those occasions when, according to McCartney, 'I do things that aren't necessarily thought out.'

Still, The Beatles had taken a fall, but survived the heavy tirade of critical flak that was hurled at them. And, at the beginning of February 1968, left Britain for India, to complete their course in transcendental meditation, begun the year before in North Wales, and interrupted by Brian Epstein's death. It was to prove an unhappy trip for all of them . . . and each one became more and more disillusioned with the Yogi's teachings, so much so that Paul and Ringo came home early. The tranquillity and peaceful atmosphere of India did give McCartney the opportunity of writing several new songs, including 'Rocky Raccoon', (co-written with John Lennon and with a little help from singing star Donovan), 'Birthday', 'Mother Nature's Son' . . . and 'Junk' and 'Teddy Boy', which were later to be featured on his first solo album, 'McCartney'.

Back in Britain, the next Beatle project on the agenda was the formation of their own company, Apple – named by Paul after a painting of an apple by his favourite artist Magritte.

The idea was founded on good intentions: to set up a creative empire where The Beatles would use their considerable money and their philanthropic ability, to promote and develop new artistic talent of all kinds – an organization dedicated to helping writers and composers, musicians and inventors, artists of all kinds. The group would provide the financial backing so that talented people had the chance to be heard, to be seen and to get their ideas off the ground, *without* having to ask 'the men in suits', as Paul called them, for money. 'We want to help other people,' he said, 'but without doing it like a charity and without seeming like patrons of the arts.'

The first venture was to set up a boutique in London's Baker Street area, with clothes made by a Dutch design team called The Fool. It closed down within six months with a loss of over £100,000. Later the group changed its name from Beatles Ltd. to Apple Corps to show a sceptical world that they really did mean business, and had confidence in their own beliefs. They also set up a business office in London's Wigmore Street.

The whole idea of Apple, though, was destined to failure. The Beatles wanted something they could control themselves . . . but they were out of their depth. Although having tremendous musical talent, when it came to business acumen, they were naive, and lacking ability. No-one would take overall responsibility. With four great egos clashing together, no-one was allowed a free hand on his own. The people they had initially wanted to help – people like they had once been themselves, in need of a lucky break – helped themselves to whatever was going, taking advantage of The Beatles' generosity. Freeloaders abounded when Apple moved its headquarters to Savile Row. They lost money with such regularity and speed, that by 1969, John Lennon announced he was down to his last £40,000. 'Apple is losing money,' he said. 'If it carries on like this we'll all be broke in six months.' In a year, the company had lost £1,000,000 . . . and for the first time in a long, long time, The Beatles were overdrawn at the bank.

Lennon would later say: 'Apple was full of hustlers and spongers. The staff came and went as they pleased and were lavish with money and hospitality.

'People were robbing us, living on us . . . £18,000–20,000 a week was rolling out of Apple and nobody was doing anything about it.'

He added later: 'Apple was the manifestation of Beatle naivety, collective naivety: We said, "We're going to do this to help everybody," and all that, and we got conned. We really didn't get approached by the best artists, we got all the bums from everywhere else.'

Drastic action had to be taken – and it arrived in the burly form of American business troubleshooter, Allen Klein, who had been recommended to the group by Rolling Stone Mick Jagger. Allen Klein had heard Lennon's pleas in the Press and had decided to take action of his own. He believed he was the right man for the job, and also desperately wanted to become the manager of the world's most famous group.

This time, however, Paul McCartney was against Klein's intervention. He wanted his own father-in-law, Lee Eastman – the well-respected American lawyer – to take over the running of The Beatles' affairs, and for a while, the two Americans worked closely together sorting out the complex legal situation. It was only when John, George and Ringo – against the better judgement of Paul McCartney – appointed Klein as The Beatles manager, that the rift in the group widened. Paul had been outvoted on the appointment, but he strongly disagreed with Allen Klein's business methods and wanted no part of the deal. There was a way out, but it would mean suing his friends.

'I didn't like Allen Klein, but they wanted to go with him,' said Paul. 'I figured that was a bad thing to do and would lose us everything we'd gained. Later that turned out to be true and everyone got rid of Allen Klein, and said, "thank you" to me for it. But I had to go through all this craziness. It seemed I was pitted against *them* for my own gain – it was actually for the common good.'

Apple, however, did have its successes. The record side of the company thrived and accumulated a formidable stable of stars, including Mary Hopkin, and Badfinger, for whom Paul wrote and produced; Jackie Lomax, Billy Preston and James Taylor. There were single ventures, too, with artists as diverse as the MJQ and the Black Dyke Mills Brass Band, and, of course, The Beatles' solo projects, particularly by John Lennon with Yoko Ono, and George Harrison.

Naturally, The Beatles were the label's biggest asset. They gave Apple Records its first Number 1 in the fall of 1968, with the release of the group's longest-ever single, at 7.15 minutes long, and one of their biggest-selling of all time – the McCartney composition, 'Hey Jude'. It proved, that despite all the problems at Apple Corps, The Beatles could still make great music.

'Hey Jude' was written with John's son, Julian, in mind.

'I happened to be driving to see Cynthia Lennon,' Paul told Paul Gambaccini. 'I think it was just after John and she had broken up, and I was quite mates with Julian. And I was vaguely singing this song . . . and it was like, 'Hey Jules'. And then I just thought a better name was Jude, a bit country and western.'

John Lennon believed the song had been written for him and Yoko, with whom he was now living following the marriage failure with Cynthia. He told Paul it was very avant-garde. 'It's one of Paul's best,' said John.

The Beatles' first Apple album, 'The Beatles' (commonly known as 'The White Album'), proved to be an assortment of songs, some good, some not so good, and some that should never have made the recording studio. However, it marked another innovation for the group because they decided to make it a *double* album package. It was an adventurous move. Until then, only classical LPs had been issued as double albums. But John and Paul had a backlog of songs they wanted to use, and George chipped in with several of his own. In truth, there was enough good material to make one excellent album, the rest was throwaway, which in better times would have been democratically thrown out by all concerned. But The Beatles were breaking away from each other . . . and nobody cared.

For the first time, there was a clear distinction between Lennon and McCartney songs on the album; between Paul's commercial instincts and John's 'determination to create electronic sound poems', as Philip Norman had suggested. Instead of being a group performance as a whole, the album came together as a series of solo projects, using the individual Beatles as session musicians. It was a poor follow-up to 'Sergeant Pepper', but that was *always* going to be a hard act to follow. Yet, taken out of the context of the album and set alone on their own merits, some of the songs *were* equal to those on 'Pepper': Lennon's inventive 'Happiness Is A Warm Gun', the wistful 'Julia' and 'I'm So Tired'; Harrison's emotive 'While My Guitar Gently Weeps'; and McCartney's 'Back In The USSR', 'Ob-La-Di Ob-La-Da', 'Blackbird' and 'I Will'. The end, however, for the world's greatest group was in sight. They now lacked the one thing that had kept them going in the past against all the odds – *direction*. And as four creative egos strained, Ringo Starr walked out. It was just the jolt to the system they needed to make them realize things were going wrong, and after much coaxing, the diminutive drummer returned to the fold.

'We made the double album,' said Lennon. 'It's like if you took each track off it and made it all mine, and all George's . . . it was just me and a backing group, Paul and a backing group. We broke up then.'

With John becoming increasingly more involved with Yoko's artistic ventures and his own avant-garde musical excursions, it was left to Paul McCartney to bring The Beatles together again. He came up with an exciting idea that appealed to John and George and Ringo for their next combined musical scheme. They would return to their roots, rehearse a set of numbers and then give a special 'live' performance, before an invited audience, as a purely private occasion. Throughout the planning, the rehearsing, the recording *and* the live climax to the project, they would film everything, warts and all, for a full-length documentary movie on the life and times of The Beatles. It was ambitious, it was cheeky . . . but it might work, and it might keep The Beatles together as a musical unit. Paul figured it was certainly worth a try. But as they worked on the songs, recording over a hundred old and new, things started to go wrong. Relationships within the group, between the four individual Beatles, crumbled and fell apart. The whole idea seemed to be going nowhere, fast. It was becoming a giant bore.

In an effort to bring some kind of co-ordination to the group, Paul took it upon himself to provide the motivation, the drive and leadership. The others rejected it. They objected to his bossiness, telling them what to do, and even how to play their own instruments.

'In order to get things together, Paul would try and get everybody organized,' admitted George Martin. 'And would be rather over bossy, which the boys disliked. But it was the only way of getting them together.'

The film was originally called 'Get Back', but the nearest The Beatles came to a live performance in concert, was a remarkable rooftop jam session, above the London skyline atop Apple headquarters at 3 Savile Row . . . until they were requested to stop playing by a sheepish policeman, after complaints from neighbours.

In the end The Beatles grew tired of the whole project, and it simply petered out. Dozens of cans of film were put on a shelf to gather dust, until eventually Allen Klein sold the rights to United Artists. The recording tapes were put to one side too; no-one really knew what to do with them. No-one wanted to get involved, certainly none of The Beatles, who went off to pursue their own solo ventures. Ringo was becoming increasingly involved with acting; George was experimenting with electronics; Paul was recording Mary Hopkin, and had several other recording projects under supervision and was working towards a solo album; John had Yoko, and was involved with experimentation of all kinds – music and art. Whenever Paul was in John's company after he had met Yoko, he felt he had to write or even say something avant-garde.

In the spring of 1969, McCartney made one last effort to bring the warring factions within the group together, and to unite The Beatles, suggesting they make an album – 'like the old days'. Reluctantly, the others consented, and George Martin was contacted to produce it. They started recording in June.

'Paul came to me and said, "Let's get back and record like we used to. Will you produce an album like we used to?" So I said, "Yes, if you will allow me to, I will." And that's how we made "Abbey Road". It wasn't quite like the old days, because they were still working on their own songs, and they would bring in other people as musicians to work for them, rather than being a team. The one side that Paul and I worked on was the connected one and that had slightly reluctant contributions from John, because he didn't really like production – he liked good old rock 'n' roll. So one side was to please him, as a kind of collection of songs. The other side was to please Paul.'

It proved a remarkable album when released in September and even outsold 'Sergeant Pepper'! But it failed in its attempt to stop the rot within the group. The end was nigh!

By the time 'Abbey Road' hit the record shops, John Lennon had been out on his own, experiencing the buzz and apprehension of working on stage in front of a live audience again. In July, he had enjoyed chart success with his solo single, 'Give Peace A Chance', fronting The Plastic Ono Band with whom he had recently performed at a rock 'n' roll festival in Toronto, Canada. The band had been quickly put together for the engagement and included John and Yoko, Alan White on drums, Eric Clapton on guitar and Klaus Voorman, The Beatles' old friend from Hamburg, on bass.

On the flight back to Britain after a great reception from the Canadian audience, John realized that he didn't need The Beatles any more; they had become surplus to his own requirements. He could make it on his own; Toronto had proved it. He announced to his close circle of friends his decision to quit the group.

At the next Apple meeting, however, Paul McCartney played the ace card he believed *must* bring the group back together again. He had seen how excited Lennon had become after the concert in Toronto. Live gigging had brought back the old sparkle and breathed new life into him. This was the solution.

'I think we should get back on the road,' said Paul. 'Go and do the clubs. Sod it, let's go back to square one and remember what we're all about.'

Lennon's reply stunned him . . . and silenced the meeting.

'I think you're daft,' he said. 'I wasn't going to tell you, but I'm breaking the group up. It feels good; it's like a divorce.'

Paul couldn't believe what he was hearing. He thought it must be a passing phase, after all, hadn't George and Ringo walked out in the past, yet always returned later? John would. But Lennon was adamant! It was all over. But he agreed he would not make a public announcement of his intentions, in case it jeopardized any of the negotiations Allen Klein was finalizing on the group's and Apple's behalf. He kept his word.

Paul, meanwhile, had his own problems.

With the release of 'Abbey Road' in America, Detroit disc jockey, Russ Gibbs, made the astounding claim that Paul McCartney was dead! And he subsequently backed his claim by revealing a series of cryptic clues The Beatles themselves had set down on various record releases. On 'Strawberry Fields Forever' for instance, a musical phrase played backwards at the end of the record, was supposedly John Lennon singing 'I buried Paul' when played forwards. On the cover of 'Sergeant Pepper', The Beatles are standing by Paul's recently dug grave, while on the inside cover, Paul is wearing a badge with the legend 'OPD' – 'Officially Pronounced Dead' – it didn't matter that it was really an emblem of the Ontario Police Department. The song, 'A Day In The Life', tells the gruesome story of Paul's death.

According to Gibbs, The Beatles and their manager had decided to cover up the whole story and had brought in a young Scot, called William Campbell, to impersonate McCartney. The death-mongers had insisted he had undergone extensive plastic surgery to make him look like Paul.

'Abbey Road' only fuelled the fire, as the cover purported to depict a funeral procession, with The Beatles walking across the road in single file: John was the clergyman, George was the grave digger, Ringo was the undertaker. Paul, in a suit walking barefoot between them, (apparently a Mafia symbol of death), was the corpse. The Volkswagen car parked near to the crossing had the number plate '28 IF', which was translated as meaning Paul would have been 28 years-old *if* he had lived! There were numerous so-called signs on several other Beatles tracks.

When the reports of his death were circulated around the world, Paul had disappeared to his Scottish farm to record material for his forthcoming solo album. His non-appearance in London added to the intensity of the mystery and rumours. When he was finally tracked down, he dismissed all the scaremongers by saying: 'The rumours of my death have been greatly exaggerated. However, if I was dead, I'm sure I'd be the last to know.'

Events were putting a serious strain on McCartney, and inevitably his work suffered. It suffered even more when shortly after the death story began to subside, Northern Songs, The Beatles' publishing company, was taken over by ATV. It was announced that The Beatles were to sell all their shares in Northern Songs to ATV at a price 'in accordance with the terms laid down by the Take-over Panel!'

Allen Klein, realizing that there was a lot of money gathering dust along with the tapes of the 'Get Back' venture, brought in Phil Spector to try and sort them out . . . and knock the twenty-nine hours of taped music into some kind of shape for release, hopefully, as a single album.

When Spector finished the mammoth task in hand in the editing room, an acetate of the proposed completed album was sent to all four Beatles for approval. McCartney was furious when he heard it. He hated the way Spector, someone he had always admired in the past for his excellent work in the music industry, had over-produced his stirring ballads, 'Let It Be', and especially 'The Long And Winding Road', by the introduction of strings and a full chorus in the background. It certainly wasn't what *he* had intended when he wrote the songs – their strength and appeal were in their simplicity and needed no fantastic production to get home their message. Paul immediately demanded that Allen Klein restore the original versions to the album. He declined, and McCartney failed to get his own way.

By now, he'd had enough of the back-biting and the bitching that surrounded The Beatles.

When the album was finally released in May 1970, under the title 'Let It Be', it became The Beatles' epitaph.

Seven days later when the movie of the same name was premièred in Liverpool and London, none of The Beatles attended either ceremony.

Two weeks prior to the release of 'Let It Be', Paul McCartney had issued his own solo album, called simply, 'McCartney'. In the ensuing press release, he announced to the world that he had left The Beatles . . . through 'personal differences, business differences, musical differences.'

On December 31st, 1970, he started High Court proceedings to end The Beatles partnership. It was the end of a beautiful friendship.

George Martin said: 'The great thing about The Beatles was that they were of their time. Their timing was right. They didn't choose it, someone chose it for them, but the timing was right, and they have left their mark in history because of that . . . they expressed the mood of the people, their own generation.'

10

Lennon and McCartney

PAUL MCCARTNEY'S MUSICAL partnership with John Lennon was not a partnership in the true sense, more a collaboration of two great talents, although everything they wrote – either separately or together – was credited to *Lennon and McCartney*. It was an agreement they had made when they first started writing songs, back in 1957, and a simple handshake became a binding contract.

In the early days of writing, John and Paul were heavily influenced by the rock 'n' roll music of Elvis Presley, Chuck Berry, Little Richard and the great pioneers of rock. Yet, they also admired tremendously the styles of the American pop composers, Leiber and Stoller, Mann and Weil, Felice and Boudleaux Bryant and Goffin and King – and they learned their songwriting from them all – and hoped one day to emulate them. All the time, they firmly believed that the best songs were written by teams; they liked the idea themselves, and so Lennon and McCartney became a team. The name sounded right – it had style.

For much of the time, they wrote separately, coming together only when they were stuck for inspiration and needed help, or to present a new song for the other's approval. They were their own critics and often the other would deliberately change a line or a phrase, virtually for change's sake. But they were learning from each other's tentative steps in song development. Paul, the more musically adept, encouraged John to expand his own music by introducing a larger variety of notes and chords to his compositions; John helped Paul to expand his lyrical vocabulary and to experiment with words.

The formula stayed with them throughout their work

together. 'They were always songwriters who helped each other out with little bits and pieces,' said George Martin. 'One would have most of a song finished and play it to the other and he'd say, "Well, why don't you do this?" That was just about the way their collaboration worked.'

'John and I were perfect for each other,' said Paul. 'I could do stuff he might not be in the mood for, egg him on in a certain direction he might not want to go. And he could do the same with me.'

McCartney, however, has always been suspicious of a songwriting formula.

He told Vic Garbazini: 'The minute I've got a formula, I try and change it. People used to ask us what comes first – the music or the words? Or Lennon and McCartney, who does what? We all did a bit of everything. Sometimes I wrote the words and sometimes John did; sometimes I'd write a tune and sometimes he would.'

He added, putting everything into perspective: 'But when you think of Lennon and McCartney, you assume all the songs were written together. They weren't actually, probably eighty per cent were written apart, and twenty per cent together, that's about the right split.'

In those early days John and Paul looked to America for inspiration. 'We took all the American influences and stewed them up in a British way,' he admitted. And they learned how to construct songs, how to use hooks for effect, how to repeat lines for emphasis. They experimented with harmonies and guitar riffs, serving a long but valuable apprenticeship, copying what they had heard. Adapting. Changing. The black American girl groups were another influence; from them they borrowed their style of lyrical formations, emphasis and rhyme, although in those days, lyrics weren't too important to them, and they would simply sing out any old words that came into their heads and sounded right, as long as they fitted the melody line and construction of the song. McCartney went round for days singing 'scrambled eggs' to the tune of 'Yesterday' before he attempted to write a more poignant lyric. In later years, however, McCartney would return to this free-form approach of writing, using words as lyrical sounds and rhymes purely to gain effect more than meaning, when composing material for Wings or his own solo ventures. 'Jet' and 'Let 'Em In' are two perfect examples of the effectiveness of words and sounds that mean very little as story-telling lyrics.

'We didn't care about lyrics as long as the song had some vague theme: she loves you, he loves her, they all love each other,' said John. 'It was the hook line and sound we were going for.'

From the emerging Tamla Motown stable, they got atmosphere and presence.

By now they were developing and devising subconsciously a way of being able to copy and mimic other writers' styles to use in their own composing. They also took the things they liked in other writers' work, and liberally adapted them for their own songwriting in the same way that their stage act and overall musical sound, borrowed much from many other sources which they remoulded into something of their own, with great success.

Paul put it bluntly: 'We used to nick songs and titles.'

But whatever they begged, or stole, or borrowed, John and Paul improved.

Later on they would acknowledge the great debt they owed to the forefathers of rock 'n' roll by writing songs directly influenced by the people they admired so much, like Chuck Berry, Fats Domino, Little Richard and Elvis Presley. Carl Perkins inspired them to compose 'One After 909' and 'What Goes On'; 'Please Please Me' was originally written in the style of Roy Orbison; and 'Oh Darling' was a celebration of the work of Paul Anka. Buddy Holly figured prominently in their musical influence, and his style of writing songs reared its head in the McCartney-penned compositions, 'I'll Follow The Sun', 'World Without Love', 'Nobody I Know' and 'I'll Be On My Way'.

As they progressed, John and Paul's music and lyrics reacted to their quickly changing lives. They were writing in an ever-changing world and their music reflected the changes going on all around them. They were quick to seize upon anything they thought useful; newspaper articles, television, fashion, trends. And, as they matured and grew up, so too did their songs, though at first their early efforts were of very poor quality and often banal. Yet, undeterred, they continued to write at an amazing pace as if trying to prove something to themselves and each other. They wrote at first using guitars, but later both preferred to use a piano because it was far more appropriate to their needs. On occasions, however, they would often whistle segments or phrases of a new idea, a half-written song, to each other, hoping the other one would pick up the thread, elaborate and develop it further. And they disciplined themselves to write, often writing for the sake of writing, in an effort to learn their trade. It came in handy in later days, when The Beatles had deadlines to meet to complete the writing of new material for albums. When recording, they would often find that they had only enough new material for three-quarters of the LP and then specifically sat down to write for that album. They gave themselves a time limit in which to compose and then knocked the resulting songs into shape with the help of the rest of the group . . . and George Martin.

Once they had mastered the art of songwriting, the results were spectacular. They broke all the rules, made new ones, and then broke them all over again.

The music of Lennon and McCartney revolutionized popular music throughout the world by expanding its horizons and bringing respectability, and a whole new acceptance from a wider audience.

Like the American pioners of rock 'n' roll before them in the 1950s, whose music they adored and regularly refurbished, John and Paul inspired a whole new generation. But unlike those same American founding fathers of rock 'n' roll, Lennon and McCartney bridged the huge gap between musical generations. As someone once wrote: 'Once Lennon and McCartney's music hit the public arena, it was public property.' It became international and spoke all languages. Lennon and McCartney owned it no longer; it belonged to the world.

For too many years, Britain had been the poor relation of American popular music. Rock 'n' roll had been created in the USA – and what America did today, Britain followed tomorrow. John and Paul's music changed all that by breaking down the barrier to America – to open up a whole new and vast territory. And yet, they did it with America's help, by absorbing everything that was best in American music, repackaging it in their own style and presentation, and selling it back across the Atlantic. It was different.

They stayed way ahead of the field because they knew their own limitations – and stuck rigidly to them. As Lennon once said, if a song didn't work – 'drop it'. They experimented in writing on each of their albums, using audience reaction as their test case. Each album progressed musically from the one before and developed, apart from 'The Beatles' and 'Let It Be', yet there were innovations on each of these albums. But in that way, their songwriting never went stale, never stayed in a rut. It was allowed to breathe and expand. They also never stopped looking for ways to improve. Journalist and writer Charlie Gillett commented: 'They listened to a vast number of current releases, read newspapers, looked at photographs, remembered bits of slang from their youth. And from it all, they produced a commentary of their times, picking up ideas so fast that it sometimes seemed they had thought of them first.'

When the soul-boom started to erupt in Britain, McCartney wrote 'Got To Get You Into My Life'; he was one of the first people to experiment with reggae on 'Ob-La-Di Ob-La-Da' – he took the expression 'Ob-La-Di Ob-La-Da' from a Jamaican friend, Jimmy Scott, who had been using it for years in his band, Jimmy Scott And His Ob-La-Di, Ob-La-Da Band. It means literally, 'Life goes on'.

John and Paul never stopped listening to their contemporaries to see what the opposition was doing, and they were always being influenced by other artists. McCartney admitted that he was inspired by The Beach Boys to come up with the whole 'Sergeant Pepper' idea, and he later borrowed from the American group's surfing sound to write 'Back In The USSR' (the original title of 'I'm *Backing* The USSR' was thought too strong even by Beatle standards), which was inspired by Brian Wilson's 'Surfin' USA', which in turn was inspired by Chuck Berry's 'Sweet Little Sixteen'. The musical merry-go-round had turned full circle.

The Who provided the spark that made Paul write 'Helter Skelter', which in turn motivated cult-leader Charles Manson to organize the brutal Sharon Tate – La Bianca killings in Los Angeles in 1969. The American psychopath misinterpreted the meaning of Paul's song which he thought was telling him the end of the world was at hand. 'Helter Skelter' became Manson's name for the race war.

Paul said: '"Helter Skelter" came about because I read in the *Melody Maker*, that The Who had made some track or other that was the loudest, most raucous rock 'n' roll, the dirtiest thing they've ever done. I didn't know what track they were talking about, but it made me think, "Okay, got to do it." And I got totally off on that one little sentence in the paper and I said, "*We've* got to do the loudest, most raucous . . ." and it ended up as "Helter Skelter".'

In turn, their contemporaries fed off Lennon and McCartney's inspiration. The Byrds, Creedence Clearwater Revival, Cream, and later the Electric Light Orchestra. There were many more . . .

John Lennon admitted that The Rolling Stones copied virtually everything The Beatles pioneered. After their album, 'Sergeant Pepper's Lonely Hearts Club Band', The Stones produced, 'Their Satanic Majesties Request'; after 'All You Need Is Love', The Stones produced 'We Love You'.

But it was John and Paul who inspired Mick Jagger and Keith Richard to start writing songs of their own, after Lennon and McCartney had been asked to write a song for the London-based group to record. They came up with 'I Wanna Be Your Man'.

John Lennon told the story: 'We were taken down by Brian Epstein to meet them at the club they were playing in Richmond. They wanted a song and we went to see what kind of stuff they did. Paul had this bit of a song and we played it roughly to them, and they said. "Yeah, okay, that's our style." But it was really only a lick.

'So Paul and I went off in a corner of the room, and finished the song off while they were sitting there talking. We came back and Mick and Keith said, "Jesus, look at that, they just went over there and wrote it." You know right in front of their eyes. We gave it to them. It was a throwaway. Ringo sang it for us – and The Stones did their version. It shows how much importance we put on them. We weren't going to give them anything great.

'Anyway, Mick and Keith said, "If they can write songs so easily, we should try it." They say it inspired them to start writing together.'

From the start of their own songwriting partnership, the two opposite poles that were Lennon and McCartney – two totally different and complex characters – manifested themselves in their writing. Lennon's wit and sarcasm, his aggression and bitterness; the rebel, found a genuine expression in his songs. And yet, he was capable of writing some of the most tender of love songs. Was it all an act? McCartney seemed to walk through life with a smile on his face, no matter what happened. Like Charles Dickens' character Mr Micawber he was convinced that something would turn up. It was a message conveyed in his songs. As they matured, they developed their own identities as songwriters and went their separate ways. McCartney was the romantic, the dreamer. John was the cynic, the realist. These qualities, in the main, permeated into the characters they created in their songs. For Paul, Desmond and Molly, Rita, the banker, barber and the fireman from Penny Lane, Honey Pie, and even Maxwell, were creatures of hope with a genuine warmth. John's creations, Mr Mustard, Polythene Pam, Sexy Sadie and Henry the Horse, were slightly out of focus, grotesque and figures of pity.

'Paul contributed a lightness, an optimism . . . while I would always go for the sadness, the discords,' said John. It was a point proved on several of the songs on which they collaborated together. On 'We Can Work It Out', McCartney wrote the optimistic verse, while John contributed the pessimistic middle – 'Life is very short . . .'. On 'A Day In The Life', John's verse is harsh, cold and stark, while Paul's middle section is alive, vibrant.

Back at the beginning of their association, they wrote at Paul's house or Julia's, or maybe George Harrison's. Later, on the road, they would write in the back of the van, or on the tour coach. In Hamburg, they often wrote in the Seaman's Mission, and later at John's house in Weybridge, where Paul composed amongst others, 'Here There And Everywhere', 'Good Day Sunshine' and 'Eleanor Rigby'. Later still, the studio became a favourite spot.

Early on, John and Paul chose the usual subjects of boy meets girl, boy loses girl, boy finds another girl, as their themes for their songwriting. They wove stories of adolescent love and teenage dreams, although as if to distance themselves from any thoughts of love they might have, they often wrote in the third person, becoming the narrator of the song, rather than the subject; as if telling a story to a friend rather than being part of it on a one-to-one basis: 'She Loves You'; 'I'm A Loser', 'You're Gonna Lose That Girl', 'Hey Jude', 'Every Little Thing', 'And Your Bird Can Sing', 'I've Just Seen A Face'. It was more often a case of 'And I Love Her', than 'I Love You'. But love in all its facets became – and remained – the main subject, particularly for Paul.

'It's always been traditional to have love as a theme for songs,' he said. 'It's nice.' And for McCartney, relationships between people have always been the subject of much of his work, although: 'I never usually write a song and think, "Right, now this is going to be about something specific." It's just that the words happen. I never try to make any serious social point. Just words to go with music.'

His songs are about life: 'I think politics should be kept for the politicians,' he said in his Beatle-days. 'I don't write or do anything seriously. I always want to do it for a laugh.' His attitude, however, changed briefly in the early 1970s, when he wrote and recorded, 'Give Ireland Back To The Irish' as a reaction to Bloody Sunday in Northern Ireland.

During the halcyon days of The Beatles, Paul McCartney found his inspiration to write in many forms. It was deep-rooted in his family life. A secure and loving home and family background meant a lot to Paul; in love, he found hope for the future. He had a happy childhood and often returned to those days to conjure up his memories of youth. 'Penny Lane', where his father took him for haircuts – 'It's part fact, part nostalgia,' said Paul, 'for a place which is a great place.' 'Magical Mystery Tour' and memories of his trips to nowhere in particular out into the Cheshire countryside on a charabanc. 'Yellow Submarine', a product of his imagination inspired by Saturday morning pictures.

Paul's family played its part, too. The McCartney matriarch, Aunty Jin, has been featured in several of Paul's songs – there is a great warmth and affection between the two of them. Paul wrote an instrumental for her called 'Aunty Jin's Theme' which was later revised with words, under the title of 'I've Just Seen A Face'. Uncle Ernie, Uncle Albert and Brother Michael would later feature in McCartney songs.

His father, Jim McCartney, was also a major influence. Paul was tremendously proud of his dad's musical achievements with his own band – Jim Mac's Band – who played during the 1920s and '30s . . . and that whole era of syncopation and vaudeville has been regularly featured in Paul's music. He always had a great love for the razz-matazz of showbusiness, and Hollywood musicals, and from an early age developed a liking for Fred Astaire and Jack Buchanan. It was dad's era, too. In truth, Paul would have felt very much at home as an all-round entertainer, singing and dancing the soft-shoe shuffle, a point which gathered momentum in 1973 on his TV spectacular, 'James Paul McCartney'. The influence rubbed off on 'When I'm 64', a teenager looking at retirement with rose-tinted spectacles; the flapperish 'Honey Pie'; 'Your Mother Should Know' and the '30s-style ode to his sheepdog, 'Martha My Dear'.

Whimsy and fantasy also played their parts in shaping McCartney's music, through 'Rocky Raccoon' and 'Mother Nature's Son', although there were several others.

'A lot of my songs are made up – it's the kind of song I like to write, like "Maxwell's Silver Hammer". It's just a silly story about all these people I've never met – I don't think I'd like to meet some of them. It's just like someone writing a play, you don't have to know these people, you just make them up,' said Paul.

Loneliness is another subject, personified in 'Lady Madonna', 'Blackbird', 'Fool On The Hill' and 'Eleanor Rigby' with its Dickensian atmosphere and sepia-tinted portrait of life.

'With a lot of songs I do, the first line is it,' said Paul. 'It's all in the first line and then you have to go and write the second line. With "Eleanor Rigby", I had ". . . picks up the rice in a church where the wedding has been" – that was the one big line that started it off.'

Characters came next. McCartney explained: 'I was sitting at the piano when I thought of it. And I got this name in my head – Daisy Hawkins . . . I don't know why. Then the name Father McCartney came to me . . . and all the lonely people. But I thought people would think it was supposed to be my dad, sitting, knitting his socks. So I went through the telephone book and got the name McKenzie.'

'Eleanor Rigby' was another song that Paul revised for his movie 'Give My Regards To Broad Street'. In the film's setting, the song evoked pictures of a nineteenth century England, of Dickensian London and days gone by . . . the song captured the period to perfection. Prior to the movie's release, McCartney elaborated further on the song.

'The name Rigby was from a shop in Bristol where I saw above the window, Rigby & Co . . . and Eleanor was probably subconsciously taken from the name of actress Eleanor Bron, who we were working with during that time.

'The lonely people line is something I'd seen while I was growing up in Liverpool . . . lonely old people in flats on their own.' Back to his childhood once again.

He concluded: 'I took the song down to John's house in Weybridge. We sat around laughing, got stoned, and finished it off. There was never an Eleanor Rigby.'

John contributed much of the last verse to the song.

But there were other forms of inspiration that moved Paul to write: 'Eight Days A Week' was written about Brian Epstein and the amount of time he used to spend working. Eppy was also the subject of a song Paul wrote, which put together with another song of John's, became 'Baby You're a Rich Man'. It was Paul's title. He penned 'Paperback Writer', '. . . because I love the word *paperback*'; 'She's Leaving Home' came from a newspaper cutting – 'it's a much younger girl than 'Eleanor Rigby', but the same sort of loneliness. That was a *Daily Mirror* story again: this girl left home and her father said, "We gave her everything. I don't know why she left home." But he didn't give her that much, not what she wanted when she left home.'

'Golden Slumbers' was written at his father's home in Heswell. Paul was doodling on the piano one day, when his step-sister Ruth – Jim McCartney had got married again in 1964 to one Angela Williams – showed him a music book containing the traditional song 'Golden Slumbers', written over 400 years ago by Thomas Dekker. Paul was drawn to the song, but not being able to read music, couldn't play it. So he did the next best thing – he composed his own melody line to fit the words. Later, he retained one verse by Dekker and wrote a new set of words for the rest.

'Carry That Weight' was written as a reaction to the responsibility of keeping The Beatles together after Epstein's death, while 'You Never Give Me Your Money' was a commentary on the financial dealings and backroom squabbles over Apple and the group breaking up.

Paul showed his complete mastery of songwriting and tremendous versatility by writing all kinds of songs – there were very few subjects he avoided – and in all styles. Happy songs . . . 'Fixing A Hole', 'Good Day Sunshine' – 'it was a warm and breezy summer, and I used to go to John's house to write. It was a happy-go-lucky summer song' – 'Getting Better', which he started to write whilst out walking his dog, Martha, one day when he suddenly realized spring had arrived.

He wrote some of the best rock 'n' roll to come out of the 1960s from 'I Saw Her Standing There', which someone once hailed as the definitive British rock 'n' roll song, to the raucous, 'She Came In Through The Bathroom Window'. And some of the most haunting ballads of all time, from the simplicity of 'Yesterday', 'I Will' and 'I'll Follow The Sun', to the awe-inspiring 'Long And Winding Road' which shares the same theme of loneliness with 'Let It Be'.

'Let It Be' is a song about being alienated from other people, Paul once admitted, and added: 'The feeling of not having a home or a base to return to – "When I find myself in times of trouble, Mother Mary comes to me" – that would be me having major panics and probably missing having a mother, because my mum died when I was fourteen, and missing that person to be able to go and cry on.'

His songs covered the complete musical spectrum and he admitted: 'I've never felt I'm in any one musical category.'

And yet, not all of McCartney's material is good – far from it. There is a lot of over-indulgence in his writing and many songs are puerile in both music and lyrical content: 'Helter Skelter', 'Why Don't We Do It In The Road' – which Lennon called his favourite Paul McCartney song – and 'Birthday' are written for effect, based on under-developed musical phrases and riffs alone, and 'Oh Darling' is simply a 12-bar blues revisited. Other songs seem to lack depth and direction: 'Rocky Raccoon' stands up on its words alone, the music becomes a dirge and goes nowhere after a solitary verse is repeated over and over again, and becomes tedious; 'Mother Nature's Son' meanders; 'Baby You're A Rich Man, palls after the first musical phrase; while 'I've Got A Feeling' stagnates as a song. Some of his material on the other hand seems under-played and incomplete in content: 'Wild Honey Pie' 'Blackbird' and particularly 'All Together Now' seem to be thrown together as compositions and would have benefited greatly from a little more time, trouble and effort spent on them.

Of the two composers, Lennon and McCartney – Paul McCartney emerged from the partnership as the more commercial of the two. He had an ear for a good melody line and a finely honed tune, and he wrote for a much wider audience than the confines of The Beatles, which tended to be Lennon's one failing; he was too insular in that respect.

Lennon refused to widen his musical horizons, until he went out on his own.

George Martin saw it coming – 'Paul's songs get to the average man,' he said – and admitted that he was 'able at the drop of a hat to produce an attractive, commercial melody with words to match.'

McCartney acknowledged the compliment: 'If you have a song you want me to write, I can manage it. I'm quite proud of the fact that I can do it. It's like someone who can strip a car down. I'd be just as proud of that. It's just that music is the same for me as any talent. It's no big deal. I'm glad I can do it.'

John Lennon, however, wrote for his own amusement much of the time, or at a touch, for The Beatles. He tended towards laziness . . . if often took McCartney's keenness to make him write at all.

But if proof of Paul McCartney's commercialism was in any doubt, of the last eleven Beatles singles released in Britain from 1966 to 1970, McCartney's songs accounted for eight A-sides: 'Paperback Writer', 'Yellow Submarine', 'Penny Lane', 'Hello Goodbye', 'Lady Madonna', 'Hey Jude', 'Get Back' and 'Let It Be'; of the others, George Harrison wrote 'Something'; John Lennon wrote 'Ballad Of John And Yoko; and John and Paul collaborated on 'All You Need Is Love'.

Towards the end of the association, John and Paul wrote alone in the studio or at home. Paul wrote complete songs; Lennon composed bits and pieces, phrases, incomplete sentences. McCartney would often play his half-finished efforts to friends and acquaintances for their reaction and approval, as he could no longer rely on his partner's coherence. But left to his own devices, Paul did tend to become far too sentimental in his writing, and romantically over the top. He needed another equal ego to bounce off.

John Lennon summed the whole thing up: 'We wrote together because we enjoyed it a lot sometimes and also because they would say, "Well, you're gonna make an album, get together and knock off a few songs" – *just like a job.*'

For McCartney, however, songwriting was never a job. It has remained a vocation, a hobby, a way of life, a passion ever since, and something he enjoys doing immensely.

It was inevitable that the partnership would eventually come to an end. When the two opposite poles met at the beginning, they were drawn together by their love of music. But when that love was replaced by something else – in John's case, Yoko Ono – the association was doomed. As Ray Coleman said: 'The partnership only grew irrevocably apart when they found other partners.'

Yet, the name of Lennon and McCartney was responsible for some of the most successful and aesthetic music of the twentieth century. The name stood for class and quality . . . and genius.

Someone once wrote that John and Paul's 'legacy remains the most significant in the whole of rock history.'

Arranger Milton Okun added that they 'took rock music to the outer limits of achievement and then went on to create a new music all of their own.'

Writer, producer and broadcaster Tony Palmer simply called them 'the greatest songwriters since Schubert.'

But it was left to John Lennon to capture the whole ideal perfectly. He described Lennon and McCartney as . . . 'Two fuckin' brilliant songwriters.'

PART TWO:

Tomorrow

11

Mr and Mrs McCartney

Paul McCartney was effectively unemployed when he walked out on The Beatles in April 1970.

'The truth was that when The Beatles broke up, I was out of a job,' he said. 'For me it was like building the whole thing from square one.'

McCartney, like the rest of the group, had slowly introduced a series of solo projects into his work schedule away from The Beatles. He had tried his hand at composing film scores – writing the music for the Boulting Brothers' movie 'The Family Way' – and Apple was supposedly created to enhance the group's solo ventures.

His great protégée at the time was singer Mary Hopkin who had been recommended to him by Twiggy. The London model had seen Mary on the television talent show, 'Opportunity Knocks', was greatly impressed with her talent, and telephoned Paul to see if he could do anything for the young Welsh girl. McCartney's response was to sign her to Apple Records and produce her first British hit single, 'Those Were The Days' which went on to top the charts in the fall of 1968. He wrote and produced her follow-up single, 'Goodbye' and produced her first album – 'Postcard' – on which a version of 'The Honeymoon Song' by Theodrakis appeared. It was one of Paul's favourites and one of the songs he sang himself in Hamburg, and on early Beatles engagements. It was a gentle ballad that allowed him to show off his voice!

The Iveys were another act Paul produced and wrote for, and as Badfinger, they had a hit in 1970 with McCartney's 'Come And Get It', the theme tune from Ringo's movie 'The Magic Christian'.

Yet . . . with the demise of the Fab Four, Paul had to start all over again.

His first solo album, 'McCartney', on which he sang and played all the instruments, had been recorded in both his Scottish and London homes, although Morgan Studios in London was used to mix and finish off the project. It had been released just after he had announced his decision to leave The Beatles. Indeed, to coincide with both events, Paul issued a press release explaining the situation, and outlining his reasons for leaving the group. Lennon was furious. He had honoured *his* word and agreed to keep quiet about his leaving the group several months before. Now, he accused McCartney of walking out on The Beatles as a giant publicity stunt, to sell copies of his new album.

'I was a fool not to do what Paul did,' said John, 'which was to use it to sell a record. He's a good PR man, Paul, we're all hurt that he didn't tell us what he was going to do.'

He added with venom: 'Paul hasn't left, I sacked him.'

The release of 'McCartney' had been one of the reasons Paul decided to get out when he did. He could see Allen Klein manipulating the group over agreements with royalties and commissions. Okay, so he was making money for the group, but at what cost overall to The Beatles? A showdown had been coming for some time. Later, Paul would explain: 'Klein says, "What The Beatles made in six years, I made them in nineteen months." All I say is, okay, where is it?'

Matters came to a head when Allen Klein, supposedly backed by Lennon, Harrison and Starr, refused to let Paul release his solo album *before* The Beatles had issued the long-awaited and controversial, 'Let It Be' LP, for which a release date had already been set and circulated. In the end, after much discussion and argument, McCartney got his way . . . but it was a struggle.

'We didn't want to put out "Let It Be" and Paul's LP at the same time,' said John Lennon. 'It would have knocked the sales. There has to be timing. We're not idiots.'

Paul told the London *Evening Standard*: 'We all have to ask each other's permission before any of us does anything without the other three. My own record nearly didn't come out because Klein and some of the others thought it would be too near the date of the next Beatles album.' He added: 'I had to get George, who's a director of Apple, to authorize its release for me.'

The album itself was a strange mixture of half-finished songs and ideas. If 'Sergeant Pepper' had been a product of magnificent contrivance and production, then Paul's solo project was a product of simplicity. It was a do-it-yourself album in every way, and *under*-stated.

'I had all these rough things and I liked them all and thought, "Well, they're rough, but thev're got that certain kind of thing about them,"' he said.

From among the musical bric-à-brac, instrumentals and snatches of incomplete songs, the album threw up a half-developed love song to his wife, 'The Lovely Linda'; a piece of typical McCartney whimsy, in 'Junk', which had been written in India and earmarked for the 'Abbey Road' album; 'Hot As Sun', written way back in 1958; and two outstanding songs, 'Every Night', and a ballad that oozed class in the same mould as 'Let It Be' and 'Hey Jude' – 'Maybe I'm Amazed', which in essence was a hymn to Linda McCartney.

The critics, however, didn't like the album and 'McCartney' was panned. Apparently, they were expecting too much. Yet, it still managed to top the album chart in Britain and America. Lennon called it 'rubbish'.

Throughout the year, Paul McCartney had made many overtures to Allen Klein, and John Lennon, George Harrison and Ringo Starr, to release him from the partnership agreement with The Beatles. They all refused. In the end, he was faced with the only course of action open to him . . . to sue. At the end of 1970, he started High Court proceedings against them, officially to dissolve The Beatles. It was an agonizing decision to make.

The case came to court the following February when the newspapers had a field day reporting the evidence of John Lennon and George Harrison and Ringo Starr, which revealed the true extent of the arguments, the petty squabbles and bickering within the group. The world's Press went to town holding front pages for the stories. The financial side of The Beatles' affairs made fascinating reading when it was revealed in court, that in eight-and-a-half years, *without* taking into account their revenue from songwriting, The Beatles had earned £17,500,000. Allen Klein said that £9,000,000 had been earned in the past nineteen months!

Paul's case was that basically he didn't trust Klein. In court, his statement read: 'I grew increasingly to distrust Allen Klein on the grounds of his proneness to boast about his ability to make spectacular deals which he proved unable to fulfil; his tendency to sow discord; his untruthfulness; and his unscrupulous efforts to hold himself out as my manager and gain commission in other fields, not covered by his agreement.'

At the end of the 11-day hearing, an official receiver was appointed to handle The Beatles' assets, and Allen Klein was removed from further management of the group. Mr Justice Stamp said: 'A receiver, in my judgment, is needed so that there may be a firm hand to produce order. I have no doubt that a receiver and manager ought to be appointed.'

Paul McCartney had won the day, but his victory was accompanied by a bitchy campaign in the music Press by John Lennon, decrying his old songwriting partner for what he had done to The Beatles. He seized every opportunity to make a vitriolic attack on McCartney.

Back in court, Mr Justice Stamp pointed out that Allen Klein's company ABKCO had taken at least £500,000 commission more than the 20 per cent specified in the original agreement. It had received: '. . . commission grossly in excess of that specified in the appointment,' said the judge.

At the beginning of that year, Klein had been found guilty by a New York court of failing to make and file tax returns relating to employees' tax.

On April 26th, 1971, The Beatles officially came to an end as a partnership when John, George and Ringo dropped their appeal against the receivership – although it took until 1975 before the complex financial dealings were sorted out. Two years later, they would sue Allen Klein themselves, alleging fraud and mismanagement, although Klein in turn, brought actions against all four Beatles and ended up with a payout of 5,000,000 dollars! In 1979, however, he was found guilty of filing a false tax return for 1970, relating to the sale of Apple promotional albums. He was given a two month jail sentence and fined 5,000 dollars.

With evidence still being given in court over the dissolution of The Beatles, Paul McCartney's first solo single, 'Another Day', was released. It was a song very much in the vein of 'For No One', about a lonely career girl looking for someone to love, and almost immediately, it landed McCartney in trouble.

The authorship of 'Another Day' was attributed to *Mr and Mrs McCartney* (Paul and Linda), which meant that Linda would be able to claim half the share of royalties earned through sales of the single, without it going to Northern Songs, McCartney's music publisher, now owned by ATV. Lew Grade, head of the company, was incensed! Northern Songs Chairman, Jack Gill, intimated that Linda McCartney was not, in fact, capable of composing songs with Paul.

ATV took McCartney to court, alleging that 'Another Day' was Paul's song and as such, *he* should receive the entire writing royalty payment due. They had to prove that Linda McCartney had no musical ability as a writer and that could be hard.

The McCartney lawyers made the simple point that it was Paul's prerogative to write with whosoever he chose, regardless of musical ability. They won the case!

'Another Day', meanwhile, went on to reach Number 2 in the British charts, and 5 in America. McCartney was back in business!

When Paul McCartney announced his decision to quit The Beatles, he listed his reasons for breaking away as 'personal differences, business differences, musical differences . . . but most of all *because I have a better time with my family*.' Now, perhaps, he would be allowed to enjoy his family life.

Paul had become an 'instant' family man when he married New Yorker Linda Eastman on March 12th, 1969. Linda had been divorced and had a young daughter, Heather, by her previous marriage, whom Paul later adopted. Daughter Mary – named after Paul's late mother – was born on August 29th, 1969; Stella arrived on September 13th, 1971; and their son, James – named after Paul's father – was born on September 12th, 1977.

Paul met Linda for the first time in May, 1967, at the Bag O'Nails, a London club and hang-out for musicians and showbusiness celebrities. A photographer by trade who specialized in the rock industry, Linda was later invited to attend the 'Sergeant Pepper' photo session, before she returned home to America. They didn't meet again for almost a year, until the spring of 1968, when Paul and John Lennon arrived in New York to promote the newly formed Apple. Linda accompanied her friend, Lillian Roxon – the celebrated rock journalist – to the Apple launch party, and later that evening, was taken out on the town by Paul. A further trip to America by McCartney shortly afterwards, cemented Anglo–US relations.

Back home in London, Paul invited Linda and daughter, Heather, to join him . . . and they started living together in the autumn. Within the year, they were married.

Linda Louise Eastman had been born in New York on September 24th, 1941. Her grandparents on her father's side, were Russian immigrants, and her father – Lee Eastman – changed his surname by deed poll from the family name of *Epstein*. He was a well-known and wealthy New York lawyer, specializing in the world of art and showbusiness. His clients included Hoagy Carmichael, Tommy Dorsey, Hoppalong Cassidy, and the artist Robert Rauschenberg. Linda and her younger brother, John – who would later join his father in business – were brought up in the splendour of homes in Scarsdale and Park Avenue. At an early age, she was forced (her word) to learn the piano . . . and hated every minute!

Her mother died in a plane crash when Linda was eighteen and her father later re-married. But her mother's death affected the teenager deeply.

After High School, Linda studied history and art at University in Denver, and later married geology student John See. Their daughter, Heather, was born on December 31st, 1963. However, the marriage soon foundered, and after the break up, Linda moved to Tucson, Arizona, where she studied photography at a local college. Within a year, she returned to New York where she landed a job as an assistant on *Town and Country* magazine.

Linda's first love was photography, and in what spare time she had, trying to hold down a job *and* bring up a young daughter, she could often be found at rock concerts, particularly at Fillmore East, photographing musicians. It became an obsession. She got her first big break in the business when she shot exclusive pictures of The Rolling Stones, and sold them on a freelance basis to newspapers and magazines. After that, she decided to branch out on a freelance career, and in 1967 flew to England on a commission to photograph The Animals, Steve Winwood and Traffic. It was in London that she chanced to meet her future husband.

After the do-it-yourself approach of the 'McCartney' LP, Paul decided to get help with the follow-up album and attempt a lavish production job, in an effort to silence the critics. The end result was 'Ram' by Paul and Linda McCartney, which was recorded in New York and featured the New York Philharmonic Orchestra, and session musicians Hugh McCracken (guitar), Dave Spinozza (guitar) and Denny Seiwell (drums), besides Paul and Linda. It was released in May 1971, with the album cover depicting Paul holding a ram by the horns, symbolic of the title. When Lennon issued his 'Imagine' album four months later, a give-away photograph inside showed John in an identical pose to Paul on 'Ram', grasping a *pig* by the ears. The similarity was vicious.

Prior to the release of 'Ram', however, McCartney trailered the new album in the music Press: 'The "McCartney" thing was a whole different trip that I had to go through,' he said. 'This one, though, is really *my* music. Real sweaty rock.' It didn't impress the critics. They didn't quite see it Paul's way and slammed the album, with the *New Musical Express* calling it – 'the worst thing McCartney has done'. There were certain sections of the music Press who seemed intent on getting their own back on McCartney. They still blamed him for breaking up The Beatles. Now they would show him. But it wasn't just the rock media who accused him, it was the public to a certain extent, *and* three ex-Beatles.

Still, the album went on to top the British Hit Parade and made Number 2 in America.

Although a definite improvement on 'McCartney', the 'Ram' album again featured a mish-mash of McCartney songs, many light and fanciful. There were several very good ideas, but few of them had been developed and exploited to their full potential. A lot of the material was throwaway. There were, however, some spectacular successes: 'Uncle Albert/Admiral Halsey' with its memorable 'Hands Across The Water' hook, was later to become an American chart-topping single, although Paul refused to issue the song as a single in Britain because he didn't want to be accused of 'selling the past', and 'Back Seat Of My Car' was released instead. McCartney admitted to having an Uncle Albert, too: 'He used to quote the Bible to everyone when he got drunk.' 'Heart Of The Country' a rockabilly number in the style of an old rocker, Carl Perkins, showed just where Paul's heart was at. But the undoubted highspot on the whole album came with the brilliantly put together, 'Back Seat Of My Car', which proved – if any proof were needed – that McCartney was maturing as a composer. This was a song to rank alongside Paul's greatest triumphs with The Beatles; to join the same stage as 'Hey Jude' and 'Let It Be', 'Yesterday' and 'Eleanor Rigby'. A McCartney classic.

On three other songs, however, John Lennon looked deeper into the lyrical content, believing 'Dear Boy', '3 Legs' and 'Too Many People' to be snide, behind-the-back digs at him, through McCartney's music, and was especially abusive about the line 'too many people preaching' on the last song. He also thought Paul was attacking him through the words of 'Back Seat Of My Car'. McCartney actually admitted that he had been getting at his former songwriting partner through his songs, but only on 'Too Many People'. John was reading too much into the others.

'That was the only thing I was saying, referring to John at the time,' said Paul.

Lennon's reply was to launch a blistering attack on McCartney on his next album, 'Imagine'. On the track 'How Do You Sleep', John wrote, through his lyrics, that the only good thing Paul had written was 'Yesterday', and called his music, 'muzak'. He added: 'Those freaks was right when they said you was dead'.

And he kept up a bitter and abusive tirade against Paul McCartney in the British and American music Press, still smarting over Paul's decision to take The Beatles to court! At times he called his former colleague – 'the Engelbert Humperdinck of rock.'

McCartney was bewildered: 'I sat down and pored over every little paragraph. "Does he really think that of me?" I thought. At the time, I thought – "it's me. I am. That's just what I'm like. He's captured me so well. I'm a turd, you know." I sat and thought: "I'm just nothing." But then, people who dug me, like Linda said: "You know that's not true. You're joking. He's got a grudge, man, the guy's trying to polish you off.' Gradually I started to think, "Great, that's not true. I'm not really like Engelbert Humperdinck. I don't just write ballads." And that kept me hanging on. But at the time, it hurt me.'

Criticism from the media also took its toll, and Paul had second thoughts, then . . . 'it became a challenge to me. I thought either I was going under, or I was going to get something together.'

On television, several years after John Lennon's death, Paul revealed: 'Once we were equal. When we were working together, we were considered pretty equal – we were producing equal amounts. But when the split of The Beatles happened and John moved away to New York, and the business stuff made us very bitchy with each other, John became the tough one with the experimental edge, and I became just the soppy one, writing the odd ballad. And John, of course, contributed to that by slagging me off and calling me Engelbert Humperdinck – which I thought at the time: "Who needs this?" But I didn't want to come back at him and say, "Let me tell them about *you*!" Cos I knew we'd just have a big media row and I just wasn't up to that. I'm really glad now I didn't get into that.'

When The Beatles were in the throes of splitting up, Paul had suggested that they should start all over again, get back to their rock 'n' rolling roots, to become a small band once more and play the clubs. 'Just like the old days!!'

'I wanted to get in a van and do an unadvertised concert at a Saturday night hop at Slough Town Hall, or somewhere like that,' said Paul. 'We'd call ourselves Ricky And The Red Stripes or something, and just get up and play. John thought I was daft.'

Indeed, towards the end of the partnership when Paul saw the success John was having, playing live again, with The Plastic Ono Band, McCartney, too, had the desire to get a band together and play.

Now he was out on his own, there was nothing to stop him achieving his desire. The tightness and the discipline of a band behind him, could only help Paul to regain himself, and boost his confidence. The last two years of in-fighting had certainly taken their toll, and McCartney's music had suffered badly with all the hassles going on around him. Paul, a born worrier, couldn't take too much more. Linda believed he needed to work again; the adrenalin created by a live audience would definitely help. A band would be the ideal vehicle for his music, too, it would inspire him . . . and could only improve his writing. It would be a new and exciting challenge.

After recording 'Ram' in New York, Paul approached drummer Denny Seiwell to become a permanent fixture in the new group he was forming, which would include Paul himself on bass and guitar and piano, and – as if blatantly courting the wrath of the rock media – his wife Linda would play keyboards. The line-up was completed by an old mate from the Midlands, former Moody Blues guitarist and author of one of Paul's favourite songs, 'Go Now' – Denny Laine.

They were together in the summer of 1971, to record their first album – for which most of the material was recorded in just three days, a long cry from the 700 hours The Beatles took to record 'Sergeant Pepper' – after much rehearsal in the barn at Paul's Scottish farm. Later, Paul announced to the world that the group would be called Wings. He admitted that they nearly became The Dazzlers, and then Turpentine. 'People will either like us, or they won't like us,' he said. 'If they don't like us, it's too bad.'

When the first Wings album, 'Wildlife' was released, in November – very few people *did* like them. The LP was once again attacked by the Press for its content, and it fared only moderately well in the charts, reaching 11 in Britain; 10 in America. It remains one of the lowest-selling albums of all ex-Beatles' efforts.

Of the eight tracks showcased, the group featured an old Everly Brothers song – 'Love Is Strange', given a reggae treatment, while 'Bip Bop' was inspired by Paul's daughter Mary. 'Dear Friend' had the potential to go on to greatness, but it meandered out of control. The rest of the songs were very run-of-the-mill offerings, that went nowhere. Only 'Tomorrow' stood out head-and-shoulders above the rest, but once again, Paul had failed to develop the song fully. With just a little more effort, 'Tomorrow' could have become one of the great Paul McCartney songs. Paul's interpretation of the song on 'Wildlife' – sung in a very matter-of-fact manner – summed it up. As one of the local music papers observed: 'Great song, could be brilliant.' David Cassidy covered the song on a single and handled it far *better* than McCartney.

Still, Paul was undeterred, and at the beginning of the New Year, added guitarist Henry McCullough – a former member of Joe Cocker's Grease Band – to the Wings' line-up. And he was about to achieve another long-held ambition . . . to tour again.

McCartney was going back on the road.

12

Wings

WITH HENRY MCCULLOUGH in the new Wings' line-up on lead guitar, the group rush-released a new single in February. 'Give Ireland Back To The Irish' was Paul's first, and to date last, political statement on record – expressed in condemnation of the Bloody Sunday riots and shootings in Northern Ireland. Cynics, however, regarded the release as McCartney's attempt to jump on John Lennon's political bandwagon. John and Yoko's 'Happy Christmas War Is Over' had recently been issued in America to become another Lennon-esque anthem to peace. But unlike John's offering, Paul's single was hurriedly banned by the BBC and IBA in Britain. Even so, it made the lower reaches of the chart, though McCartney had expected better things. Quite simply, the song wasn't very good, sentiment or no. And, as if in contempt of the BBC's decision to ban the record, Paul openly defied the Corporation to 'ban-this-if-you-dare', with the release of Wings' follow-up single, a McCartney-written version of the nursery rhyme, 'Mary Had A Little Lamb'. He wasn't winning many friends with the media.

Feeling he had to justify the record's release, Paul said: 'Everybody's wondering why this lamb is hanging around, cos Mary loves lambs. To me that's like a heavy trip, those lyrics. It's very spiritual.'

He added that he recorded the song because his daughter, Mary, liked hearing her name being sung – 'she perks her ears up at this tune.'

The record was issued . . . 'as a single from your old chums Wings'. McCartney wanted to be loved. The single made Number 6 in Britain, despite the outcry from the critics. In America it crept into the Top 30.

Earlier in the year, Paul achieved one of his most recent ambitions – to play live engagements again, and he turned the clock back a full dozen years to the heady days of The Beatles . . . and a clapped out van, touring the Liverpool clubs. Wings hired a brand new van, and a caravan, loaded up their cars and set off in search of adventure, and a few engagements. Paul was putting into practice the plans he had had for The Beatles in 1969 – a low profile series of unannounced performances around the country. Lennon had turned him down; now actions were speaking louder than words.

Just like a travelling circus – the Wings entourage included Paul, Linda and their children, Denny Laine, Denny Seiwell, Henry McCullough, three dogs and two road managers – they would stop at university towns, approach the students' union, and ask to play in the hall for 50p a time entrance fee. But there had to be no advance advertising, and definitely *no Press*. Who in their right mind would turn down the chance to see an ex-Beatle, *a legend* in the flesh, Paul McCartney and his new group for . . . 50p? No-one did.

Nottingham University was the first stop, and on February 9th, 1972, Paul McCartney and Wings made their live début in front of 700 curious students.

In two weeks, they visited York, Hull, Newcastle, Lancaster, Leeds, Sheffield, Manchester, Birmingham and Swansea. Paul enjoyed it all immensely . . . Ricky And The Red Stripes were in business.

On television, several years later, McCartney romanced about that first Wings' tour to Russell Harty: 'We had to get a band broken in so that you knew each other, so that you could all play the songs. We did a lot of going back to square one, playing small gigs. We used to play at student union gigs – 50p on the door. It was only because after The Beatles and all that fame, it reminded me of the early days. Because it was 50p on the door, you'd be handed a big bag of coins. With The Beatles, we made a lot of money, but we never saw it, it just went down a big hole. It was a crazy time, but the only way I could think to keep going. I didn't want to do the Andy Williams-thing – "Well, we've seen him in *The Beatles*, now dig him at Lake Tahoe."'

He was also very apprehensive about that tour, as he told Paul Gambaccini: 'The main thing I didn't want to face, was the torment of the rows of Press people with little pads, all looking and saying, "Oh, well, he's not as good as he was." So we decided to go out on that university tour, which made me less nervous.'

With the success of the university gigs, McCartney and Wings repeated the whole operation in the summer with a seven-week, 26-date tour, taking in nine European countries. The travelling circus journeyed from country to country in a multi-coloured, London double-decker bus, carrying a banner on each side with the legend: WINGS OVER EUROPE. They would often cater for themselves, drinking wine and beer, and eating fruit, cheese and bread. It was the simple life . . . and a great musical safari.

This time, however, Wings were besieged by reporters. Paul told one newspaper: 'I'm starting all over again, and working upwards. It's like boxing . . . you don't fight Cassius Clay in your first time out. A year ago I used to wake up in the morning and think, "I'm a myth. I'm Paul McCartney" . . . it scared the hell out of me.' He added: 'My ideal is to play off the back of a bus, like a travelling circus – "The Flying McCartneys".' And again: 'Doing this tour is like playing Hamburg, eight hours a day with The Beatles.'

Linda added: 'We've no managers or agents . . . just a gang of musicians touring around.'

The group played a mixture of material from 'Ram' and the 'Wildlife' album, some new songs of Paul's, and some old standards including 'Blue Moon Of Kentucky'. But the happy-go-lucky troubadours' tour was soured when Linda McCartney's ability as a musician and keyboard player, and her value to the group, was brought into question by several journalists.

Paul was quick to defend his wife: 'We like having Linda in the group. She is a great influence on us. She's no Billy Preston, but I would not like a very technical keyboard player, because they tend to want to take over. Linda isn't a pro, but if people don't like it, they shouldn't come next time. I couldn't care less. We love her playing with Wings.'

The Flying McCartneys, however, came down to earth with a bang in Sweden, when they were busted by the police for possessing cannabis – Paul, Linda and Denny Seiwell were fined £800. But the tour continued, taking in concerts in Holland, Belgium and Germany. It proved – a few hiccups apart – a resounding success.

Yet Paul was in trouble once again at the end of the year, when the group's new single – and their best to date – the raunchy, 'Hi, Hi, Hi', was banned by the BBC because it was believed the song was connected with drugs. The B-side, 'C-Moon', the shambling-along, reggae rocker, said to have been inspired by Sam The Sham's 'Woolly Bully', was played instead. The single became a double-A in Britain, reaching the Top 5. America presented no such ban, and 'Hi, Hi, Hi' made the US Top 10.

Drugs reared their head again at the beginning of 1973, when a local policeman discovered marijuana growing in the greenhouse of Paul's Scottish farm. The singer, who swore an American fan had sent him a packet of seeds and he had no idea what the packet contained, was fined £100.

Still, 1973 proved to be another eventful year, and highly successful, too, in the life of Paul McCartney. It saw him breaking new ground once more, when a new side of his persona was revealed in the television spectacular, 'James Paul McCartney', screened in May. For the first time since the break-up, Paul performed Beatles material on stage, including 'Yesterday' and 'Long Tall Sally'. But the special showed Paul to be hooked on the razz-matazz of showbusiness as he became the all-singing, all-dancing, romantic rocker, owing more to Fred Astaire than Freddie King. He composed the song 'Gotta Sing, Gotta Dance' for the show and performed it himself with the dancers.

The previous month had seen the release of a new album, 'Red Rose Speedway', credited to Paul McCartney *And* Wings. Once again, it was a slight disappointment and featured a lot of inconclusive material. The songs were stronger than before, though, and things were getting better; even the reviews were kinder.

The undoubted star track on the album came in Paul's spectacular ballad 'My Love', gaining much from 'The Long And Winding Road'. It was so obviously *the* number from the whole package and was released as a single in March. As if to prove its quality, 'My Love' was later recorded by some of the biggest names in international showbusiness.

'My Love', the single, topped the American Hit Parade along with the album; in Britain both made their respective Top Tens. But a most important landmark was reached with the song's release. Following the take-over of Northern Songs by ATV in 1969 – and the subsequent renegotiation of McCartney's own contract with the company – 'My Love' was the first song Paul actually owned himself! Although he had written 'Yesterday' and it had sold millions of copies worldwide by The Beatles, and by many other artists, he didn't own the music copyright! It was a situation that was to gall him for years to come.

Following the success of the album, Wings embarked on their first official British tour in May. It proved a sell-out. Audience reaction was superb and the critics were beginning to like McCartney, too.

It was becoming a good year.

It got better in June with the release of Wings' second single of 1973, the theme tune to the new James Bond movie 'Live And Let Die', which Paul had been commissioned to write the year before. It was a smash hit in Britain and America and later won a Grammy Award for Best Arrangement Accompanying Vocalists, *and* was nominated for an Oscar. 'Live And Let Die' re-united two old colleagues. For the first time since 'Abbey Road', George Martin produced a record featuring Paul McCartney . . . but it would be another seven years before they worked together again in the studio.

With so much going for Paul McCartney, it was inevitable that there had to be some trouble looming on the horizon, knowing his track record. It came in August when Henry McCullough announced he was leaving Wings after a studio disagreement with Paul. The announcement came at completely the wrong time, too, after McCartney had made arrangements for the group to record a new album – much of the material for which had been written earlier in the year at the Scottish farm – at the EMI Studios in Lagos, Nigeria.

There was worse to come. The day they were due to fly out to Africa, Denny Seiwell telephoned the McCartneys to tell them he wouldn't be making the trip. He had quit the group, too.

In one fell swoop, Paul McCartney's Wings had been clipped.

Undaunted, Linda and Paul and the children, and Denny Laine, made the trip themselves. They rented houses near to the airport and started work in the studio each day at 4.00 p.m., finishing well into the next morning.

Commenting on the departure of McCullough and Seiwell,

Paul said: 'When we are recording, I can play the lot myself.' On the resulting album . . . *he did*!

But, there were more problems in Nigeria.

Local idol Fela Ransome-Kuti made a blistering attack on McCartney's intentions for recording in Nigeria, accusing him of stealing African music. Paul was fuming, but pointed out that they were not using a single African musician on any of the tracks he was laying down in Lagos. He added that Wings had already made a name for themselves throughout the world, so why should they need to steal anybody else's music. 'I've done perfectly well without your music so far,' said Paul. 'Nobody's gonna steal your bloody music.'

Shortly afterwards, Paul and Linda were attacked on the streets as they made their way home, by a gang of muggers, who threatened to kill them. They were accosted on a dimly lit sidewalk and bundled into a doorway where, at knifepoint, they were robbed of money, jewellery, a camera and tape recorder.

'One of them had a knife,' said Paul. 'He said he would kill us if we didn't hand over everything we had. He was waving a knife about, so I decided it wasn't the time to try and reason with him.'

On another occasion, McCartney had difficulty breathing in the studio, and thought he had a collapsed lung. He rushed outside to get some fresh air – 'and there wasn't any!' Then the humidity hit him, and he fainted. Linda was convinced he was dying, but the doctor diagnosed overwork, and too many cigarettes. Paul was told to cut down on both.

Yet, the problems only seemed to improve the intensity and quality of the McCartneys' and Laine's work together, even if they had to play all the instruments between them. Somehow that helped, too. It brought them closer, and stimulated the small team to produce an album of the highest quality. The pressure only seemed to heighten McCartney's own brilliance as a composer.

They returned to London in September to put the finishing touches to their new material, knowing they had something special. They were all excited.

As a trailer to what was to come, a new Wings single, 'Helen Wheels' – recorded in Lagos – was released in October which Paul described to *Rolling Stone*. '"Helen Wheels" is our Land Rover. It's a name we gave our Land Rover, which is a trusty vehicle that gets us around Scotland. It takes us up to the Shetland Islands and down to London. The song starts off in Glasgow, then it goes past Carlisle, goes to Kendal, Liverpool, Birmingham and London. It's really the story of a trip down – little images along the way.'

Two months later, the album 'Band On The Run' was released. And for once the critics were unanimous in their praise. This was McCartney at his best. Every track on the album proved a winner, just like the good old days of Beatlemania. 'Helen Wheels', however, was only featured on the American album and failed to make the cut for the British market.

'Band On The Run' exuded class! Each song was to prove a masterpiece of writing. The *New Musical Express* called the album a *'milestone.'*

Paul had drawn his inspiration for the set from a number of sources, as usual. The title track had been suggested by a chance remark by George Harrison sometime before at a lengthy Apple meeting, when he said, 'if we ever get out of here'. McCartney picked up the line, and around it embroidered a fine and masterly song, with changes of tempo and style around every corner. He had woven a colourful story and introduced the listener to more of his lovable characters in the form of 'Sailor Sam' and the 'Jailer Man'. The title track suggested the theme of the album being a prison break, which Paul acknowledged 'relates to me escaping.' And he admitted that there was a linking theme to the record rather than it being a concept album alone.

'Jet' took its name from one of McCartney's Labrador puppies, while 'Bluebird' was McCartney whimsy at its best. On 'Let Me Roll It', Paul once again showed his talent at being able to capture the identical style of any artist or writer he cared to imitate musically. This time it was a gentle tribute to John Lennon And The Plastic Ono Band. The style and sound were identical to John's.

But the outstanding track on the album, was for once, not a classic Paul McCartney ballad, but a song called 'Picasso's Last Words (Drink To Me)'. A story song, with most of the lyric supplied by one of Paul's favourite painters, and inspired simply by Picasso's final words. It was very effective.

Like 'Sergeant Pepper' with The Beatles, 'Band On The Run' was to become Paul McCartney's definitive album. All the promise and potential he had shown in the past manifested itself in just nine songs (ten on the American version).

It topped the charts in Britain and America and went on to sell over 6,000,000 copies around the world. Two singles – 'Jet' and 'Band On The Run' were lifted from the LP, with both reaching the Top Ten in Britain and America, while 'Band On The Run' went on to top the US chart. The album also picked up two Grammy Awards and became the first Paul McCartney LP to be released in the Soviet Union.

But it did much more. It was a breakthrough for Paul. At last he was finally able to lay the ghost of The Beatles which had haunted him for nearly three years – 'the worst three years of my life!'

But now, he was *Paul McCartney*, not just an ex-Beatle.

13

Wings Over the World

PAUL McCARTNEY HAD already started again from square one after leaving The Beatles and setting up his own group. Now in 1974, with the demise of Wings, he was back on the ground floor and faced the prospect of having to begin once more.

Wings was dead. Long live Wings.

It seemed ironic, however, that at the pinnacle of the group's success with 'Band On The Run' topping charts all over the world, and being showered at last with huge critical acclaim from all quarters, Wings virtually ceased to exist following the departure of Denny Seiwell and Henry McCullough. They certainly couldn't tour.

McCartney was used to the set-backs by now, but he still had ambitions for his group, and in his own meticulous manner set about recruiting new members for Wings Mark II. He eventually chose guitarist Jimmy McCulloch, a former member of Thunderclap Newman and Stone The Crows, and after hectic auditions, drummer Geoff Britton was taken on. Britton in fact, was better known as a sportsman – being a karate champion – than for his musical track record, which had seen him working with Wild Angels and East Of Eden. But to the public, he was unknown.

In June, the new band left Britain for Nashville, Tennessee, to rehearse and record, and to make a movie called 'One Hand Clapping', which would be a documentary insight into Wings at work and play. It was shades of 'Let It Be' all over again, but this time, the script had been re-written to include a happier ending. The film was never released.

The environment of Tennessee proved conducive to Paul's writing. 'When I'm in a place, it's not uncommon for me to write about where I am,' he said.

One song written – and recorded – at that time, concerned Paul's visit to the bars of Printer's Alley, a colourful district of Nashville similar to London's Soho, or Sydney's King's Cross. There he met Waylon Jennings, who in the '50s had been a member of Buddy Holly's group The Crickets, and now was an established giant of country music. The two stars spent a pleasant evening together talking about music, and on more than one occasion the conversation turned towards Buddy Holly.

From that one experience, Paul's thoughts were transferred to words and music through the song 'Sally G', which in October was issued as the B-side to a Wings' single 'Junior's Farm' – another Tennessee inspired number, composed whilst staying at Junior Putnam's farm in Nashville – comprised the A-side. At the beginning of 1975, the single was flipped over with 'Sally G' becoming the featured A-side . . . and re-released.

During the Nashville sessions, recorded at the Sound Shop Studios, Wings were joined by country and western stalwarts Chet Atkins and Floyd Cramer. Together they recorded a song dear to Paul's heart, though not one he had written himself. 'Walking In The Park With Eloise' had been composed by his father in the pre-Second World War days of Jim Mac's Band. The number was issued as a single in October, featuring Wings plus two, under the collective name of The Country Hams.

Wings returned to America at the start of the new year, to undertake recording sessions in New Orleans, where they had the unenviable task of making a new album in follow up to 'Band On The Run'. The group had undergone yet another change of line up, with Joe English replacing Geoff Britton on drums. A misunderstanding in the American city had led to the karate champion's premature departure, but he later went on to find some kind of fame, representing his country in the martial arts! He had also played on three of the tracks earmarked for the new album, when Paul took the group into Abbey Road studios to start work on the record back in November.

The new album – 'Venus And Mars' – was completed in the Wally Heider Studios in Los Angeles and released at the end of May. It was well received by the Press and McCartney told *Melody Maker*: 'It's getting better because I reckon I've made some bum records in the last couple of years.'

'Venus And Mars' was a workmanlike album, although in no way could it emulate the magnificence of 'Band On The Run'. To be fair, it didn't even try to compete with its predecessor. But it did top both the British and American album charts, and showcased Paul's ability at writing an assortment of different kinds of songs . . . from the gentle ballads of "Love In Song', and 'Treat Her Gently', through the Fred Astaire-inspired vaudevillian, 'You Gave Me The Answer' which Paul called 'fruity', to the pure unadulterated pop music of 'Listen To What The Man Said'. There were several blues 'n' soul influenced numbers, with 'Letting Go' and 'Call Me Back Again' to the fore. 'Rock Show' was written with one intention in mind, as the perfect opening number for Wings' forthcoming concert tours. It succeeded in conveying exactly the right kind of atmosphere Paul required. 'I really wanted it to be sweaty!'

The suitability of 'Rock Show' as an opening number became obvious in the fall of 1975 when Paul McCartney and Wings embarked on their most adventurous project to date – a massive world tour, to take in the next thirteen months: Wings Over The World.

To augment the Wings' sound on stage, McCartney brought in a brass section, comprising well-respected session musicians – Thaddeus Richard on saxophone; Tony Dorsey on trombone – who had played on the 'Venus And Mars' recordings; Steve Howard, trumpet; and an old mate from Liverpool, Howie Casey, on saxophone, who had been featured on 'Band On The Run', delivering the atmospheric solo on 'Bluebird'. Paul and Howie went back a long way, to the days when Casey led his own group on Merseyside, Derry And The Seniors, and later appeared with King Size Taylor And The Dominoes.

The tour opened in Britain on September 9th at the Gaumont Theatre in Southampton. Wings, after much rehearsal, came over as a highly efficient and tight outfit, playing twenty-eight numbers in two hours. The set included Beatle favourites 'Yesterday' and 'Lady Madonna', together with material from several Wings albums and singles. The British tour once again became a sell-out.

Next came engagements in Australia in November, which should have been followed by two concerts in Japan. But after a previous drugs conviction, Paul discovered he was barred

Top: Paul and Linda making a rare television appearance on the Mike Yarwood Christmas Show in 1977, and celebrating their long-running No. 1 hit, 'Mull of Kintyre'. *(Universal Pictorial Press)*

Above: On the set of the feature film *Give My Regards to Broad Street. (David Morse)*

Next page: The McCartney family leaving for a holiday in Barbados, April 1980. The children are Stella (left), James and Mary. *(Press Association)*

CITY OF LIVERPOOL
At a Special Meeting
of the Council of the City of Liverpool
held in the Council Chamber within the Town Hall
on Wednesday the 7th day of March, 1984
PRESENT
The Chairman Councillor Hugh Dalton and a
full Council
AND RESOLVED
THAT, in pursuance of the Local Government Act 1972, the
Honorary Freedom of the City of Liverpool
be conferred upon
PAUL McCARTNEY M.B.E.
in recognition of the eminent service rendered by him
to the City as musician and composer and in recognition
of the world-wide acclaim of his musical talent

Previous page: November 1984: Paul being presented with the Freedom of the City of Liverpool. Derek Hatton looks on. *(Press Association)*

Top: Paul McCartney leading 72,000 fans at the Wembley Live Aid concert in a chorus of 'Let It Be'. Joining him on stage are David Bowie, Alison Moyet, Pete Townshend and Bob Geldof. *(Press Association)*

Left: 'So what's all the fuss?' From the 'Spies Like Us' video, 1985.

from entering the country. The Japanese dates were cancelled. The story would have unhappy repercussions and make world headlines a few years later. In the meantime, they returned to Europe in March for concerts in Denmark, Germany, Holland and France. In Paris, Jimmy McCulloch broke a finger, and the long-awaited American section of the tour had to be rescheduled at the last moment.

Prior to the European tour, however, Paul McCartney had taken Wings back into Abbey Road studio once more to record material for a new album release. Knowing that the tour would effectively keep them away from recording for several months, they needed a constant supply of new material on the market.

'Wings At The Speed Of Sound' was the result, surfacing to coincide with the Continental concerts. It was the first album to feature each member of the group singing lead vocals on a particularly designated track, apart from Paul, of course. Linda débuted on Paul's song 'Cook Of The House' – complete with the sounds of bacon sizzling in the pan – which Paul had written during the Australian concerts, in Adelaide. 'Must Do Something About It' showcased Joe English; 'Time To Hide' was written and sung by Denny Laine, while Jimmy McCulloch shone on his own song, 'Wino Junko'.

Amid the hastily put together tracks, were three jewels in a crown of lightweight indifference: 'Let 'Em In' which saw Paul using the names of family, friends and people he admired, to form part of the lyrics, including reference to 'Brother John' (Lennon). The song was later released as a single and topped the US chart; 'Silly Love Songs', which became the second single taken from the album to top the American Hit Parade, was a plea from McCartney's heart in support of ballads and sentiment! 'Warm And Beautiful' had hymn-like qualities, reeking of Sunday schools and Paul's north country upbringing of brass bands and Whit Walks. He would revise the style and haunting symbolism in the 1980s on the masterful 'Waterfalls'.

The re-arranged Wings Over America tour finally got under way on May 3rd, with a standing-room-only concert at Fort Worth. For the next seven weeks, the large entourage, comprising five 32-ton trucks, to carry the equipment – 15,000 watts of amplification, elaborate light shows, lasers and visual effects, plus a gigantic sound system – and twenty-seven road crew, slipped speedily across the States to take in thirty concerts in twenty-one cities. The entire tour surpassed everyone's wildest expectations and became a huge triumph for all concerned, with Wings playing to capacity business *everywhere*. Concert tickets, which could have been sold a dozen times over, exchanged hands on the black market for twenty times their face value! Wings-mania was running rife!

The tour went even way beyond Paul's greatest expectations. In Seattle, at the King Dome Stadium, Wings set a new world record for attendance, when 67,100 people saw their concert – the largest audience to see a single act in an indoor arena! The entire show was filmed, to be released subsequently as the movie, 'Rockshow', for cinema distribution . . . although it wasn't premièred until 1980. An earlier film documentary of the tour – 'Wings Over The World' – was shown as a television special in 1979.

It was the second time in his career that Paul McCartney had conquered America! But this time the success tasted even sweeter. Paul said: 'Everything I have done since The Beatles split has been leading up to this.'

He completed the globetrotting in the fall with a further series of concerts in Europe including an engagement in Venice, in aid of the UNESCO appeal, before an audience of 30,000, and a final British thrash at Wembley.

By the end of the tour, Paul McCartney and Wings had been seen by over 2,000,000 people in ten countries.

In December, the entire tour programme was reproduced 'live' on the triple album, 'Wings Over America', featuring every song in the show. It had been edited down from 900 tapes taken from thirty different shows! It became the first triple album to top the American Hit Parade, *and* the world's biggest-selling three LP set of all time, until eclipsed by Status Quo in 1982 with their 'From The Makers Of . . .'.

With wife Linda pregnant, expecting their son, James, in the summer of 1977, Paul and Wings set off for the Virgin Islands, where plans had been laid for them to record their next album on board the boat *Fair Carol*, and to that end, a twenty-four track studio had been installed. Three other luxury yachts had also been hired for the duration, as floating accommodation for the group and families. Later, Paul explained that they wanted to create idyllic working conditions, somewhere that he hoped would take the sweat out of work. 'I hate the grind of trying to seek inspiration,' he said.

The album had been started several months before in London, to where Linda, Paul, Denny and Joe returned in the autumn. Jimmy McCulloch had become another statistic on the growing Wings casualty list. Paul and some others had become tired of Jimmy's antics on the road. On many occasions, McCartney had had a quiet word with the guitarist about his general behaviour. When Jimmy chose to ignore the friendly warnings, he was politely asked to leave the group. In 1979, he was found dead in mysterious circumstances in a London flat – and the tragedy was that he never achieved his full potential as a musician.

But before the album was completed, Joe English, too, became another casualty when he left the group, leaving Paul McCartney back on the starting grid once more. Yet, like the phoenix, Wings was swift to rise from the ashes. In November the group released a new single. It was a simple, catchy song, written by Paul McCartney and Denny Laine. It would later make history. Paul called it 'a kind of glass-of-ale-in-your-hand-leaning-up-against-the-bar, tune. A cross between "Sailing" and "Amazing Grace".'

As the punk and new wave ideals took a firm grip on the music industry, no-one could ever have predicted just how much impact 'Mull Of Kintyre', featuring the Campbelltown Pipe Band, would have made on the public in Britain. It became the Christmas hit of 1977, topping the chart for an incredible nine weeks, and the first British single to sell over 2,000,000 copies, to become the biggest-selling record of all time in Britain, taking over the title from . . . 'She Loves You'. The record was to hold that distinction until 1985, when Band Aid's 'Do They Know It's Christmas?' succeeded to the crown. McCartney, who was featured on the B-side of the Band Aid single, said: 'I'm delighted "Mull" has been overtaken by such a worthy record. I hope it sells twice as many.'

The album 'London Town', released the following March, bridged the gap between the departure of Wings Mark II and the arrival of Wings Mark III, when McCartney announced that guitarist Laurence Juber and drummer Steve Holly would become permanent fixtures in Wings for all future projects, which would hopefully include another major tour.

The album, which had been recorded on the floating studio

in the sun the summer before, was an enigma. Like much of McCartney's work, it was good in parts, but there were far too many throwaway items. Paul seemed content with aping the various styles of music that had become particular McCartney favourites, although it looked as if he was taking a folksy detour along the way, which was ultimately the influence and treatment behind 'Children Children', 'Remember Your Children', 'Don't Let It Bring You Down' and 'Mouse Moose And The Grey Goose' all of which had been co-written with Denny Laine. Vaudeville was revisited with 'Famous Groupies' with its delightful and well observed lyrics.

The album also had its highspots, with 'Girlfriend' – later to become a big hit for Michael Jackson – and 'With A Little Luck', a well-constructed pop song, and another American chart-topper, standing out.

Laurence Juber and Steve Holly made their Wings début on the spring single of 1979, 'Goodnight Tonight', and were later featured on the next album project.

'Back To The Egg' arrived in June and showed McCartney coming to grips with what was going on around him in the musical world. He'd made his own concessions to the punk revolution with 'Spin It On', and 'Old Siam Sir', which Roy Carr and Tony Tyler described as: 'Jimi Hendrix signs up for the cast of "The King And I".' The album contained Paul's usual whimsy on 'We're Open Tonight', while 'After The Ball' and 'Million Miles' owed far too much to 'Amazing Grace'. The classic McCartney ballad like 'Yesterday' or 'Hey Jude' was missing, although he came close with 'Winter Rose' and 'Love Awake', while 'Baby's Request' took the listener back to the 1940s style of lounge-bar entertainment. Paul said he originally wrote the song for the Mills Brothers.

The hit of the whole set was 'Getting Closer', but there were two other interesting items: 'So Glad To See You Here' and 'Rockestra Theme'. For these two tracks, Paul had contacted some of his superstar friends in the music business, and put together the ultimate super group – The Rockestra, featuring such star names as Denny Laine, Laurence Juber, Dave Gilmour (Pink Floyd), Hank Marvin and Pete Townshend on guitar; John Bonham (Led Zeppelin), Kenney Jones (The Who) and Steve Holly on drums; John Paul Jones (Led Zeppelin), Ronnie Lane and Bruce Thomas on bass guitar; Paul McCartney, Gary Brooker and John Paul Jones on piano;

Linda McCartney and Tony Ashton on keyboards; Speedy Acquaye, Tony Carr, Ray Cooper and Morris Pert on percussion; with Howie Casey, Tony Dorsey, Steve Howard and Thaddeus Richard comprising the brass section.

'Back To The Egg' as a package, failed to inspire because it was too patchy. As an epitaph to Wings, which the album became, it was a poor finale. The two singles lifted from the album – 'Old Siam Sir' and 'Getting Closer' hardly registered in the charts.

Still, Wings did go out with a vengeance in November, when they embarked on their first tour for over three years with nineteen concert dates around Britain, followed in December by an appearance in London in one of a series of special charity shows for the people of Kampuchea. The gig was notable for an appearance by a re-vamped Rockestra. McCartney had been approached earlier in the year by the Secretary-General to the United Nations, Kurt Waldheim to help raise funds for the plight of Kampuchean refugees. Paul responded in typical style and did much to help organize the London charity engagements with promoter Harvey Goldsmith.

As part of the British tour, however, Paul McCartney also played two special concerts in Liverpool. One was to raise money for a famous old Merseyside theatre, the Royal Court, while the second was for the staff and pupils of his old school, Liverpool Institute. The school's headmaster, who had actually taught Paul geography in the 1950s, said it was a marvellous gesture on the part of a famous old boy.

'It's a way of saying thank you,' said Paul, 'for some very happy years. Everyone seems to knock their school days, but for me, they have fond memories.'

The British tour turned out to be another spectacular triumph for all concerned, with the group playing to capacity business everywhere. The boisterous audiences were treated to a tight set, featuring some old Beatles songs, several Wings standards, and some newer material thrown in for good measure. It was interesting to see that McCartney opened the show with 'Got To Get You Into My Life' and included the old Eddie Cochran standard, 'Twenty Flight Rock' in the programme. McCartney was bathing in musical memories and wallowing in nostalgia. More than twenty years before, 'Twenty Flight Rock' was the song he taught to

John Lennon at the church fête in Woolton, when the two boys met for the first time. Wings also showcased their new Christmas single – 'Wonderful Christmastime', although on the cover of the record it was credited solely to Paul McCartney. Paul had wanted to write a memorable Christmas song that would be released and re-released every year, dusted down, and bought by young and old alike, in the same way Irving Berlin's 'White Christmas' had endeared itself to the world. This, unfortunately, wasn't the one!

Plans for Wings to emulate the success of 1976, by undertaking a major world tour during 1980 after the triumph of the British engagements the year before, were dashed as early as January.

Arriving in Japan at the start of an eleven concert schedule on January 16th – it had taken three years for McCartney to secure a visa to visit the country, following previous convictions for drug possession and the cancellation of two Japanese concerts in 1975 – Paul McCartney's reputation with drugs had preceded him into Tokyo, and his luggage was searched to reveal a substantial amount of cannabis.

He was arrested immediately, and taken off in handcuffs to prison. The sell-out Japanese tour, for which the local promoter estimated over 100,000 tickets had been sold, was in jeopardy. After Paul had been incarcerated for just nine hours . . . the tour was called off.

For McCartney a nightmare was about to begin. His clothes and belongings were taken away from him and he was imprisoned *without* bail – and rumours abounded that he could face up to ten years in jail, if found guilty of *drug smuggling*. Linda and the children booked into a hotel and she enlisted the services of a local Japanese lawyer to help secure the release of her husband.

In all, McCartney spent ten days in jail. He admitted later it was hell! He was awakened at dawn and later subjected to extensive interrogation on his drug activities, before being forced to spend the rest of the day sitting on a prison mat. At night, he was expected to sleep on a straw mattress and suffered terrible headaches. To keep his thoughts together and his mind active, he compiled a mental diary of his experiences, as paper and writing material were banned from the prison. He was not allowed access to a musical instrument, either, so he couldn't compose. Instead, he spent much of his time singing with his fellow prisoners. He *was* allowed one bath a week and took it in the communal tub with the other inmates. On other occasions, he washed in the same water that supplied the lavatory.

Paul spoke of his ordeal later: 'At first I thought it was barbaric. I was woken at six in the morning, then had to sit cross-legged for roll-call. It was like "Bridge On The River Kwai".'

Ten days after his arrest, McCartney was deported from Japan. He had been released because he had brought the drugs into the country for his own personal use – not to re-sell or peddle them to others. He was lucky.

Back in Britain, he sat down to write up the mental notes he had made in jail and hoped to publish it as 'Japanese Jailbird'. He wrote everything down he could remember; the names of the people who had been nice to him inside, the names of those who had not. Every single thing that happened was written down in the 20,000-word manuscript. In the end, he decided he had better leave well alone. The diary was never published.

The Japanese episode later cost him £200,000 in compensation to the local promoter, plus over £100,000 in legal fees and living expenses.

But it also marked the end of Wings as a group – they would never re-form, never play together again. Now it was strictly Paul McCartney out on his own.

Talking later about Wings, he said: 'The Beatles did a lot more than Wings were ever gonna do. But let's look at it from another angle: have we done anything in ten years? We've done amazingly well, actually. We were daft enough to follow The Beatles.'

It was interesting to note, that in the first two years of Wings' existence, Paul McCartney earned more money than he ever did with The Beatles!

14

McCartney

1980 STARTED BADLY . . . it continued tragically. Paul McCartney was visibly shaken by his experiences in the Japanese prison. Yet, it gave him plenty of time to be alone by himself, to think, to take a long, hard look at himself and take stock. To find out exactly where he was going . . . and work out what to do next.

He decided that when he was finally released, he would go it alone once more, and complete the solo album he had been writing and planning for some time.

Back at his home, he was incarcerated once again, only this time out of choice as he worked hard to finish off the new album. He played all the instruments himself, just like on the first solo job, 'McCartney'; sang all the vocal tracks and harmony, mixed the entire package and produced it himself, too.

'I hired a 16-track machine and a couple of microphones to plug straight into it,' he said. 'I had no mixing console . . . no trick machines.' He played drums in the bathroom or the kitchen to get the echo he required. It was an old trick John Lennon and he had employed back in Forthlin Road, Allerton, when they started writing their own songs together. The acoustics were always better in the bathroom.

'McCartney II', as the album was called, was a huge personal success for Paul and had critics drooling and reaching for superlatives. It was a do-it-yourself-delight . . . and topped the British Hit Parade. Paul set out his stall with eleven outstanding tracks, occasionally returning to some old faithful ideas and standbys. On 'Temporary Secretary', he went back to an idea he first used on 'Paperback Writer', utilizing the lyrics as if writing a letter . . . this time to the Alfred Marks

Bureau. The music, written on a three note sequence, captured perfectly the staccato rat-a-tat-tat motion and jumpy rhythm of a typewriter. 'One Of These Days' was a delicate ballad in the mould of 'Mother Nature's Son', but not as flimsy and whimsical. A song full of Paul's trademarks . . . optimism and hope, and very much underrated. In tended to be overshadowed by other more obvious material, particularly 'Waterfalls', which was the magnificent superstar of the whole show.

'Waterfalls' – the title was taken from the name of Paul's home – was a hauntingly beautiful song, with a simple message: 'I love you, I need you, so take *good* care of yourself, don't do anything silly, and keep out of danger.' It was written originally for his children, and although the lyrics drift towards the obscure at times, the immense quality of the music and melody line carry it through.

The Sunday Times wrote: '"Waterfalls" . . . is what I and others have been waiting for McCartney to do all through the '70s.'

The song was an obvious single and it was duly released to make the British Top Ten, although for some strange reason, it failed to register in America. It deserved better, as one journalist admitted: 'It was the best thing Paul McCartney had done since The Beatles.'

The first single to be taken off the album as a tester for things to come was the brassy and bold rock 'n' roller with the great hook – 'Coming Up', which reached Number Two in Britain and topped the US chart. The single was noted for the superb video promotional film that accompanied its release. The film featured a large rock group – The Plastic Macs – playing the song straight. No gimmicks . . . until you looked closer. Apart from Linda's contribution on vocals, Paul played all the characters in the group himself. It was a brilliant piece of editing by the film-makers, as they cut to McCartney as 'Hank Marvin' on guitar, as 'Ginger Baker' on drums, as 'Frank Zappa', 'Roy Wood', 'Buddy Holly', *and* a wicked tongue-in-cheek caricature of 'Beatle Paul', complete with Hofner violin bass guitar, and collarless jacket. But Paul's portrayal of Ron Mael of Sparks on keyboards, was uncanny, second and third looks were needed to see beneath the disguise.

Despite all rumours and reports to the contrary, Paul

McCartney had patched up his differences with his friend, John Lennon. The two songwriters often kept in touch by trans-Atlantic telephone, and had met briefly on occasions in New York and Los Angeles. Yet, towards the end of the 1970s, a much-publicized event took place in New York. McCartney, in town on business, grabbed a guitar and made for the Dakota building where John lived, to see his old adversary. When he rang up to John's apartment on the internal intercom, Lennon told him: 'I'm sorry, but you can't just drop in on people in New York like you did in Liverpool,' and sent him away.

On the night of December 8th, 1980, while returning home from the recording studio, John Lennon was gunned down on the streets of New York city by Mark David Chapman. Within half an hour, he was dead.

There could be no Beatles' reunion now. It was the tragic and unnecessary end to a beautiful era. The whole world mourned.

McCartney was devastated. In a later statement on John's death he wrote: 'He was a great man and will be missed by the whole world, and he will be remembered for his art, music and contribution to world peace.'

Later still he added: 'There's something about sudden death. There are so many things left unsaid. I would just liked to have seen John the day before and just straightened everything out with us. We found we could talk to each other as long as it was about kids and stuff like that.'

He told interviewers: 'He was pretty rude about me sometimes, but I secretly admired him for it. There was no question that we weren't friends. I really loved the guy.'

In another interview he revealed: 'People say we were worlds apart, but we weren't. We actually did know each other. We actually were very close. We had a ding dong in the Press, especially after the Apple stuff. Yoko told me how very complimentary he was about me, but he just didn't want to be the cloying sycophantic sort of guy saying in public, 'Oh, Paul's terrific – he's really great.' There was a very competitive thing between us. Yoko says a lot of the slagging off was John taking the mickey.

'I talked to Yoko the day after he was killed and the first thing she said was, "John was really fond of you." He was very jealous, and so was I. The last telephone conversation I had with him, we were still the best of mates.'

After John's death, Paul kept a low profile. 'I really was scared for a few weeks afterwards. There are crazy people everywhere. My attitude is to try and push it out of my mind.' With Wings in cold storage, he toyed with the idea of putting a super group together for an album and major concert tour, working with people like Phil Collins, George Duke, Eric Stewart and Stanley Clarke. And then decided against it. He was on his own.

At the start of 1981, Paul left Britain for the island of Montserrat, where after holidaying, he got down to the serious business of making a new album. In the studio, he was reunited with George Martin who had been contacted and asked to produce the new project. Paul was going back. The two hadn't worked together since George produced Paul's 'Live And Let Die' single.

Said Paul: 'I wanted to work with George Martin again. I felt there was something missing from the previous albums.'

George added: 'I never thought I would work with Paul again, because he is a pretty good producer in his own right.' Later on British television, he revealed: 'One of the things that worried me when we started working together was, do you think it's a good idea? Why spoil a beautiful friendship? Because he had been used to working by himself for seven or eight years, and wasn't used to having a producer telling him what to do, I wondered how he'd react to it.

'He said, "We know each other so well, I don't think it will be a problem."

'I said, "First of all I'd better look at your material and see what the songs are like." He said, "Do you mean I've got to pass an audition?" So I could see that might have been a problem. In fact that worked out fine and we got into a method of working, where we weren't rubbing each other up the wrong way too much. There's got to be a certain amount of abrasion.'

The result of their collaboration was a new album called 'Tug Of War', which took over eighteen months to complete. On release in April 1982, it became the best McCartney had offered, for overall quality, since 'Band On The Run'. It featured a galaxy of star names as sidemen – Eric Stewart, Andy Mackay, Stanley Clarke, Ringo Starr and Carl Perkins. Stevie Wonder duetted with Paul on the emotive 'Ebony And Ivory', which was issued as a single a month before the album went on sale, and went on to top the British and American charts.

'I originally rang Stevie up,' said Paul. 'I had written the song, "Ebony And Ivory" – it's about black people and white people living in harmony. I admired him so much, and he said, "Yes" . . . he was interested in doing it. I'd never worked with him before, but it had always been a bit of an ambition to work with him.'

'Tug Of War' showed that McCartney had lost none of the sparkle, and it was an album that was well worth waiting for. It was put together with love and care, *not* simply hashed together like earlier efforts. It showed. No two songs were the same, and the LP displayed a whole range of different styles and performances, from the jazz-funk of 'Take It Away', 'Dress Me Up As A Robber' and 'That's What You're Doing' – which was co-written with Stevie Wonder and created out of a studio jam session – through the humorous country rock of 'The Pound Is Sinking', to the rockabilly shindig of 'Get It', which he sang in partnership with another old friend and music idol, Carl Perkins. There were strong ballads, too, in 'Wunderlust' with its anthem-like quality, and 'Somebody Who Cares', with its changing melodic construction and lyrical phrasing. On 'Ballroom Dancing', Paul returned to his childhood memories of playing kids' games – dressing up as pirates, Arabian nights, Cowboys and Indians, and Knights in shining armour. The whole song was set against the backdrop of his teenage years, of going out for the night to the ballrooms of Liverpool – Litherland Town Hall, the Grafton, the Grosvenor, where acute shyness prevented a young lad from chatting up the girls and asking for a dance. But, as George Harrison had reminded him on many occasions, you *had* to have at least one dance, the last waltz, with a girl, or else you couldn't really say you had been to a dance! The Beatles cut their musical teeth on a good many dances, too.

The previous May, Paul and Ringo had contributed a performance to George Harrison's song, 'All Those Years Ago', which had been released as a single, featuring the former Beatles, as a tribute to their friend John Lennon. Now, on 'Tug Of War', McCartney composed his own special song to Lennon's memory with the emotional and moving, 'Here Today'. The song showed an outside world just how much love and affection Paul had for his partner. There was a very strong bond between two of Liverpool's likely lads.

'I sat down one day and this idea occurred to me that if John was here today, and I was singing, "Oh, yes, I knew him well and he was a terrific guy," he'd say – "What a load of rubbish." It was his character. So that's what the song is about. It says . . . "And if I said I really knew you well, what would your answer be? Well, knowing you, you'd probably laugh and say that we were worlds apart" . . . and that kind of thing.'

The spring and summer of that year saw Paul back in the studio. The success of 'Tug Of War' had given him a new lease of life, he was eager to work again and refused to rest on the laurels of his success. This time, however, he joined another old friend, Michael Jackson – who a year or so before had covered Paul's 'Girlfriend' – to duet with him on 'The Girl Is Mine'. It was the first hit single featuring Paul McCartney since The Beatles' 'Something', that he neither wrote nor produced. Michael Jackson handled the writing, while Quincy Jones produced the record. It became a Top 5 success in Britain and America.

The musical association with Jackson came to fruition in 1983, with the release of the jointly written, 'Say Say Say', from McCartney's new solo album, 'Pipes Of Peace'. The video they made together to promote the single turned out to be a mini-epic in film terms. It was shot on location in the Santa Ynez Valley in California and cost 500,000 dollars to make. Set in the old West, the plot showed Michael and McCartney as a couple of con-men running their own Medicine Show, and selling Mac And Jac's Wonder Potion to unsuspecting townspeople . . . the profits of which, however, like latter-day Robin Hoods, they donated to a local orphanage!

But even this movie masterpiece was surpassed shortly afterwards with the release of Paul's next single, the title track from the new album – 'Pipes Of Peace'. The accompanying video was brilliant. Set in 1914 in the trenches on the Western Front, McCartney played dual roles of an English soldier and his German counterpart, meeting during the famous Christmas Day armistice, when both sides came together to exchange festive greetings, and spirit, across a barren, shell-ravaged no-man's-land at the height of the First World War.

Yet, although being depicted as the anti-war song and a powerful anthem to peace, 'Pipes Of Peace' was also a rich love song in all its glory. It was the perfect opening track with which to introduce the album, while as a single, it went on to top the British chart in its own right.

The album, however, demonstrated Paul McCartney's vast experience as a songwriter and recording artist, and showed a master craftsman going steadily about his business. It was an exercise in growing up. Paul had matured over twenty years . . . and it oozed from his songs. The album exuded class and originality and integrity. At last he had got it right!

Of the eleven tracks recorded with another complement of top-class sidemen, including Ringo Starr, 'So Bad' and 'Through Our Love' stand out as a testimony to something that McCartney loves to do, and needless to say, does so well . . . writing poignant love songs. 'So Bad' was inspired by the family, while 'Through Our Love' captures the optimism that love *will* triumph over everything else in the end.

'Pipes Of Peace' was Paul's last album before becoming involved in another very special project, writing and starring in his first full-length feature movie since 'Help' – 'Give My Regards To Broad Street'. It would take nearly two years to complete, and bring Paul back again into confrontation with . . . the critics. Nothing had changed.

Paul McCartney had emerged from a difficult period since The Beatles had broken up – and survived through the ever-changing face of music, to establish himself as one of the elder statesmen of rock 'n' roll, respected and admired by everyone around him. And yet . . . he was *still* able to make outstandingly successful hit singles and albums, and to beat all the newcomers at their own game. As music progressed, Paul McCartney led the charge. But he could still rock with the best of them.

Commenting on his durability and his uncanny ability to keep one step ahead of the chasing pack, McCartney was compared to Cliff Richard, Elton John and David Bowie during the course of a radio programme on new wave music. With typical modesty, Paul admitted that he was still driven on by keenness and ambition. 'All the people mentioned are all ambitious. I don't mean that in a bad way, I mean it in a good way. They are keen to do stuff. And I think that is really important. You motivate yourself. If you want to get out there and be a kind of long lasting musician, you see to it that you are.'

On the evening of Saturday, July 13th, 1985, Paul McCartney proved his durability to a massive watching audience . . . and consolidated his place in the annals of rock history.

At a few minutes after 10.00 p.m. (local time), McCartney brought the British contribution to the spectacular Live Aid Global Juke Box concerts to a rousing finale at Wembley Stadium. His appearance at Wembley had proved a major coup for organizer Bob Geldof, and had been anticipated and relished by the watching British audience of over 72,000 in the stadium, the 90,000 Americans packed into Philadelphia's JFK Stadium seeing the London connection relayed by satellite – and a world-wide television audience of many hundreds of millions. It had also fired the imagination that maybe this just might be the time, the place, and the cause to bring together on stage the three surviving Beatles with Julian Lennon standing in for his father. And rumours were rife that a dream would become reality.

At the end of the day, though, it wasn't to be. The rumours proved groundless and a reunion never took place. Still . . . the presence of Paul McCartney was well worth the wait.

Sitting almost starkly at a grand piano, playing without accompaniment, and completely unannounced, Paul McCartney took to the concert platform in darkness, and opened up with his own anthem to loneliness – 'Let It Be'. It was an emotive and emotional return to the live stage for Paul, who admitted to being petrified. Amazingly, technical problems with the microphones and sound system almost marred this perfect ending to a perfect day, and virtually obliterated the first full verse and chorus of the classic ballad.

And yet, within seconds of him singing the first bars, over 72,000 voices packed into the London arena rose as one, and joined together as a vast choir with Paul McCartney at its head, leading the way. 'And when the broken hearted people, Living in the world agree . . .'

Nothing had changed!

15

The Man

PAUL McCARTNEY WAS always the most down to earth member of The Beatles. Always charming in company, good mannered, a diplomat and the master of good sense and tact. He was looked upon by the others as the PRO of the group, and he would hate to hurt anyone's feelings.

Paul was always polite and pleasant, and showed tremendous humility and warmth, *and* great respect for others. Always Mr Nice Guy with his feet very firmly on the ground. He possessed a mischievous sense of humour, too, typical of Liverpool.

He has retained all of these qualities ever since, and in recent years, has gone out of his way on occasions to make himself accessible to the public and Press alike. He appreciates more than most, how his fans feel, too, and identifies with them; after all he was a fan himself once and he still is star struck. Paul gets a tremendous kick out of working with the legends of rock 'n' roll, and looks upon it as a great privilege to be able to appear with the likes of Carl Perkins, Michael Jackson, or Stevie Wonder. As a youngster, he would often be found outside the stage door of the Liverpool Empire Theatre waiting to secure autographs from the stars appearing there.

When The Beatles were in the midst of their breakup, Paul's father-in-law Lee Eastman, offered him the advice that no matter how successful he became, no matter how big a star, or how rich and famous, he should always endeavour to . . . 'stay ordinary'.

Paul McCartney has kept faith with Eastman's words ever since. Indeed, when he married Linda in 1969, Paul virtually turned his back on the showbusiness merry-go-round of party-time and razzle dazzle. He'd done it all before. He needed it no longer. 'We're bored with it all,' he said.

Today, as always, Paul McCartney finds his strength and stability in the warmth of a loving family. It was something he always had as a youngster growing up in Liverpool. And, no matter how hard the times, there was always a deep feeling of security.

The McCartney family was very close. Paul remembers that his parents 'didn't have too many friends – they had relatives, aunties, uncles and cousins,' and there was always an atmosphere of friendship, harmony and mutual trust in the household.

He told writer Diane de Dubovay: 'Being able to discuss your problems with people you love. There's not a lot better than that in life . . . that was always there for me.'

He has cultivated the same kind of loving atmosphere with his own family.

From father Jim McCartney, Paul learnt the true values of life, and despite being classed as one of the ten richest people in the country, Paul McCartney has made every effort in his private life to retain normality, and a sense of those values. It is something he firmly believes in, and instils into his own children.

'Actually we've taken a very conscious approach. Our kids have been brought up in the state school system,' Paul told *Woman's Own*. 'They don't go to private schools. It's not that we are against people having privilege, but I figure if we did that with our kids, they'd have privilege and then more privilege.

'They're being brought up just like ordinary kids. They go to ordinary schools. They do exams just like everyone else. They do everything ordinary.'

The McCartney children travel to the local village school by bus – and are expected to help around the home. Paul proudly admits that Heather, Mary and Stella have developed into very good cooks just like their mother.

McCartney's decision to send his children to state school, was taken several years ago when the family still lived at the London home in St John's Wood. Heather was attending a private school in the capital, when, after seeing some of the other pupils looking, as Paul described, 'like prostitutes', he decided it was time she should move on. Shortly before taking the ultimate decision, however, a heated argument with

Heather had revealed just what kind of company the girl was keeping at school.

Paul admitted: 'She told me that her friends had told her not to worry. They said that if I gave her any more trouble, she could go to the papers and tell them all about me. Just realizing that she was mixing with children who had this mentality was very worrying.'

Before long the McCartneys had moved out of London and into the country.

Home for Paul and Linda McCartney and their children is a five-bedroomed farmhouse. Paul designed the house himself with special emphasis placed on plenty of windows so that the family can enjoy the splendid views of the rolling countryside all around them, and a large, round kitchen, full of light.

The house is often littered with children and animals and plants and newspapers, books and toys. It's a practical house and possesses that special atmospheric quality that makes a house a home. It is well lived in and has its own identity. It feels *right*. When it rains, there is usually more mud on the inside than on the outside. It is also difficult to avoid tripping over the many animals that share the home with the humans. Paul and Linda keep a dozen horses; all the family ride, although Linda is the fanatic and she spends much of her spare time training and breeding and showing Appaloosa ponies. One of the other horses on the farm is Drake's Drum, the thoroughbred Paul bought for his race-loving father as a present in the mid-'60s. The former steeplechasing charger lives out his days in splendid retirement. The farm also contains some sheep, geese, ducks, deer, chickens, pheasants and dogs. The McCartneys also grow their own vegetables.

'We are vegetarians and will not eat anything that has got to be killed. We have our own free-range hens, but wouldn't dream of killing them for food,' said Linda.

The only luxury is a swimming pool.

Since John Lennon's murder, however, Paul has had the house fitted with bullet-proof glass and surrounded the estate with double fences and floodlighting. All very necessary precautions in his case. In the autumn of 1984, police foiled an attempt to kidnap Linda McCartney and hold her for a ransom of £10,000,000. Paul dismissed the attempt: 'I try to lead a normal life with Linda and the kids. I don't like talking about my security measures. Any talk of a kidnap plot is bound to give ideas to nutters.'

As if to keep to his principles of retaining a healthy and normal life, Paul can often be seen by neighbours, jogging through the countryside on many mornings.

There is also another home in Scotland, where the barn doubles as a recording studio, which Paul purchased as a 183 acre dairy farm in 1966. He added to his holdings by a further 400 acres of land adjacent to the farm in 1971. The farm is often the family home when the schools have broken up for the holidays.

Normality for Paul McCartney is being able to share a drink with the people he can count on as his friends. He likes beer . . . and watching television. His favourite programmes include 'The World About Us', 'The Living Planet', 'Eastenders', and most nature-based shows. He admits to watching games shows, quizzes and sport on television. Linda is especially keen on football! Paul McCartney is also *not* averse to *washing up*. It was something he had to do at home in Liverpool and now he takes pride in doing the dishes.

'I'm not too careful about image,' he said. 'If I were careful, I'd try to avoid that "family man" and "he lives on a farm". Because you know that kids and the farm are ammo, and they say, "Here's old family man Paulie, back with the sheep, what a yawn." If I were really concerned with it, I'd live in London and always be down the clubs, popping pills just to show them how hip I was.'

In 1963, Paul along with John Lennon, George Harrison and Ringo Starr, filled in one of those inevitable questionnaires that were given wide coverage in the music Press of the day, listing 'favourite foods', 'likes', 'pet hates' and a whole catalogue of lifelines. Under 'likes' McCartney listed . . . 'music and TV'.

Very little changes over two decades. Today, Paul is still very much involved with both. His horizons, however, have widened to take in a passion for carpentry, sheep shearing, and, not surprisingly, farming. One Christmas, Linda bought him a tractor as a present . . . to help on the farm.

Another great love is painting, and Paul admires the work of Magritte and Picasso and has invested in some of their paintings.

His tastes in music, though, have become more catholic, and now envelop a much wider range of choice, including Fred Astaire, Buddy Holly, rock 'n' roll, classical music, Pink Floyd and The Sex Pistols. Stevie Wonder is a particularly favourite singer.

Back in 1963, Paul's musical tastes covered . . . 'R & B and modern jazz', while his favourite singers included the likes of Ben E. King, Chuck Berry and Little Richard.

These days, Paul McCartney has developed a passion for recording, and loves the whole process attached to making records. He loves working in the studio, writing and playing around. He spends many hours simply putting down any tracks that come to mind, bits and pieces of material, half-finished songs and phrases, guitar riffs, weird and wonderful sounds. Anything that some day might be used again in a song or on a recording. He records everything he does, and adores it. It is one way of channelling his creativity.

Paul also likes the whole idea of record production. George Martin has called him 'a pretty good producer in his own right' – and in the past, besides his work with Wings, he has produced a number of singles and albums by other artists including Mary Hopkin, Ringo Starr and his brother Mike McGear (McCartney) and *his* former group, Scaffold.

Despite paying supertax on his vast earnings, Paul McCartney is very patriotic. He's proud to be British and calls his wife 'honorary British'. He hits out at people who ask him why he hasn't become a tax exile like so many of his contemporaries.

'I just hate the idea that you have to live where it's convenient for your money,' he says. 'We like it in England. We love the country. It's a great place to bring up children.'

He also gets annoyed when people speculate about his wealth and how much he actually earns. He will never reveal his true worth – indeed, he admits to not knowing how much money he possesses – and in any case, no-one has the right to know.

'My own father didn't tell my mother how much he earned,' says Paul.

Paul's upbringing has made him rightly protective of his earning capacity. It is very personal to him. He is proud of the fact that his father taught him thrift and never to borrow money. Perhaps it stemmed from the fact that for most of his working life, Jim McCartney fought hard to make ends meet and never had enough money for life's little luxuries. But he made sure Paul and his brother Michael never wanted for anything in those days. He didn't want either of them to go short if he could help it.

Up until 1966, during the riotous days of Beatlemania, Paul was only allowed £50 a week spending money from the group.

Even today, he still firmly believes that he *has* to keep on working because if he ever stopped . . . he could lose everything he has worked for! It would be pretty difficult to accomplish, because his money has been well invested.

After The Beatles split up, Paul McCartney relied heavily on the advice and counsel of his father-in-law, Lee Eastman, to guide him. And he steered him through a rough and very painful period of time as McCartney was branded the villain who actually dared to break up The Beatles. Paul listened to what Eastman had to say and acted accordingly on what he was told.

When he set up his own company, McCartney Productions Limited, he took over a small, dingy office on the fourth floor of a building on the edge of London's Soho Square. When Eastman saw it, he advised his son-in-law to invest by buying the whole six-storey building. Paul, who is often hesitant when making decisions, although once he has made up his mind he sticks to his decision, took Linda's father's advice.

Later Eastman asked McCartney what else he wanted to invest his money in. Paul didn't know.

'What are you interested in?' said Lee.

'Music,' came the reply, 'particularly Buddy Holly.' So money was invested in *music*. The first music publishing company MPL took over was the E.H. Morris catalogue which administered the songs of Buddy Holly. And every year since then, Paul has organized and run an official Buddy Holly Week.

Lee Eastman rationalized that it was far better for his son-in-law to put his money into something he enjoyed, and with which he could become actively involved, than to buy up investments for the sake of it . . . that would be meaningless to Paul.

Today, through shrewd investing, Paul McCartney is one of the most prominent music publishers in the world, owning the rights to a vast catalogue of songs and music, including several Broadway musicals – 'Annie', 'Mame', 'Grease', 'Peter Pan', 'Hello Dolly', 'Bye Bye Birdie' and 'A Chorus Line'. He also owns such perennials as 'Tenderly' 'Autumn Leaves', 'Stormy Weather' and 'After You've Gone', as well as big band hits, jazz standards and the old favourite, 'Chopsticks'. He is the proud owner, too, of 'Your Feet's Too Big', one of the songs The Beatles used to feature in their stage act in the Hamburg days, and a number they played for George Martin at their Parlophone audition in 1962.

McCartney, however, *doesn't* own many of his own songs, like 'Yesterday', 'Eleanor Rigby' and 'For No One', which were first taken over by ATV Music when Northern Songs, The Beatles' music publisher, was bought out at the end of the 1960s. It has become a bone of contention for Paul ever since the take-over, and on several occasions he has tried to buy back the catalogue, particularly in 1981 when a bid of £21,000,000 failed . . . and shortly afterwards when a joint offer by McCartney and Yoko Ono was rejected.

The years, though, saw McCartney appear to mellow with time. He became less bitter, or so it seemed. On television in the fall of 1984, he admitted that his attitude had changed to the events which robbed him of some of his most famous music.

'I've got past getting angry,' he said. 'When you look at the justice of it. You come down from Liverpool, you get in with a publisher and he's good for you, and you get successful. If you don't happen to know how to get your own songs, you can't blame him (the publisher) for doing whatever he does.

'I don't own "Yesterday" and I don't own "Here There And Everywhere". I think if you talked to a lot of people in the streets: "Did you know Paul McCartney doesn't own 'Yesterday'?" They'd say, "Why? What happened?" When you think that I wrote it, recorded it, went out and sold it . . . obviously, I *deserve* to own it.'

In the summer of 1985, the rock industry – and indeed the business world – were stunned, when in August it was announced that ATV Music, owners of Northern Songs and publishers of over 250 Lennon and McCartney songs, written between 1964 and 1970, had been bought out by . . . Michael Jackson, in a reputed deal worth over 40,000,000 dollars. In a long-running series of negotiations lasting several months, Jackson had beaten off the likes of Coca Cola, CBS, and EMI for the lucrative publishing package. Paul McCartney and Yoko Ono had offered £25,000,000 for control of the company.

In one British newspaper announcing details of the takeover, a spokesman for McCartney was reported as saying: 'He will be absolutely devastated.

'Paul has been trying to pull this off for so long. When he hears what has happened he's going to be very, very upset – particularly as it's Michael Jackson. He and Paul have become good friends.'

The catalogue of songs Michael Jackson picked up covered all the Lennon–McCartney songs except four. 'Love Me Do' and 'P.S. I Love You', which are owned by McCartney himself through MPL, and 'Please Please Me' and 'Ask Me Why', owned by the late Dick James.

Yet, although he doesn't officially own the titles from a publishing point of view, Paul McCartney still receives massive royalties from the songs through performing rights. When 'Help' was issued for use in an American television commercial in 1985, the price for just one year's use was over £100,000. A similar fee was paid for the television advertising rights for the use of 'We Can Work It Out' in Britain.

When it comes to money, though, Paul McCartney runs a very tight ship at home. He doesn't flaunt his money and for this reason, on occasions, he has been accused of meanness. In truth, he regularly gives large amounts to an assortment of charities in secret, without fuss, publicity or ballyhoo. His only request is that his name be kept quiet and off the list of patrons. He was, however, more than happy to lend his name, and everything it stands for, to the Band Aid and Live Aid appeals during 1984 and 1985.

In private, McCartney rarely carries large amounts of money on him and several times he has been caught short.

On one occasion, he took Linda into town for a morning to do some shopping, while he visited his usual local barber for a hair cut. The idea was for them both to meet up later in a nearby public house, to enjoy a quick drink, before returning home. When they reached the pub and ordered their drinks, they suddenly realized they had spent most of their money and thought they didn't have enough to cover the bill. They wouldn't hear of it when the barman offered the drinks on the house. A frantic search through pockets and bags revealed just enough coppers to pay their way. At other times, Paul has been spotted in the local town, in second-hand record shops, looking to snap up bargains.

And yet . . . when it comes to his professional life, Paul has been known to be wildly extravagant, spending thousands of pounds on promotion campaigns and video projects.

For the Wings Over America tour, he insisted that everything – every single move the band made – be filmed and photographed. He even took an official artist along on the tour to make a special artistic record for posterity. It all cost a fortune.

In 1978, Linda bought an antique statuette of a 'flying lady' at an auction, with which Paul was so taken, he decided it would be perfect for the cover of the group's forthcoming 'Wings Greatest' album. An idea was spawned to picture the statuette standing forlorn in drifting snow, and a suitable photo session arranged. The resulting photographs failed to convey the picture Paul had originally envisaged. The snow simply didn't look right! So, he decided to do it all for real. The family and a team of twelve were flown to Switzerland for a week, all expenses paid, where the seven-day long session took place. To add realism to the picture, a snow-plough was hired to create a suitable snowdrift, and the whole scene was photographed from the air, in a specially chartered helicopter. The episode cost thousands.

Paul McCartney is very proud of his north country roots and has a warm love and affection for his home city of Liverpool, regularly visiting aunts, uncles and cousins who still live on Merseyside. He has been hurt on several occasions by accusations made against him, and the other ex-Beatles, for *not* doing enough for the city in its hours of need.

However, all was forgiven in November 1984, when Paul McCartney received the Freedom of the City of Liverpool, to join under fifty other recipients, including William Gladstone and Bessie Braddock.

At a civic ceremony to mark the occasion, Paul was moved: 'It's a great honour and I'm well chuffed. I like to think it's the people who have given it, and if that's the case, it's the greatest honour of all.

'I want to thank the 'Pool itself because we couldn't have made it without you.'

Asked how he had felt over the years as he got richer, while Liverpool's fortunes declined, he added: 'It can given you a bit of a guilty feeling because you don't know where you got it from. I like to think it's clean money. Nobody is forced to buy the records and I don't rip anybody off. I keep a lot of people in work.'

It's a well-known fact that Paul and Linda McCartney's marriage is one of the most stable in showbusiness. It is legendary. They are as close as they have always been. Indeed, since their wedding, in 1969, they have rarely been parted. The longest they have been separated was the ten days Paul spent in prison in Japan in 1980.

Says Paul: 'Our marriage isn't an idyll, we have our rows. I'd characterize our relationship as rather volatile. But we're not bored. We do have wonderful children and a lovely marriage. And yes, I expect it to go on for ever.'

The closeness of his marriage, and the family ties, were the reasons Paul gave when turning down a sensational offer of nearly £1,000,000 in 1984, for him to appear in just eight episodes of TV's 'Dallas'. For £110,000 per episode, Paul would have played the part of a wealthy British landowner visiting Texas to look at property for investment.

'The kids wouldn't have been able to accompany me,' he said. 'Unless I took them out of school.

'If I went on my own it would have meant being separated from them, and I didn't like the thought of us being apart, so I turned the offer down.'

The offer would also have taken McCartney a step nearer to achieving another ambition he now holds, to become a serious actor, after the success of his acting in 'Broad Street'. And he would dearly love to follow in the footsteps of such other singing stars who made their names – and a secondary lucrative career – in acting, like Sinatra and Crosby, and more recently David Bowie, Sting and David Essex.

'Acting does appeal to me,' he says. 'I'd like to do a bit of character acting.' And adds: 'I'd rather be a 103 year-old fellow who just sits there. That's what I really fancy. I don't even know if I could do it, but I like having a go at these things.'

At the end of 1963 with The Beatles on the verge of worldwide musical domination, Paul McCartney was asked to comment on his newly-acquired success. He said: 'Security is the only thing I want. Money to do nothing with; money to have in case you wanted to do something.'

Twenty-one years later, his attitudes had changed very little. 'You reach a point when you say what was I trying to get famous for? To get a guitar, a car and a house. That was it – I could never think of anything beyond those.

'I've got a guitar now, and a car, and a house – and so it's then that you think – well, what's it for? To give you the freedom to do just what you want to do; *to live just as you feel.*'

16

Paul McCartney

SOMEONE SUGGESTED THAT Paul McCartney's secret of success as a songwriter lay in the fact that prior to setting out on his own solo career away from The Beatles, he had actually taken the trouble to do a little market research, to find out exactly what kinds of songs people wanted to hear. When he was given the results, so the rumour goes, he consciously tailored his work to the tastes of his supposed market. It has been successful ever since. However, in a radio interview, he put it another way when talking about his writing.

'You sort of put yourself in the mode of remembering who you are. Remember, you are the kid who used to get on the bus, and go down to Lewis's, and buy your little thing in your brown paper packet . . . and look at it, read it all the way home: *the record*. And you used to get that thrilled and involved with the record because you knew you loved these people, whoever they were, whoever the band was.

'So when I write . . . I tend to do that. I'm not looking for what the public will want, I'm looking for the public in *me*. It's me just sitting down there and saying, "I've got my heart on a string and everything's a flutter," cos that seems to fit, and it seems to be that kind of nervousness of love, a little flutter. I just try to get stuff that seems good and seems to fit and that feels right. But if you're lucky, these things write themselves.

'But where does a song come from? I've been asked that millions of times, and every composer you ever hear says – "Well, I sit down and it sort of comes through. I'm a vehicle." And it's true, you are. You sit down and have a bit a fun . . . you love playing around on the old piano or the guitar. Suddenly, this little idea comes through . . .'

For Paul McCartney to talk openly about his own songwriting is very rare. He prefers to let others analyse his music while he gets on with the job. He has never categorized his writing because he is consciously aware how much more there is to music than an array of labels, or tags, or pigeon holes.

'When I get in my car and turn on the radio, I want to hear some good sounds,' he says 'So whatever I write, I write for that. What are the alternatives?'

He adds: 'I'd say I've done some songs that are really good; some I think didn't quite come off; some I hate. But I've done enough to satisfy myself that I'm okay. That's basically all I'm looking for, like most people.'

With the break-up of The Beatles, Paul McCartney was out on his own as a songwriter. Although they had not written together as a team for some time, he no longer had the support of John Lennon to help him out, or for that matter, the other Beatles to bounce his ideas off. He was by himself in a world that had suddenly become tougher and far more cynical. He had to grow up quickly to survive . . . if he wanted to survive.

Towards the end of his days as a Beatle, Paul's music was showing far greater maturity. His ear for commerciality was finely tuned, and in certain respects, he was leaving John in his wake. But with the split, and the ensuing aggravation – the bickering and in-fighting and the strain of High Court proceedings – his music started to suffer dramatically and fell away. The songs on his first two solo albums were criticized by the rock Press for being of mundane quality, despite the fact that both albums threw up several songs of which The Beatles would have been proud – 'Every Night', 'Maybe I'm Amazed', 'Uncle Albert/Admiral Halsey', 'Heart Of The Country' and 'Back Seat Of My Car'. But instead of presenting material to fill only half an album, like he had done in the past, sharing songs with John Lennon and George Harrison, he now had the entire showcase to complete by himself. In the beginning, he couldn't do it to such a high standard that was expected from Paul McCartney. Those early efforts were often hurried, seldom seen through to their ultimate ending, simply put together to fill space, and thrown away. Yet . . . they became a release for Paul, a safety valve that needed turning as he sought his own musical independence. They were fences he needed to climb; statements that he needed to make. Far from learning how to walk though, Paul had to learn the art of cantering before he could gallop.

'With the breakup of The Beatles, I was a little unsure in some of the material and I think it showed,' he admitted. 'But I don't agree with anyone who says the songs weren't good.'

Once he *had* sorted himself out, once the problems had been resolved, and Paul had found his true self again, his work started to improve, gaining much from the experience. It grew in confidence . . . and has been growing ever since, developing, gaining discipline and tightness . . . and maturing like good wine.

Paul McCartney is the first to admit that there is no special pattern to his songwriting. Miraculously to the layman, the songs just happen. Linda revealed: 'He doesn't lock himself away. We can be sitting, watching television and he might get up and play, and all of a sudden, there's another song there. I'm amazed how it comes to him.'

Other times, however, he has to work hard at his trade. 'About a third of my songs are pure slog,' he says.

On occasions, inspiration can come through the subconscious. 'No Values', one of the original offerings on his 'Give My Regards To Broad Street' movie, came to him in a dream. He was on holiday at the time.

'I was dreaming I saw The Stones on stage and saw Mick singing this song called, "No Values",' he said. 'I remembered the chorus – a very catchy chorus. I saw it and woke up and said, "Great, I love that song The Stones do – 'No Values'." And then I thought, "No, there isn't one." I just dreamt it. I certainly wasn't sitting at a piano trying to write a song.'

After he checked it out that The Stones hadn't written or recorded the song, he set about writing down everything himself.

Whenever the going has got rough – and there have been several occasions – Paul has been steered through the bad times by his devotion to Linda and the children, and the family, who have remained a constant source of inspiration for material. Without them, he might well have foundered a long time ago. His post-Beatle songs have developed a warmer edge to them . . . something that has come out of contentment, peace of mind. And it is easy to see which of these songs have been culled from the family's influence: 'Love In Song', with its magnificent hook . . . 'Happiness in the homeland'; 'So Bad', 'Warm And Beautiful', 'Waterfalls', and 'Through Our Love' are just a few. He wrote a song, 'Heather', to his eldest daughter, although it has yet to be released on any record.

It's interesting to note that when John Lennon returned to the recording arena, after a lengthy absence when his days were spent sharing the joys and warmth of family life, bringing up his son Sean, and he released the 'Double Fantasy' album, he, too, had mellowed as a writer. His songs had lost that bite and subtle cruelty of old, and numbers like 'Beautiful Boy', 'Woman' and 'Starting Over' were softer. The contentment and serenity of a loving family had brought a new depth of quality to his work that was missing in the past. The irony was that at times McCartney was trying to break free from the chains of his 'silly love songs' hopefully to emulate Lennon in his songwriting. The wheel had turned full circle: John Lennon was emulating Paul McCartney.

Paul McCartney's songs are an expression of his life in every way, evoking all the things he holds dear. Love, happiness, family values, warmth and comfort. Many are autobiographical – he pleads for the simple life in 'Heart Of The Country' and for forgiveness on 'One More Kiss'. He writes about what he sees and hears, and feels and senses, although very little about his music builds up an in-depth picture of his true personality. He writes in fantasy rather than reality, and personal experiences play little part. He hides the truth on purpose. His songs reveal his personality to be more of a photo-fit picture than a true photograph.

'I remember George Harrison saying to me, "I couldn't write songs like that." He does it more from personal experience. I do some from personal experience, but my style is to veil it, whereas John's was to show it there, the naked truth. Mine is to draw a bit of a veil across it. If I was a painter, I'd probably just mask things a little bit more than some people. It's just my style,' he said.

It is easy to see just how high in esteem McCartney holds his rock 'n' roll heroes. He has paid homage to them time and time again, in his songs when writing with Lennon for The Beatles, and beyond. Gene Vincent's style was captured on '3 Legs', 'Spirits Of Ancient Egypt' and 'Let Me Roll It'. He paid tribute to Ben E. King on 'When The Night' and celebrated Buddy Holly on 'Eat At Home'.

Carl Perkins was a particular source of material during The Beatles days. The group featured many of the American's rockabilly songs in their act, and recorded several on albums. The influence was carried over with Paul's songs 'One More Kiss' and 'Heart Of The Country', which are lifted straight out of the Carl Perkins' songbook. On the album 'Tug Of War' the two stars recorded 'Get It' together, and each admired the other's performance.

It is hardly surprising that Paul McCartney has retained many of the themes and subjects he had developed with The Beatles, to fire his imagination in new songs. And loneliness keeps creeping into his own catalogue through 'Another Day', 'London Town', 'Lonely Old People', 'Man We Was Lonely' . . . as if he constantly needs reminding what might happen if he didn't have the love of a family behind him. He has also borrowed ideas from his former group. On several McCartney songs, including 'Mrs Vanderbilt' and 'Cafe On The Left Bank', he has returned to a descending guitar phrase used extensively on a number of Beatles numbers, but most effectively as the instrumental link between 'Carry That Weight' and 'The End' on 'Abbey Road'. He probably wrote it himself, although George Harrison has used it on several occasions, too, and a similar lick appears on 'Badge', the song he wrote with Eric Clapton for Cream. On others, Paul liberally dips into The Beatles' bag of favourite chords, riffs and musical sentences that first saw the light on Lennon and McCartney songs. Little phrases and musical sequences permeate the mind on several of Paul's items, begging the question: Where did I hear that before? But they are gone in a moment. A phrase on 'Baby's Request' comes straight off 'Do You Want To Know A Secret'; 'No Words' contains pieces from 'Nowhere Man' and 'You Never Give Me Your Money'; 'Long Haired Lady' smacks of 'Baby You're A Rich Man'; a piece from 'Rocky Raccoon' resurfaces on 'Mamunia'; while 'Oh Woman, Oh Why' is 'Why Don't We Do It In The Road' second time around, and 'Let Me Roll It' sees the return of 'Oh, Darling'.

McCartney has carried over another talent he learned with John Lennon, that of being able to combine two half-written songs or musical phrases, to make one entity. They did it together on 'I've Got A Feeling', 'Baby You're A Rich Man' and 'A Day In The Life'; Paul has done it on 'Uncle Albert/

Admiral Halsey', 'Miss Momma America' – 'they ran into each other by accident,' he said – 'Little Lamb Dragonfly' . . . and possibly 'Band On The Run' which appears to have been several songs run together. But he has also retained the habit of putting throwaway material on his albums to fill up holes – 'Dark Room', 'Be What You See', 'Glasses' and 'To You', have never been fully exploited as songs.

Paul also re-visits his own post-Beatles songs at times – whether subconsciously or as a deliberate ploy – to refurbish ideas and patterns further on totally different songs, like a musical pedigree. 'Silly Love Songs' is an extension of 'Girlfriend' which is an extension of 'Take It Away' in musical construction. The connection is even stronger between 'Baby's Request' and 'One More Kiss'.

One of McCartney's greatest talents has been an ability to absorb musical influences, develop them, and make them work for him on a different level, but in a completely positive way.

Since the days of The Beatles, he has had this uncanny knack of being able to write songs in virtually any style of music he cares to . . . and has done it often. He has also been able to mirror sounds, mimic trends, and accommodate the musical requirements of the world through pastiches of his own – from a natural affinity to Tamla Motown on songs like 'Beware My Love' and 'Sweetest Little Thing', to the jazz-funk of Earth Wind And Fire on 'Dress Me Up Like A Robber' and 'Take It Away'; from the gospel-sounding 'Million Miles' and 'After The Ball', to the rhythm and blues of Alexis Korner on 'On The Way' and 'Nobody Knows'; and to capture such individual styles as The Isley Brothers ('The Man'), Crosby, Still, Nash and Young ('Deliver Your Children') and Pink Floyd with 'Loup (1st Indian On The Moon)'.

'The kind of thing I am involved with has been changed anyway, to a large extent by the arrival of new music over the last – I don't know how long, really – because it's an ever-changing process in its time,' said Paul. 'I don't think that you can put it into little compartments and say: "During the last ten years the new wave British groups have ousted the old establishment." For me, the whole thing is always changing . . .'

If McCartney has his faults, however, they can often be found in his lyrics. On many of his songs, the words are virtually meaningless and obscure – 'Lady Dynamite', 'Jet', 'Backwards Traveller' – but he sometimes does it on purpose, preferring to use patterns of words for their sounds and rhymes for effect rather than any positive meaning they might convey: 'Spin It On', 'Bip Bop' and 'Spirits Of Ancient Egypt', are other examples. There are many more, and it seems that on occasions, if McCartney could get away with scat singing on songs, he would.

Paul likes whimsical phrases as seen on 'Junk' and 'Bluebird', and at times, he abandons all hope of grammatical correctness with his lyrics, in favour of getting his message home – phrases on 'So Bad' and 'Live And Let Die' leave a lot to be desired. Perhaps John Lennon summed it up best of all: 'Paul is quite a capable lyricist who doesn't think he is. So he doesn't go for it.'

George Martin countered: 'Paul could write some great lyrics,' . . . and at times *he* delivered the goods brilliantly, as witnessed on 'Pipes Of Peace', 'Tug Of War', 'Here Today' and 'No More Lonely Nights'.

On one occasion, the obscurity of his lyrics got one song banned, when the BBC refused to play the Wings single, 'Hi, Hi, Hi' . . .

'The daft thing about all that was our publishing company, Northern Songs, got the lyrics wrong and sent them round to the radio station and it said, "Get ready for my body gun", which is far more suggestive than anything I put – "Get ready for my polygon",' Paul told Paul Gambaccini . . . although the BBC stated the ban was enforced because they believed 'Hi, Hi, Hi' could be construed as a drug song.

Humour has always played a large part in McCartney's music, from the black comedy of 'Maxwell's Silver Hammer' in the early days, to the jokey 'The Pound Is Sinking' and the jolly 'Mrs Vanderbilt', through to 'Smile Away' and the bawdily observed 'Famous Groupies'. He has carried a wry smile and a gentle touch of comedy through his many excursions into the realms of vaudeville, too, with 'Uncle Albert/Admiral Halsey' – complete with Noël Coward voices – 'You Gave Me The Answer' and 'Average Person'.

Like all good writers, Paul McCartney draws his inspiration from many sources, from what he reads: 'Venus And Mars was inspired by an Asimov novel, 'Magneto And Titanium Man' came from a *Marvel* comic, and 'Bogey Music' was created from the 'Fungus And The Bogeyman' book of Raymond Briggs; from the environment in which he finds himself: 'My Carnival' was written in New Orleans at Mardi Gras time, 'Wunderlust' was the name of one of the boats Paul hired in the Virgin Islands when recording the 'London Town' album, and 'Front Parlour' was conceived and written in the front room of his home. And the peace and tranquillity of life on his Scottish farm has helped his music enormously at times. He composed almost all the music featured on the 'Band On The Run' album at the farm, and several other songs first saw the light of day in Scotland.

Yet of all the varying styles and the vast assortment of songs he has written, Paul McCartney is best known – and best-loved – for his love songs and ballads. Despite almost non-stop criticism from the rock Press that he can *only* write ballads – although his track record over many years has put paid to that theory – Paul is proud of his ability to write about romance, and love in all its varying aspects. His songs possess a remarkable quality of being able to express the feelings everyone has experienced in love and life at one time or another. His songs speak the language of the people; they put emotion into words and music. And often a Paul McCartney song has been able to say so much more in a few lines of music and words than a thousand words can convey on the written page.

He wrote 'Silly Love Songs' as a reaction to the critics who accused him of only writing 'sentimental slush'.

'Originally, I wrote this song at about the time when the kind of material I did was a bit out of favour, and you had Alice Cooper doing "No More Mr Nice Guy", and that kind of parody,' he told Andrew Harvey. 'I rather picked up a feeling in the air that ballads were regarded as soppy and love as too sentimental.

'I thought, so what's wrong with silly love songs? I was striking a blow for nice, sentimental love songs.'

Since breaking away on his own, Paul McCartney has written several songs in collaboration with other musicians, including his wife, Linda, his brother Michael McCartney (Mike McGear), Denny Laine, Stevie Wonder and Michael Jackson. Yet, at the end of a major television documentary on his work, Paul McCartney was asked if he missed working with John Lennon.

'I doubt whether John and I would have got back together writing,' said Paul. 'I think because of his breaking up The Beatles and his association in other fields, with Yoko for instance, I think it would have been very hard to come back together.

'I liked working with John and I certainly do miss having someone like that around. John was a special writer. I think his stuff has got a lot of depth and he was very easy to write with. Our partnership had broken up with the end of The Beatles, it just came full circle.'

A few months later, Paul added: 'Linda and I writing together wasn't ever a serious musical collaboration. I didn't even feel that writing with Michael Jackson was a collaboration in the same way it was with John. That was a songwriting partnership . . .

'We were very special.'

17

From Penny Lane to Broad Street

PAUL MCCARTNEY ALWAYS fancied the idea of writing a musical. Indeed, in the early days, several of the songs he composed were set aside to be part of a musical venture at some later date, including 'When I'm 64'.

'I wrote the tune for that and I was vaguely thinking it might come in handy for a musical comedy or something,' he said.

Somehow, he never quite got around to doing it and over the years, the idea wore off. There was no self motivation.

'I always had my sights vaguely set on a musical, probably because people used to say to John and myself, "When are you going to write your musical?" Lennon and McCartney sounds like a musical-writing team.

'But I've never been attracted to the field really. I've often thought one of these days will be right and I'll feel like doing it, but I don't like to do anything unless that fire in the belly is there.'

His music did, however, appear in a musical in 1974 when 'John, Paul, George, Ringo . . . and Bert' – by award-winning writer Willie Russell – was staged in London's West End at the Lyric Theatre. The show told the story of The Beatles against a backdrop of Lennon and McCartney songs, all of which were sung by a young, unknown Scottish folk singer, who later went on to enjoy outstanding worldwide success – Barbara Dickson.

Paul wasn't enamoured with the production because it gave a distorted view of the group and put the blame for the break up of The Beatles firmly on his shoulders. 'It set me down in history as the one who broke the group up,' he said. 'The opposite is true.'

When it came to writing for the much wider global stage of movies, though, Paul was rarin' to go. It was a different ball game altogether.

The Beatles' first film, 'A Hard Day's Night' – the original title was going to be Beatlemania until Ringo came up with a better one – was made in 1964 on a budget of under £200,000. Because the producers looked upon the group as just another popular musical act of the day, and made the movie around them, they simply absorbed the music The Beatles were writing at the time and slotted it around the documentary-type plot. Nothing was composed specially for the film, apart from the title song which John wrote one evening, in response to producer Walter Shenson's promptings, that it would be a good idea to have a title track to run over the opening and closing credits.

Of the nine songs featured on the soundtrack, Paul contributed to just three – 'She Loves You', 'Can't Buy Me Love' and the stylish love poem to Jane Asher, 'And I Love Her'.

The situation regarding musical content was repeated the following year when The Beatles made 'Help' for which to this day, Paul McCartney admits to not having read the entire movie script.

Once again, a loose plot, based on a frantic Marx Brothers-type chase through such locations as Austria and the Bahamas, was dressed up with Beatles music. George Harrison contributed 'I Need You', while McCartney chipped in with 'Another Girl' and 'The Night Before'. Lennon handled the title track once more after the movie's name was changed from 'Eight Arms To Hold You' to 'Help.'

For their next movie outing, however, Paul remembers that none of The Beatles wanted to get involved with the 'Yellow Submarine' animated feature film. The idea of seeing themselves portrayed as cartoons was one they didn't relish. So, when they were approached by the film-makers for an original score, they virtually turned them down.

'We were very irresponsible,' said Paul. 'We didn't really want to write the music.'

At that time, the group was firmly ensconced in the world of flower power and psychedelia in the studio making 'Sergeant Pepper', and they were reluctant to help out in any way, or get involved.

In the end, the producers of the film decided to go along

with the whole idea of 'Pepperland' and love and peace and psychedelia, and the film was made accordingly. Almost grudgingly, The Beatles contributed a mere handful of songs to the venture – of no particular importance, and not particularly good – including Paul's spoof on skiffle groups, 'All Together Now'. It was not a memorable song. Yet an abundance of established Beatles material was also featured in the movie which gave the soundtrack a touch of class and quality and virtually saved it, featuring the McCartney composed songs 'All You Need Is Love', 'When I'm 64', 'Sergeant Pepper's Lonely Hearts Club Band', 'Eleanor Rigby' and the title track. George Martin composed an original score of incidental music, which was recorded by the London Symphony Orchestra, and made up one side of the subsequently released 'Yellow Submarine' soundtrack album.

Paul McCartney's own first attempt at writing an original score for a film, came in 1966 when he was approached to provide a soundtrack for the Boulting Brothers' British film comedy, 'The Family Way', based on Bill Naughton's 'All In Good Time', and set in a Lancashire town.

He explained to Nicholas Jackson how he set about the task: 'It was easy for me and hard for George Martin, because the hardest thing in writing for films is the physical spadework of actually measuring out against the frames. It's a hard job. I just made up the themes. I just wrote the tunes and said, "Here's how it goes, George," and then explained to him how I wanted it orchestrated because I can't write music to this day. It's almost a superstition, it doesn't seem to equate . . . the noises I hear with those dots. I have a bit of a problem with that. It's like musical dyslexia.'

Writing a theme score proved a completely different kind of experience for Paul.

'I wasn't trying to write hits,' he said. 'I was just trying to write something that would suit the film, which was actually harder to do than something commercial.'

He succeeded quite well in capturing the feeling of the picture and its north country atmosphere in the music, which evoked cobblestones and cotton mills, and yet he retained the great warmth and humour that is so indicative of Lancashire. The haunting refrain of the main theme, 'Love In The Open Air', displayed a sadness in its melody that was one of the underlying themes of the entire film, while his wedding theme paraded optimism and hope for the future.

Shortly afterwards, Paul wrote his first television theme, composing the title tune for the 1968 situation comedy series, 'Thingumybob', starring Stanley Holloway. And once again, Paul returned to a well-trodden path to find his inspiration in his own north country roots and memories. 'Thingumybob' was recorded by the Black Dyke Mills Brass Band on Apple Records and released as a single, which McCartney produced himself, but neither the theme tune nor the series was memorable enough to warrant more than a season's outing on television.

Six years later, he returned to the small screen to write the theme to the adventure series, 'Zoo Gang', starring John Mills and Lili Palmer. Wings recorded the number and released it as the flip-side to the single version of 'Band On The Run'.

'Magical Mystery Tour' in 1967 promised much – and turned out to be the first of a series of spectacular failures that would dog The Beatles in later days. It proved to a cynical world that, after their enormous international acclaim and success, The Beatles were vulnerable.

The movie concept was Paul's – an idea thought up on a transatlantic flight. He had written the song, 'Magical Mystery Tour' with John, for the 'Sergeant Pepper' album, and it developed further from there into a full-scale project of its own. The Beatles would write and produce the entire film without any outside help from directors and the like. 'We didn't worry about the fact that we didn't know anything about making films and had never made one before,' said Paul. 'We realized years ago you didn't need knowledge in this world to do anything.'

The basic theme for the film was to re-create a mystery coach tour out into the country, only the movie would be filled with fun and fantasy, music and magic. With this in mind, the mystery tour coach, packed with actors, extras, musicians, camera crew and technicians, set off for nowhere in particular – travelling around the country lanes of southern England. The idea was to stop and shoot whatever happened along the way. What The Beatles failed to realize was that they would be hounded everywhere they went by the world's Press, hungry for a scoop. It made filming impossible. After two days of causing havoc on the roads, the coach trip was halted in favour of filming at West Malling Airfield in Kent, followed later by studio work. The whole set-up lacked any kind of co-ordination and organization. The Beatles naively believed they wouldn't need a comprehensive shooting-script or story-line – they could just make it up as they went along. It might have been the way they were currently working in the recording studios, writing and recording their songs, but it was an impossible way to work making a film. It was a shambles from start to finish, and the film was always destined to fail. The final production, which each of The Beatles attempted to edit, was often grotesque, and far too surreal for British television audiences who were exposed to its magic, and mystery, on December 26th, 1967. The critics panned it mercilessly.

The *Daily Express* called it '*rubbish*'.

Yet even in the midst of disaster came triumph.

From out of the débâcle of a picture came six new and original songs which showed that, although The Beatles might not be able to make good films, they had no equals when it came to making good music. The movie soundtrack showcased Lennon's 'I Am The Walrus', Harrison's 'Blue Jay Way', and the jointly composed instrumental, 'Flying'. McCartney's three songs stuck very much to his well-tried themes of childhood memories on the title track, loneliness for the mysterious and whimsical 'Fool On The Hill', and a favourite formula of vaudeville on 'Your Mother Should Know', for which the film sequence showed John, Paul, George and Ringo as four song-and-dance men resplendent in white tie and tails! Two other compositions, 'Jessie's Dream' and 'Shirley's Wild Accordion' were never recorded.

The Beatles took another tumble with their next film, 'Let It Be' – but by the time it was put out on general release in 1970, it didn't much matter any more. The movie, directed under the greatest possible strain by Michael Lindsay-Hogg, actually became a major success for all the *wrong* reasons, and won an Oscar for Best Original Song Score. Far from being a behind-the-scenes look at days in the life of The Beatles, seen rehearsing and recording a series of songs for an album, before giving a live performance at the end of the film as Paul had conceived the entity, 'Let It Be' became a documentary on the group tearing itself apart and breaking up.

Paul said: 'It shows how we were. Our personalities. Me egging everyone on saying, "Come on we've got this film to make," and these people saying, "Shut up!" It would be John and George, but not often Ringo. All the insecurities came out.'

John said: 'It was hell making the film. Even the biggest Beatle fan couldn't have sat through those six weeks of misery. It was the most miserable session on earth.'

He added: '"Let It Be" was set up by Paul, for Paul. That's one of the main reasons The Beatles finished.'

The finished movie featured twenty-two of The Beatles' songs, including some of the material they had played on stage in the early days, like 'Besame Mucho', 'Kansas City' and 'Shake Rattle And Roll', together with some newer material and a song John and Paul had penned in 1958 – 'One After 909'.

Before finally getting the 'Broad Street' movie off the ground in 1983, however, Paul McCartney had faced the biggest challenge yet in writing for the cinema, when ten years before, he had been asked to turn his highly talented hands to composing the theme for a new James Bond movie – 'Live And Let Die' – which incidentally marked Roger Moore's début as the Ian Fleming super hero. It turned into a big, spectacular production job. 'I didn't feel that I could go out and do a little acoustic number for a Bond film. What are people going to think. "Oh, Christ, what is it?" You're following something, so you've got to keep vaguely with the format,' said Paul.

'Live And Let Die' became one of Paul's great success stories, picking up a Grammy Award for its composer, and an Oscar nomination as Best Song, although Marvin Hamlish, with 'The Way We Were', stole the limelight at the Academy Awards presentation ceremony.

But right at the start of the whole project there had been problems.

George Martin explained in a radio interview that when the finished record of 'Live And Let Die', featuring McCartney and Wings, was played to Harry Salzman, who had commissioned the material in the first place, he accepted it *only* as a demo! It was then suggested that a girl singer be employed to sing the title theme, and Salzman suggested Thelma Houston, and later Shirley Bassey, to George Martin as suitable candidates.

'I was completely nonplussed,' said George. 'And in my

best tactful way I had to suggest to him that if he didn't take the thing more or less as it stood, I didn't think that Paul would like him to have the song. And I had to be very delicate about it, because I could see that egos were getting in the way. But eventually it did sink in.'

Since 'Live And Let Die', Paul has written themes for three more major films, including 'The Honorary Consul' in 1983. For Warren Beatty's 1978 movie, 'Heaven Can Wait', he supplied the telling, 'Haven't We Met Somewhere Before?', which was never used on the picture's soundtrack. He also composed the title theme for the 1986-released movie, 'Spies Like Us', starring Chevy Chase and Dan Ackroyd – who were also featured in McCartney's own video to promote the single of the same name, released in the fall of 1985.

'I saw a rough cut of the film and decided that I liked it so much, I'd love to write a song for it,' said Paul.

'Normally I don't like to write under pressure, I like to take things pretty easy, but it was good to have that challenge for me.'

In 1974, Paul filmed and produced a 32-minute documentary called 'Empty Hand', which featured Wings drummer, Geoff Britton, in karate action, in a full-scale tournament, representing his country against Japan. For the movie soundtrack, Paul composed a piece of semi-abstract percussion music which he called, 'Karate Chaos'. It has never been released on record.

In 1976, the music of John Lennon and Paul McCartney returned in dramatic style to the large screen, in the disturbing anti-war film, 'All This And World War II'. Made by Lou Reizner, the movie was in effect a jigsaw puzzle of film footage, taken by news cameramen during the Second World War, which built up as complete a picture as possible of each historic campaign, showing the many terrifying faces of war, all paraded to a soundtrack and backdrop of Lennon and McCartney's music. The commentary was taken from the lyrics of each song. It was a strong and thought-provoking piece of cinema which showed the depth and perception of The Beatles' music, even when taken completely out of its original context. Instead of using the original Beatles versions, the songs were re-recorded – and given new and personal interpretations – by a number of leading rock stars and groups, among them Rod Stewart who handled 'Get

Back', The Four Seasons ('We Can Work It Out'), Status Quo ('Getting Better'), Elton John ('Lucy In The Sky With Diamonds'), David Essex ('Yesterday'), Keith Moon ('When I'm Sixty Four'), and The Bee Gees ('Golden Slumbers', 'Carry That Weight', 'Sun King' and 'She Came In Through The Bathroom Window'). The Bee Gees also starred in the multi-million dollar film fantasy, 'Sergeant Pepper's Lonely Hearts Club Band', which attempted to bring The Beatles' album to life in Cinemascope! The movie, with its appalling plot, shattered all the illusions the original LP had created ten years before . . . and failed miserably at the box-office.

Paul McCartney had been offered several movie scripts before he started work on 'Give My Regards To Broad Street' and was actively looking for ways to become involved in making films.

'I had been looking at scripts and offers from other people, but it was always *their* project, their ideas . . . and a little bit of me,' said Paul. 'I really wanted to do something that would be more me, more to do with what I was to do with.

'So I ended up writing a script of my own.'

He wrote the script in longhand, while sitting in the back of his car as he commuted daily between the London studio and his home, during the recording sessions for the 'Pipes Of Peace' album.

'I had two hours every day in the car going to the studio and two hours going back,' he said. 'So instead of just sitting there being bored, to relieve the boredom I thought I'd write a script.'

Initially the idea had been to write for a TV special, but as it progressed, he realized he was into bigger things.

He got the idea for his movie plot from producer Chris Thomas, who had told Paul a bizarre story of how the tapes to a new Sex Pistols album had gone missing. A production assistant, who had been trusted to take the masters to the factory, left them on a station platform – and completely forgot all about them.

Luckily, to everyone's relief, they were discovered later, and no harm had been done. Yet, the spark of an idea was conjured up in Paul's mind.

'So I started off with that Sex Pistols story about the lost tapes, and imagined how it might be a little tongue-in-cheek, if *my* tapes went missing. I started to develop that as a story.'

The plot evolved into a day in the life of a superstar pop artist called 'Paul McCartney', and was based on a real day in Paul's life, with the overriding theme of the missing tapes dominating the movie. Paul showed his finished script to several people in the film industry without too many favourable comments. Then . . . 'I showed it to director Peter Webb and he said, "It'll work", and that was it,' said Paul. 'Give My Regards To Broad Street' was rolling.

The whole treatment of the film was then devised as a means of allowing McCartney to approach the musical numbers in a completely natural and relaxed way.

'Anything to do with music should be introduced in a natural way,' he said, 'in a way I would normally do it, rather than the old-fashioned musical . . . which is very dodgy.' Paul recalled musicals where the hero would simply burst into song, for no apparent reason, during the film, totally out of context to the plot . . . singing to the marvellous accompaniment of a large and lush orchestra, playing out of sight of the cameras. The falseness of that kind of situation often caused John Lennon to walk out of the cinema. Paul didn't want to make that mistake. But he wanted, wherever possible, to ensure that all the featured music was played and recorded 'live', to try to move away from the conventional method of production for a musical, filming to pre-recorded playback tapes. The 'live' feel was something Paul liked to convey on records – he loved atmosphere on records and sent for that approach on 'Live And Let Die'. It was a legacy inherited from George Martin. In the early recording days, Martin preferred to go for a 'live' approach on The Beatles' records, and often accepted as finished product, songs that sounded right, even though they might contain one or two errors. It was the overall effect that mattered, and the excitement it created.

'I've seen so many films, especially music films through the years, where you'd get the drummer – and he's a drummer you love and you're watching him – and you really know his style . . . and he's putting the sticks on the snare, and the soundtrack is on the other beat!

'We wanted to avoid the thing where you see a film and the camera goes into the guitarist's fingers, and he's not playing it. He's playing some bass solo or something. As a musician I know it annoyed me and my friends through the years.

'So to get over that we had to re-record "live".'

He added: 'We had to make everything we conceivably could "live". We didn't see much sense in miming to playback when the whole point of the film was seeing me there, singing . . . and that gave the camera and technical people a lot of synchronization problems.'

Paul McCartney wrote only three new songs for the movie, 'No Values', 'Not Such A Bad Boy', and the theme song, 'No More Lonely Nights', which developed out of a simple bass riff, played with a lot of repeat and echo. The song gave Paul a sizeable hit when it was taken off the soundtrack as a single.

'We didn't want it to be like a musical with a whole new score,' said Paul. So the rest of the soundtrack was taken from his past musical career, songs written for The Beatles, songs written for Wings, and the solo material. He wanted to choose songs that encompassed everything he had ever written over the years; material that would be a true reflection of Paul McCartney: composer.

So, with George Martin, McCartney pulled up a short list of fifty songs, from which the nine featured numbers were eventually selected. It was a hard process, and although credited to Lennon and McCartney in most cases, all the material chosen from The Beatles' era, was written almost exclusively by McCartney himself and not in collaboration – 'Here There And Everywhere', 'Yesterday', 'For No One', 'Good Day Sunshine', and 'The Long And Winding Road'. Only 'Eleanor Rigby', had a contribution from John Lennon.

He chose the songs for various reasons.

'I chose "For No One" because I suddenly realized that I'd written the song – it had taken me about a week or so to write; I'd taken it to the studio, played it to everyone, made the record, and that was it. I said "goodbye" to that song. I never ever sang it again or saw it again. It had gone. It seemed strange that I, unlike a lot of people, should have deserted a lot of good stuff from the past. So I thought – something like "For No One", I'd like to sing again. We chose all the songs like that. "Here There And Everywhere" and "Eleanor Rigby" – I realized I'd never actually done them in vision, I'd only ever sung them . . .'

Knowing, too, that they were going to feature a movie studio set in the film, Paul saw all possibilities opening up in the way of a big spectacular production number, like he remembered from the Fred Astaire pictures he adored so much. 'Ballroom Dancing' from the 'Tug Of War' album seemed a perfect choice.

'Give My Regards To Broad Street' also allowed Paul to expand his range of composing, and to encompass classical music. The Victorian fantasy sequence accompanying 'Eleanor Rigby', proved to be longer than at first anticipated. So Paul was faced with the challenge of scoring a full eight minutes of incidental music, which had to be effective. He chose a classical approach, featuring in parts acoustic guitar segments.

He told Melvyn Bragg: 'I tried to write my own type of classical score. Classical music is just a lot of tunes, or one recurring tune. But it is still generally what I do . . . it is just a different way of doing it.

'So I approached it from the same old angle, which is to get a tune I like, to voice it the way I like it, to get the dynamics . . . getting it to come and go, to recur . . . and to do all the stuff I like to happen. But the big thing was that there were no words to help me out. I couldn't keep bringing back choruses. It had to fit with the film.'

Paul enjoyed the experience immensely, and the musical sequence he composed became one of the outstanding artistic highspots of the entire film, capturing the eerie Victorian atmosphere very well indeed.

When the movie was eventually released in the autumn of 1984, it came in for some severe criticism from all sections of the Press, both in America and Britain.

The *Washington Post* said: 'You don't have to play this movie backwards to know that Paul is dead.' *Rolling Stone* called it 'disastrous'.

In Britain, the *Daily Mail* advised: 'Don't see it. Send a wreath and condolences to all concerned.' The *Daily Express* called it 'a home movie'.

Paul admitted later: 'Having written it, I was always going to walk into a wall of criticism because most of the people criticizing me are writers. We went into it to make a film, have a lot of fun, get into acting, sing some songs, to make a bit of music. To put it all together as a British film.'

He added: 'The thing about criticism is that everyone has an opinion. The critics all have opinions – nearly everyone's opinion is different.

'I wish I felt, "Well, what does it matter?" – I think a lot of people expect you to feel like that when you've got some success. They expect you *not* to be affected by it.

'When I first met Linda, she expected me not to be affected by that. She didn't think I noticed the criticism . . . but you read it, you see it – what I do is look at it and if there's something that I really hate, it's when they get near to the mark, near to the truth. *That's* when you hate it.'

There were compensations for Paul's film. The song, 'No More Lonely Nights' was nominated for a British Academy Award by the British Academy of Film and Television Arts as Best Original Song In A Film. It was beaten to the title by Ray Parker Jnr's 'Ghostbusters'.

Accompanying 'Broad Street' on general release in British cinemas was an animated cartoon feature – 'Rupert And The Frog Song' – produced by McCartney Productions Ltd. It was based on the comic character, from the *Daily Express* newspaper, Rupert Bear, the film rights to which Paul bought as long ago as 1970 with the intention of producing a full-length cartoon film. Indeed, he had written and recorded songs for the venture, including the charming, 'We All Stand Together' which was released as a single to coincide with the film. Billed as Paul McCartney And The Frog Chorus, and coupled with the 'humming version' by Paul McCartney And The Finchley Frogettes, 'We All Stand Together' became a big Christmas hit at the end of 1984.

The 12-minute cartoon film featured several well-known British character actors playing the parts of animals, while Paul took the lead role of Rupert, making his voice sound remarkably like that of a 12-year-old.

At the 1985 BAFTA Awards, 'Rupert And The Frog Song' picked up the award as Best Animated Film of 1984, while 'We All Stand Together' was acclaimed as Best Film Theme in the 1984 Ivor Novello Awards. The film was released on video in the winter of 1985 and went on to become one of the best-selling music videos of all time.

Paul said: 'Originally we made the cartoon, which is a short, but one of these days my ambition is to make a full-length cartoon of it. But that's not easy to do.'

18

The Magic of McCartney

IN A MUSIC industry often accused of being fickle and insular, where in-fighting and back-biting are the order of most days; in a business that possesses two totally different faces – a positive one for the outside world, and very often a negative face for its own little world, where change is regularly frowned upon . . . Paul McCartney, through his ability first, and his achievements second, is today one of the most esteemed members of that musical fraternity.

McCartney's contemporaries and his musical peers, talk of him in glowing terms . . . with great affection. His talent as a songwriter is well respected across the musical spectrum, from jazz to rock 'n' roll; from classical music to heavy metal; from pop to middle-of-the-road and country. And he is admired as a musical ambassador and elder statesman of the industry. Jealousy at his outstanding achievements doesn't even enter into it.

Paul McCartney is revered as a songwriter.

Francis Rossi has achieved tremendous worldwide acclaim in recent years, as the leader and inspiration behind supergroup Status Quo. He, too, has emerged as a highly talented and successful songwriter in his own right . . . and remains an ardent admirer of McCartney.

'Paul McCartney is brilliant,' says Francis. 'Certainly amongst the leading songwriters in the business. He is a masterful composer.

'McCartney writes wonderful chord sequences to his music . . . and despite an often complicated and intriguing chord structure, the melody lines to his songs are always magnificent, very catchy and obviously commercial. His strong melodies are the key to his success as a writer. He knows how to put a melody together and how to construct a mature song, to make them viable in the commercial market. He knows that market so well.

'Take a look at the frog song, 'We All Stand Together' – it is so simple, yet so effective. So catchy, you don't need any words, the melody line stands up on its own. Its power and strength is in its simplicity.

'I actually don't think he is a lyrics person as much as a music person, but having said that, his words are getting better, although on many of his songs, it is the sound of the words he uses, and not what they say or mean, that counts, that *makes* some songs.

'I have the greatest respect for him as a writer and as a musician. I think he has a great voice – and is able to sing sweetly; to call up emotion for ballads, and then in the next instant charge into raucous rock 'n' roll. He can virtually sing anything, but then his own songwriting has that ability to cover all the styles. I'm sure he writes from personal experience, particularly from the early influences. He's been around a long time, and he's getting better all the time.'

Francis Rossi readily admits that McCartney certainly helped to take popular music into another dimension with his writing.

'He revolutionized the industry,' he says. 'He allowed all the groups to say, "We'd like to write *our* own songs." John and Paul always wrote their own material and insisted on recording their own songs on singles. At that time, it was virtually unheard of in the music business. When a new act was signed to a recording contract, they were told to find themselves suitable songs to record from the various music publishers in London's Tin Pan Alley. Denmark Street was swarming with publishers and writers looking for outlets. It happened to us. When Status Quo started out, we wanted to write our own songs, but we soon realized that our material was naive and banal. We needed time to develop. Our songs lacked experience, but we were told that we must not write our own songs, we had to get them from a publisher. The Beatles changed all that . . . for the better, and it gave us all a chance to get our own material heard.

'Lennon and McCartney wrote quality songs and in doing so they gave us all a standard to aim at, to keeping plugging away with our own stuff, learning, developing . . . instead of being intimidated by others. The Beatles laid down their own guidelines and we all picked them up and followed. Paul McCartney and The Beatles made us all have a go, and gradually the industry woke up to the fact that other groups *could* write their own material; they *could* write good songs that were commercial enough to record and stood a chance of being successful. But it took time.

'McCartney also brought a freshness to the music business and definitely gave rock 'n' roll respectability. Songs like "The Long And Winding Road", "Eleanor Rigby", and "Maybe I'm Amazed" gave rock 'n' roll an acceptable face. It appealed to the markets right across the board and helped music grow up. He broke through the barriers of acceptance. With The Beatles, he was innovative, I mean, at that time who would ever have thought of a heavy rock band like The Beatles were, performing on record with a string quartet as they did with "Yesterday"? They did it. And the more they progressed, the more recording techniques they used . . . the more the industry accepted them, and let us all in.

'The music of Lennon and McCartney, through its sheer quality, also helped to establish the album market in Britain.

'You always knew that their albums would contain six or seven good class songs. You knew that whatever else happened, you would always get value for money from a Beatles album, and that was all down to John and Paul and their songs. Before them, the album market was modest by comparison, but they opened up the field and it made us all work harder to emulate their success. We all wanted to be the next Beatles, the next Lennon and McCartney, and that was healthy competition.'

As a songwriter, Francis Rossi believes that Paul McCartney can easily be compared with the great romantic composers of the past like Cole Porter or Jerome Kern.

'I rate Paul McCartney alongside the people we have come to call the "all-time greats" of writing. Although it is a different time, and he is writing for a different generation, I think his ballads particularly stand up against the best. They are quality songs – and quality songs stand the test of *any* time. There is such an endearing quality about his music; you can return to it again and again, and each time, you can find something different. Something extra to enjoy. The music endures, it never goes stale. I hate him for it . . . in the nicest possible way.

'When I hear some of his stuff for the first time, it sickens me to think, "He's done it again! Why didn't *I* think of that?" The trouble is, he can only improve. I know it's a tall order, but how can you improve on the best? He can and will. He is over forty in a business that everyone says is for young men. But Macca can still do it. He is the only person whose songs can be sung anywhere in the world, in any language, and you know instantly that it's a McCartney song. And that is a very rare talent.'

Chris Barber is one of the most respected figures in international jazz circles today. There are very few people alive who have done more to aid the development of jazz than he has. He also helped to bring rhythm and blues music to a much wider audience and indirectly helped skiffle take its first tentative steps in Britain. Indeed, Lonnie Donegan, who did more than most in Britain to launch skiffle music, was a former member of the Chris Barber Jazz Band, and recorded 'Rock Island Line' while still playing guitar and banjo in the group's line-up.

Chris Barber, who topped the British Hit Parade in 1959 with the million-selling 'Petite Fleur', first met Paul McCartney in the Cavern in Liverpool, in the very early days.

'The Cavern used to be a great jazz venue,' says Chris. 'The Beatles used to be on the bill as a support band, playing R & B. Our band never actually played there, but a lot of the bands that did, used to take the piss out of The Beatles and their music. I think that shabby treatment early on by certain jazz musicians, prompted John Lennon to make his famous outburst against jazz music in the '70s, when he called it a load of rubbish. I think he was getting his own back for those days in the Cavern.

'We got along fine with The Beatles, very well indeed. Whenever we were on tour and appeared on Merseyside, we would often drop into the Cavern for a drink and to watch the bands, after our gig had finished. We would regularly meet the boys there.'

He renewed his friendship with Paul in 1967 when the Chris Barber Jazz Band recorded McCartney's composition, 'Catcall'.

'"Catcall" came about in a funny way,' says Chris. 'Paul was buying a house in St John's Wood in London, which coincidentally, belonged to a friend of mine, who asked me to look after some of the arrangements for him. I went along to see Paul one day, in connection with the house sale, and we got talking about music. So I asked him if he had a song that might be suitable for the band to record, and he came up with "Catcall", and more or less produced the record for us. He certainly assisted *and* played left hand on the organ, and joined in with the yells and shouts on the backing track. It was a catchy number, based on a production idea like "All You Need Is Love". Really, it was a party-type number, a rave up, sing-a-long and very tongue-in-cheek. But the idea worked quite well.

'Paul wrote a lot of his material with his tongue firmly in the side of his cheek! "All Together Now", featured on the "Yellow Submarine" movie, was a send up of skiffle groups and the way the members of the groups insisted on asking the audience to join in on their songs – "Come on, all together now . . . well, when the Saints – *all together now* – go marching in – *all together now* . . ." He wrote the song like that.

'The trouble is today, too many people read too much into his music. I'm sure he doesn't. He's just having a good time.

'Paul McCartney is a good basic musician. He has a good ear. Great talent and ability. If you put all that together, you come up with a person who knows what to do. It's amazing that in this society, people who can write fifteen bars of nice music can be amongst some of the highest paid – that's how it is, but good luck to them. It's finding what the public wants.

'I admire Paul for the fact that he never flaunts his money. If he's got it, he's got it, if not . . . hard luck. He has no pretensions and he's a down to earth fellow who has got his head screwed on.'

Chris Barber also respects McCartney's talents as a writer.

'I think he's very good. He never set out to be a writer of songs or things that last forever, but he succeeded in doing just that. In pop music, it's here today, gone tomorrow – instant throwaway music. He has found the right formula. He can write to order . . . whatever is needed.

'Paul has written some of the most memorable pop tunes of their kind, of their generation, but it would be absurd to class them as symphonies.

'He is good at writing great hooks. He is the best hook writer in the business. The lyrics are not his greatest strength, though there are one or two exceptions. But hooks are what make hit records.

'Writing almost instant songs is part of his great talent. It's a disposable market, pop music, a song lasts a few months and then fades away, and that doesn't really matter because there are always more coming along all the time. Obviously a great song will come along from time to time . . . and Paul has written a couple that have become standards.

'I don't think you could ever compare McCartney with the likes of Irving Berlin or Richard Rodgers, because they wrote mainly for musicals. And a different set of rules apply. To me, though, some of Paul McCartney's songs are as memorable as theirs – "Yesterday" has such a marvellous hook.

'People have often compared Paul with the classical composers like Beethoven, but it's not the same thing at all. I don't think McCartney tries to be like them at all. Pop music is a minor art form with very little lasting quality. Paul McCartney doesn't go out to write symphonies. He knows what he does best and sticks to it. He is very much his own man, and knows his own limitations. He refuses to get involved with something he doesn't think he can do. But throughout history there have been balladeers and minstrels who have been more popular with the multitudes than the so called "classical" composers of the day. McCartney is one of them . . . he knows his market so well and is brilliant at writing for it.'

Unlike many people, however, Chris Barber is convinced The Beatles' effect on pop music in the early days was minimal.

'They certainly added a personal style to pop music, but The Beatles' music was just copied from other sources, and developed into their own way,' he says. 'I appeared with them on a radio show called "Saturday Club" in 1963, just before the boom, and they were playing a lot of rhythm and blues material. They were very much into black music and the blues. They actually did what trad jazz bands did in the '50s with skiffle. That was really country blues.

'Lonnie Donegan had a greater influence on pop music, which is often overlooked. I would say *more* than The Beatles in a way. But they certainly helped to pioneer a lot of new recording techniques.

'The Beatles were always honest about their influences, and paid homage to all the people who created that kind of music. They acknowledged their debt to them all. A lot of jazz bands who picked up on a type of American music and introduced it into Britain, claimed it as their own creation, and gave no credit to the real source. But The Beatles always came clean.

'What Paul McCartney and the group did was to open the eyes of non-pop people to pop music . . . mums and dads. It was no longer "them and us" in a sense as far as teenagers went.

'But . . . listening to pop music now, I don't hear a lot of today's music retaining a Beatles influence – except for Paul McCartney himself.'

Barry Mason's track record as a songwriter is impressive. His songs have been recorded by Rod Stewart, David Essex and Elvis Presley among many others. He wrote 'Delilah' and 'I'm Coming Home' and 'Love Me Tonight' for Tom Jones. For Engelbert Humperdinck, he penned 'Les Bicyclettes de Belsize' and 'The Last Waltz'. He is more than qualified to talk about songwriting, and knows more than most what it takes to write a hit song. He rates Paul McCartney as one of the best songwriters in the business.

'I think he's terrific,' says Barry, 'probably the greatest post-war songwriter. Who else is there to rival him? McCartney does it all, lyrics, music. I think he is certainly the greatest songwriter we have produced for a long time.

'The amazing thing about McCartney is that he *keeps* on doing it. Keeps coming up with winning songs. He doesn't have to – so he must love the whole process of writing and recording.

'All he can do now is go down. If he doesn't get to Number One in the charts – he's looked upon as a failure. He puts himself up there to be shot at.

'I think he's got tremendous enthusiasm and courage. Anybody else would have retired or turned to writing esoteric material that is specialized. *Not* Paul – he still attacks the charts, still plugs his singles, and is so enthusiastic for our business. That can only be good for the business, too.

'In the past, Paul McCartney helped to put British music on the map and he is still doing it today. As a member of The Beatles, he became the biggest single influence on British pop music there has ever been. The group broke through into America for a start. At that time, we were only 8 per cent of the world market to America's 53 per cent. To break into that market was a miracle. But they opened it all up, and changed the maps around.

'Paul, with The Beatles, was also instrumental in starting the fashion of groups writing their own material which was unknown in the industry before then . . . and although they drove a knife into the backs of many professional songwriters by taking away a market for them at the time, The Beatles also strengthened the songwriting business in this country and encouraged thousands of kids to be creative.'

McCartney's greatest asset as a songwriter, according to Barry Mason, is his talent to appeal to the masses.

'He's a people's writer. He has terrific appeal to the man-in-the-street. He has written songs that everybody likes – mums, dads, kids, trendies. And that is a true test of his quality and talent,' says Barry.

'I like him because he is romantic – unashamedly romantic. And I like emotional songs. McCartney is an emotional writer. I'd like him to do more soppy and sad songs. He's not afraid of emotion, and then again, he can write some fantastic rock 'n' roll, but I don't take rock 'n' roll seriously. I don't count them as songs. In a way it's just fun music, which I suppose is ridiculous, because they *are* equally important. It's just my own preference.

'A writer can only be judged by the times in which he writes, and the style of those times. The fashion of the 1930s for songs, was wordy, inter-rhyming, technically brilliant songs. Today, everything is much more simple and direct. But I believe that if McCartney had been writing in the '30s, he would have been just as successful, just as brilliant a songwriter, only in a totally different style.'

Mason also revealed that *he* had been influenced in his own writing by Paul McCartney.

'I wrote a song with Les Reed called "Misty Morning Eyes", which was influenced by Paul's song, "Michelle". Our song was absolutely nothing like "Michelle" in content or in style, but the atmosphere and feel to it were completely inspired by McCartney.

'Throughout his career, I know Paul McCartney has taken a pasting at the hands of the critics, but as a writer myself, I can't really criticize him, because if you like someone, you like them to a fault. It overwhelms you. I just like his songs.

'When I hear his music, I don't think good or bad, although I think if they offended me, I probably wouldn't listen again. I don't really like the songs he did with Michael Jackson, but to me that's the bad side of his enthusiasm. Paul doesn't have to do anything, and he hasn't got to expose himself creatively; he could go on to a much more refined area of music and still succeed. But he stays in mainstream pop. I'm convinced he could produce great classical pieces of music which would floor the whole world, if he wanted to.

'I think the public judge you . . . and you can't ignore public opinion. If the mass of people who are interested in popular music love what somebody does, then you've got to put McCartney up with all the rest of them. Tchaikovsky, in his time, wrote popular music and the style then was what the people liked to hear.'

American singing star Gene Pitney built up a lot of his early success internationally on the fact that he took the time and trouble to re-record his English-speaking hit singles into various other languages, for other markets . . . and he scored heavily in the charts in Italy, Germany and several Spanish-speaking territories. When The Beatles came along, they soon changed all that.

'That was one of my strong points,' says Gene. 'I was one of the few singing stars who recorded in "other" languages, or to suit a particular market. And I made many successful hit records in this way.

'When The Beatles came on to the scene, however, English suddenly became the universal language for records. They crossed over borders and opened up whole new markets around the world for themselves. They certainly opened up America for British acts. Before The Beatles' era, I was on tour in England and picked up a terrific record by Adam Faith, which knocked me out. Back in the States, I asked several American radio stations to play the record, thinking it might catch on and become a hit over here. But they all refused, not because the record was bad, but because it came from England. After The Beatles broke through, the American radio stations couldn't get enough British material to play, and they all vied with each other to try and discover the *next* British sensation. Trouble was, the established American stars missed out.

'But The Beatles' impact went a lot deeper.'

Gene Pitney first made a name for himself in the music industry as a songwriter, penning such hits as 'Hello Mary Lou' for Ricky Nelson, 'He's A Rebel' for The Crystals,

'Today's Teardrops' for Roy Orbison and 'Rubber Ball' for Bobby Vee. When he wrote songs he was constantly looking for something different, something away from the run of the mill, three chord pop tunes.

'When I first started writing,' says Gene, 'I didn't have any influences. I was looking for something unusual, using strange chord sequences, weird tempos, changes and lyrics. Something *different*. But when I took these songs to the publishers, they all said how different they were, but added: "Who would record them?". They were *too* different. The market was influenced by the Presley dominance of four chord songs. So we all went back and wrote to order – all the publishers were frightened by anything new. But along came The Beatles, Lennon and McCartney, and pow! They made music into an art form. They made music better, more acceptable. For once the lyrics had something to say. Melody-wise, the songs turned in every direction you could think of, and each of their albums experimented with sounds, and brought in different concepts.

'It's frightening to think what they did *without* any formal musical training.

'Before they made it big in America, when they were still relatively unknown over here, I was offered a batch of Lennon and McCartney songs by my publisher for possible numbers to record. I *wasn't* impressed with them. I *wasn't* impressed much later when an English PR friend of mine played me the acetate of their first album before it came over to America. Things change!'

Since then, however, Gene has been *very* impressed with Paul McCartney's music, and rates him very highly. Being a composer himself, he can recognize the qualities that make Paul so special.

'He's a great craftsman,' says Gene, 'his songs are not mechanical, they're not contrived. They are superior songs. Paul has an ability to write to such a variety of styles – so much light and shade – he goes in every single direction, which is the hallmark of a great composer. He is a natural and I would compare him for his craft with Oscar Hammerstein.

'There are very few people to match his creative talents. Of his peers, to stand alongside him, I'd match McCartney with say, Bacharach and David, and Paul Simon – but for sheer volume of material, Paul McCartney beats them all.

'After Wings, I didn't think his songs had the same impact as those he did with The Beatles. *They* had a feel to them, a vitality, a power that I believe is missing from his later work. I don't know whether he has the same kind of drive he had then. But when The Beatles were rampant, it was a stimulating period of time for creativity. But as I said before, times change.'

Choosing his favourite McCartney songs, Pitney returned to Paul's days with The Beatles, where he admitted he was spoilt for choice.

'I love the symbolism of "Eleanor Rigby" – the beautiful relationship between the lyrics and the melody is fantastic,' he says. '"Hey Jude" is outrageously magnificent. But I prefer the songs from that era, before the split, before Wings. I think he got to a point where he lost his edge and his excitement a little; maybe he needs stimulating once more.

'I would certainly like to see him write classical music. I'm sure he could be very good at it if he put his mind to it. He's got natural talent, tremendous creative ability . . . and he's naive in a sense that he wouldn't know the technicalities of writing for the classics. His strength is in his naivety. If he had been schooled in composition and told how to write to a structure, it would be ineffective.

'Maybe that's for the future; in the meantime, obviously his songwriting is the key to where he goes from here as far as longevity is concerned. He works very hard. Drives himself hard, but I feel he needs new challenges.

'What I would like to see him doing, is to direct himself towards crafting some *great* songs – not nice commercial numbers that are successful for the publishing company. But . . . gritting his teeth and going for something that is different for the times. Something unique. He is very capable of doing it. It is difficult to *top* the top, but you must always strive to do just that . . . and keep going.

'I think in the last few years, by striving hard like that, Paul has shaken off the mantle of The Beatles. In days to come, he will be remembered *not* as an ex-Beatle . . . but as *Paul McCartney – songwriter*.

Alvin Stardust came to Paul McCartney and The Beatles' rescue in 1963, and Paul has never forgotten. It was during the time in his own career, when he was known as Shane Fenton and had enjoyed success with several hit singles before The Beatles arrived on the recording scene.

The group were appearing in Alvin's hometown of Mansfield, but were unable to leave the theatre and find somewhere to eat, owing to the vast crowds of people waiting outside. The place was under siege. When Alvin dropped into the theatre to see the boys, he found them incarcerated in their dressing room.

'They were starving,' said Alvin. 'So I drove back home and got my mum to make up a meal for them. We owned a boarding-house which was often frequented by theatrical people, actors on tour and the like, and so she was used to catering for several people at a time. She packed a super hamper with flasks of soup and coffee, and lashings of salmon sandwiches. In those days, you were looked upon as being posh if you ate salmon. I think my mother was trying to impress the boys.

'When I got back to the theatre, the crowds had increased. I had to go through the chip shop next door and clamber up the fire escape to get into the building through an emergency exit in order to avoid the screaming masses outside.

'At that time in Mansfield, although I was officially called Shane Fenton, everyone knew me by my real name of Bernie. And to this day, whenever Paul and I meet, he still calls me "Bernie", and he still asks: "Where's the salmon sandwiches, Bernie?" That's the kind of guy he is – *super*. He's down to earth with a great sense of humour. Unpretentious . . . an ordinary bloke. He also happens to be one of the best songwriters in the world.

'Paul is an unusual person, and people are totally amazed at where he finds his inspiration to write. I'm sure he calls upon his vast experience to help him. It's like any writer, inspiration can come to you at any time, completely out of the blue. I doubt whether he specifically sits down at the piano with the sole intention of writing a song. Yet, he has this tremendous ability to come up with the hits, time and time again. And that's a rare talent.

'There are many writers who have had lots of hits, but they simply aren't in Paul's league. He is first, and the rest trail behind him. And there aren't many of those writers who in fifty years will still be renowned. McCartney will!'

Alvin Stardust is certain Paul McCartney's talent will see him acknowledged as a composer alongside the great classical writers, when someone sits down to write the history of music in the next century.

'The great classical composers were the pop writers of their day,' says Alvin. 'Just like McCartney. But only the good ones survived through the ages. Sure, there were many other writers down the centuries who were popular with the people and wrote nice pieces of music, but their work lacked magic, and a certain something that makes it stand out above the rest. Over the years, these composers have fallen by the wayside, and yet their contemporaries have become revered in another time, by another generation of people. Who knows why? – perhaps it's down to quality. One thing's for sure, Paul McCartney's music *will* survive. I'd rate him in the same class as many of the classical composers – and nearer to our time – I think he stands alongside the likes of Gilbert and Sullivan.

'Classical writers were the composers of *their* times – the good ones' music transcended time. McCartney is more than just a writer of *his* time – he is a writer of time in general, and I'm sure that will be proved in say two hundred years from now. It's a pity I shan't be around to be proved right!!

'Paul's greatest asset is that he is a writer for the common man,' Alvin adds. 'And I say that without denigrating the common man. One of the ways in which The Beatles turned everything upside down in the music industry in the '60s was by bringing music to the common man, and making it acceptable. Paul is still doing that – he thinks like the common man. He is one of *us*, and never writes for effect, never writes for writing's sake. He simply enjoys composing and he writes to make personal statements like 'I love you', 'Keep your chin up'.

'McCartney is a good writer of melodies and his lyrics complement those melodies. He does have his faults, but remember he is only human. Sometimes he'll write a song that doesn't come off – and he'll be knocked for it. But the good thing is that he has attempted something different and refused to be compromised. I can't say I like everything he has turned out, and some of his songs work better than others, but Paul has gone past the stage where he has to set trends. The problem is . . . he can't help it now, and others follow his lead. He is one of these people who ducks and dives. You never know if he is coming up with a socially aware statement in his songs, or if he's just having fun. Should we listen to be informed? Or just listen to be entertained? It can be confusing sometimes.'

For Neil Murray, bass player with heavy metal band, Whitesnake, McCartney's potency as a songwriter faded with the break up of The Beatles.

'Although I was a big fan of the early Beatles, it is true to say that for me, at least, Paul McCartney's solo work – including Wings – doesn't come close to the freshness and inspiration of the songs he wrote when he was collaborating with John Lennon,' he says. 'I know they more than likely wrote most of their material apart, yet they spurred each other on to try new chord sequences, melody lines and arrangements . . . and to experiment with their music.

'Lennon's power with words stopped McCartney from becoming twee or too sentimental.

'More recently, Paul has been too conservative musically, though he has a great gift for writing simple, but catchy melodies. "Yesterday" must rank as one of the best songs ever written.'

One of the great virtues of Paul's music is that it can be taken, re-arranged and translated into so many different styles – jazz, big bands, military bands. Because of its simplicity, however, it adapts superbly well into classical music, and over the years, there have been a number of interpretations of McCartney's music with variations on the classical theme.

Elena Duran, the celebrated American flute virtuoso has won many outstanding accolades within the classical music field. She is certain that because of that rare quality in his music, Paul McCartney would make a marvellous classical composer.

'I would like to see him try,' she says. 'And I would love him to write a piece for the flute. He would have terrific ideas, although I don't know whether the idea of writing classical music appeals to him, whether he has the time or the inclination. He would certainly have to write a lot more notes! But he is versatile and experienced enough to be able to do it. And do it well. A lot of people are misled by thinking a classical piece needs to be twenty to forty minutes in length. But it can be three minutes long and be just as effective.

'Classical music has taken a back seat in the 20th century. Not very much good music has been written – people can't remember it. There has been a lot written, but it hasn't been worth remembering. I'm sure he could write material that people would *want* to remember, material they couldn't forget.

'As a songwriter, Paul McCartney is the best. There will be a lot of songwriters who will write more meaningful songs – but Paul writes memorable songs. He doesn't need to be technically brilliant to be a great songwriter. His music stays with you. His qualities are his simplicity: he writes music without getting too complicated; he states things without getting too fancy, or going overboard; his lyrics stand up – the melody lines are memorable, and he has found a magic formula, and will never let it go away from him. *And* he keeps close to his audience through his music, both young and old. These are the qualities that have moulded the writer.

'However, technically as a composer, he is *not* very good. But it doesn't matter. Technically comparing him with George Gershwin . . . then Gershwin would come out on top because Paul's writing is too simplistic. He is musically naive when it comes to technicalities – but it makes him no less a composer, because he doesn't follow guide lines. He takes his ideas from lots of sources, and puts them to his own use and advantage. He is an opportunist in the best sense, and he knows exactly what his own limits are.'

Being one of the most respected and talented classical flute players in the world, having studied under Jean-Pierre Rampal and Aurèle Nicolet and later appeared with some of the most distinguished orchestras in the world, Elena Duran is highly qualified to judge McCartney's merits against the great classical composers.

'Historically, McCartney will be acclaimed as a great composer,' says Elena. 'Mozart was never recognized in his time as being one of the greats. Paul already is. A lot of successful writers who are known now, won't necessarily be acclaimed in years to come. I think Paul McCartney will.

'He has already established himself amongst the greats and whatever he does in the future, he can't destroy what he has already achieved, even if everything he did from now on was rubbish. He is already a legend in his own lifetime; a very few composers aspire to that.

'McCartney's music has opened up the whole world. I have travelled extensively in the course of my career, and I find that his music is so influential the world over. Part of the charm of his music is that his personality shines through in most of his songs. They're bright, optimistic.

'Paul McCartney has made a tremendous contribution to music inasmuch as he has brought people *to* music who wouldn't necessarily have discovered music before. He gave music to a lot of people who never had it, and he gave music back to the people.

'Two hundred years ago, everyone was much more involved in music. Music was very much part of those times. It tended to fall by the wayside in the nineteenth and twentieth centuries – Paul brought it back again, or certainly helped to bring it back. And I think he will be remembered for that. For being a good guy, a good composer, a people's musician.

'The public will remember him as a great songwriter.'

Elena Duran grew up with The Beatles – and saw them twice, firstly at the Cow Palace in San Francisco in 1965 – and again at their very last concert together as a group, on August 29th, 1966, at San Francisco's Candlestick Park. 'I was a great fan, *not* a screaming fan. I went to the concerts to *enjoy* the music. But I never thought I would meet one of them, let alone work with one,' she says. The opportunity arose to work with Paul McCartney when he recorded 'We All Stand Together'.

'When I was asked if I would like to do the session with Paul McCartney, I really didn't know if I should accept it or not,' she admits. 'When I heard that the violinist from the London Symphony Orchestra would be there, and the King's Singers, and the choir from Westminster Boys School, I had second thoughts . . . and accepted.

'I was very impressed with McCartney. He showed his great love for music on that session. He knew exactly what he wanted to communicate, and how to put it together. For me it was a terrific experience working with him and I learnt more from that one session than I had in years. He generated so much excitement, so much warmth. The session was a joy, and needless to say, he made it easy for the rest of us.

'At the start of the recording, he showed us all the pictures of the frogs Linda had drawn, and outlined the story . . . and what he wanted to convey in the music, the whole concept of the song. He made sure that the mood and atmosphere were right in the studio before we started recording. Everything had to be just so. On other classical sessions I have attended, the producer will go for a take right from the beginning, and then simply find the best track. This was different.

'I was very impressed with the way Paul and George Martin worked together. George interpreted Paul's wishes and scored the song to his specifications. But the overall statement was McCartney's. It was his show; he directed it all and conducted the choir, even though he hasn't been trained as a conductor. What came across to me, is that Paul McCartney is a terribly emotional person, it oozes out of him.

'It's funny, but the week before I made that record, I had appeared on BBC Television's "Pebble Mill" programme, and the boys from Westminster School had seen my performances. Several of the choirboys had also taken flute as their chosen instrument for their musical course at the school. When we met together in the studio, some of the boys came over to me and wanted to know all about the flute and various playing techniques. I was flattered when they asked for my autograph. Paul came over and said jokingly, "Where do you think you are?" It was a happy situation, because he was very warm and charming, and made everyone relaxed and at ease. It permeated throughout that session.

'At one stage, I had to play the lowest note you can play on the flute, as part of the score. I don't very often play it – and naturally, I was a little apprehensive. Yet in that happy atmosphere Paul had set up in the studio, you couldn't help but give of your best. He makes people want to do their best – he certainly has that charisma and star-quality aura about him.

'When I left that session, I left with a lot more energy than when I first arrived. I actually said to him, "Does it really have to end so soon?" It was marvellous. And I have such total respect for that man as a musican and as a person.'

A final word from Francis Rossi: 'Paul McCartney will go down in musical history. He will become respected like George Gershwin. McCartney's best stuff is yet to come, and it will take him on to a higher plane of musical acceptance. Wow!

'I wish he'd stop and give the rest of us a chance!'

APPENDIX I

The Songs of Paul McCartney (1)

These songs were written by Paul McCartney during a period between 1957 and 1970 and credited to Lennon and McCartney. They were all originally recorded by The Beatles, and appear on singles and albums.

LOVE ME DO
Written in collaboration with John Lennon on one of the days they played truant from school in order to write together at Paul's house in Forthlin Road, Liverpool. Paul wrote the verse; John wrote the middle eight.
P.S. I LOVE YOU
Written in collaboration with John Lennon and inspired by the black American singing group, The Shirelles.
ASK ME WHY
Written in collaboration with John Lennon and featuring the latin beat McCartney was fond of. Pre-Hamburg.
I SAW HER STANDING THERE
Written in Paul's front room at Forthlin Road. Pre-Hamburg.
MISERY
Written in collaboration with John Lennon originally for Helen Shapiro to record.
FROM ME TO YOU
Written in collaboration with John Lennon on the tour bus during the Helen Shapiro package. Legend has it that the song was composed between York and Shrewsbury and was inspired by the letters column in the *New Musical Express* called 'From You To Us'.
THANK YOU GIRL
Written in collaboration with John Lennon on tour. John called it 'a silly song'. It was originally scheduled to be the follow-up single to 'Please Please Me'.
SHE LOVES YOU
Written in collaboration with John Lennon and rumoured to be the

last song they actually sat down together to write. Composed while touring Yorkshire.
I'LL GET YOU
Written in collaboration with John Lennon and originally intended to be the follow up single to 'From Me To You'.
ALL MY LOVING
Written by Paul whilst shaving one morning, and originally started out life as a poem.
LITTLE CHILD
Written in collaboration with John Lennon originally for Ringo Starr to record.
HOLD ME TIGHT
Written in collaboration with John Lennon and influenced by Tamla Motown music. It was composed before the group made it big and was a featured song in the group's stage act in the Cavern.
I WANNA BE YOUR MAN
Written in collaboration with John Lennon for The Rolling Stones. It was penned during a visit to see The Stones on stage in a club in Richmond, and inspired Mick Jagger and Keith Richard to start writing their own material.
I WANT TO HOLD YOUR HAND
Written in collaboration with John Lennon in the basement of Jane Asher's London home in Wimpole Street.
CAN'T BUY ME LOVE
Written in collaboration with John Lennon.
THINGS WE SAID TODAY
Influenced by Bob Dylan.
AND I LOVE HER
Written in collaboration with John Lennon, who supplied the middle section of the song. Inspired by Jane Asher . . . and features subtle latin-beat.
SHE'S A WOMAN
Influenced by Little Richard.
I'LL FOLLOW THE SUN
Influenced by Buddy Holly, and features McCartney's latin-style beat.
EIGHT DAYS A WEEK
Written in collaboration with John Lennon and originally scheduled as a single. Legend has it that the song was intended to be the title track for the group's second film, which was initially called, 'Eight Arms To Hold You', before 'Help' was chosen instead. The revised song was dedicated to Brian Epstein and was about the lengthy hours he worked each day.
EVERY LITTLE THING
Written in collaboration with John Lennon, with a country and western feel.

WHAT YOU'RE DOING
Written in collaboration with John Lennon as a tribute to the work and style of Phil Spector. The featured guitar riff is reminiscent of that used on 'Daytripper'.
I'M DOWN
Influenced by Little Richard and written to replace 'Long Tall Sally' in The Beatles' stage act.
THE NIGHT BEFORE
Country rock-flavour, written for the movie 'Help'.
ANOTHER GIRL
Another optimistic number extolling the virtue of love, but with bitchy lyrics to a former girlfriend. Featured in 'Help'.
TELL ME WHAT YOU SEE
Optimistic love song, inspired by Jane Asher, with its 'I'll-always-be-there-when-you-need-me' lyrics.
I'VE JUST SEEN A FACE
Originally written as an instrumental for Aunty Jin, called 'Aunty Jin's Theme', under which title there is an instrumental version available by George Martin. Influenced by Bob Dylan.
YESTERDAY
Paul's original lyric was 'scrambled eggs', before he completed the words, and he allegedly offered the song to Chris Farlowe to record *before* The Beatles did it. Classic ballad, revised on the 1984 movie, 'Give My Regards To Broad Street'.
DAY TRIPPER
Written in collaboration with John Lennon, although Paul only contributed a small amount to the song on the verse. Legend has it that the song was written about drugs.
WE CAN WORK IT OUT
Written in collaboration with John Lennon. Paul wrote the optimistic verse; John supplied the pessimistic middle section. Reportedly the group's first anthem to peace!
DRIVE MY CAR
Written in collaboration with John Lennon, and influenced by Tamla Motown, but with cynical undertones.
NORWEGIAN WOOD
Written in collaboration with John Lennon who wrote most of the song. It is an admission, in song, by Lennon to an affair he had with another woman that he didn't want his wife, Cynthia, to know about . . . yet he felt he had to write down his feelings about the affair. Paul supplied some of the lyric.
THE WORD
Written in collaboration with John Lennon. A simple love song which proved to be the forerunner to 'All You Need Is Love'.
WHAT GOES ON
Written in collaboration with John Lennon and Ringo Starr. Country

and western-styled song, influenced by Carl Perkins. John wrote the verse; Ringo and Paul supplied the middle part.

YOU WON'T SEE ME

Inspired by – and written in the style of – the black American girl groups. Shades of early Tamla Motown.

HELLO GOODBYE

Optimistic song, with a change of style and tempo for the lengthy ending sequence which became part of The Beatles' trademark on other songs, notably on 'Hey Jude' and 'All You Need Is Love'.

MICHELLE

Written in collaboration with John Lennon, who supplied the 'I Love You, I Love You, I Love You' middle section. Written for the daughter of an American millionaire. Paul thought the melody line reminded him of a typical French style of song and wanted to put a French lyric to it. The wife of a friend of his taught French, and he asked her to help with the translation. The French lyric is identical to the English words . . . 'These are words that go together well . . .'

I'M LOOKING THROUGH YOU

Written when his girlfriend, Jane Asher, left him after a tiff, and went off to Bristol.

IN MY LIFE

Written in collaboration with John Lennon. Lennon supplied the words; McCartney wrote the tune.

WAIT

Written in collaboration with John Lennon.

PAPERBACK WRITER

Written in collaboration with John Lennon. Influenced by The Beach Boys – Paul wanted to write a song that matched the American group's counterpoint harmony – and John Lennon's success as an author, which Paul much admired. 'When we did the song,' said Paul, 'we wrote the words down like we were writing a letter. There's no story behind it.'

ELEANOR RIGBY

Written in collaboration with John Lennon, who supplied the last verse. Written about loneliness. The heroine of the song was originally called 'Daisy Hawkins'; 'Father McKenzie' was originally 'Father McCartney'.

YELLOW SUBMARINE

'It's really a children's song,' said Paul, and it was acclaimed as the Best Children's Song since Mel Blanc's, 'I Taught I Taw A Puddy Cat.' On the record, the sound effects included John Lennon blowing bubbles with a straw, and George Harrison swirling a bucket of water around.

HERE, THERE AND EVERYWHERE

Old fashioned love song, inspired by Jane Asher, with a two-line, 'thirties-style, semi-talking introduction. Written at John Lennon's house in Weybridge and influenced by The Beach Boys' 'God Only Knows'. Paul revised the song on 'Give My Regards To Broad Street'.

GOOD DAY SUNSHINE

Written at John's house in Weybridge. 'It was a happy-go-lucky summer song,' said Paul. Another song featured in 'Give My Regards To Broad Street'.

FOR NO ONE

Written while Paul was on a ski-ing holiday in Switzerland, and inspired by Jane Asher. It's a story song about a career girl, with the underriding theme of loneliness. He used the song in 'Give My Regards To Broad Street' and in the accompanying book wrote: 'This has to do with living with a woman. I was old enough to have amorous affairs rather than live at home, which is what the song is all about.'

DR ROBERT

Written in collaboration with John Lennon who wrote most of the song. Paul supplied the middle section. It's a song about a man in New York who The Beatles were told would be able to supply anything 'medicinal'. A pill doctor.

GOT TO GET YOU INTO MY LIFE

Soul-inspired, Tamla Motown influenced. Written when soul music was dominating the British charts.

PENNY LANE

A trip down Memory Lane. Originally planned as one of the songs on a theme album which would be about The Beatles' childhood in Liverpool. The album eventually turned into 'Sergeant Pepper'. Inspired by childhood memories.

WITH A LITTLE HELP FROM MY FRIENDS

Written in collaboration with John Lennon and originally called, 'Bad Finger Boogie' – the name later inspired a group signed to Apple, called The Iveys, to change their name to Badfinger. John supplied the line: 'What do you see when you turn out the light? I can't tell you but I know it's mine.'

SERGEANT PEPPER'S LONELY HEARTS CLUB BAND

The title track from the album of the same name. Paul thought it would be a good idea if The Beatles took over the persona of Sergeant Pepper's Lonely Hearts Club Band and made an album as if the Brass Band was making it, *not* The Beatles. He thought it would inspire the group and bring a little zest and excitement back into their work.

GETTING BETTER

Written in collaboration with John Lennon. It was based on a catch-phrase Jimmy Nicol – the session drummer The Beatles used for part of their Australian tour when Ringo Starr collapsed with tonsillitis – used to say all the time . . . 'it's getting better'. Paul wrote the song one day after walking his dog, when he suddenly realized spring had arrived. John wrote the middle section.

FIXING A HOLE

Paul explained the meaning of the song to a journalist: 'This song is just about a hole in the road where the rain gets in; a good old analogy – the hole in your make-up which lets the rain in and stops your mind from going where it will. It's you interfering with things . . . If you're a junky sitting in a room *fixing* a hole, then that's what it will mean to you, but when I wrote it, I meant, if there's a crack, or the room is uncolourful, then I'll paint it.'

SHE'S LEAVING HOME

Written in collaboration with John Lennon. A song about loneliness. Paul was inspired to write it after reading a story in the *Daily Mirror* about a young girl leaving home, and her father couldn't understand why, after they had given her everything, she wanted to leave. McCartney transferred his thoughts from the newspaper story into the song. John supplied most of the chorus hook lines. 'All those lines like, "We sacrificed most of our life . . . We gave her everything money could buy . . ." those were the things Mimi used to say,' said John.

WHEN I'M SIXTY FOUR

Written in collaboration with John Lennon, as a vaudeville-type tribute to Jim McCartney. Paul wrote the song when he was sixteen, about old age and retirement. It was originally intended to be part of a future musical comedy. John supplied lines like . . . 'Vera, Chuck and Dave' and 'Doing the garden, digging the weeds'. It was the type of song Jim Mac's Band might have played in the 1920s.

A DAY IN THE LIFE

Written in collaboration with John Lennon. Originally two separate songs. The main verse was supplied by John, inspired by a story he read in the *Daily Mail*, about the death of his friend Tara Browne, the Guinness heir. He actually propped up the newspaper on to the piano rest and started composing the song as he . . . 'read the news'. Paul's contribution was the middle section, but he gave the song its definition with the haunting phrase . . . 'I'd love to turn you on'.

ALL YOU NEED IS LOVE

Written in collaboration with John Lennon and composed specially for the 'live' international television programme, 'Our World', as part of the celebrations for Canada's Expo 67. Four hundred million people saw the show in twenty-six countries. 'All You Need Is Love' was Britain's contribution.

BABY YOU'RE A RICH MAN

Written in collaboration with John Lennon. Two songs combined together to make one – Lennon's 'One Of The Beautiful People'; McCartney's 'Baby You're A Rich Man'. A song about Brian Epstein, originally intended for the 'Sergeant Pepper' album.

LOVELY RITA
Inspired by a comment from an American lady, visiting Britain, who said: 'Oh, I see you've got *Meter Maids* over here.' Paul said: 'I was thinking vaguely that it should be a hate song, but then I thought it would be better to *love* her, and if she was freaky, too, like a military man, with a bag on her shoulder. A foot-stomper, but nice.' He added: 'The song was imagining if somebody was there taking down my number and I suddenly fell for her.'

However, in September 1985, when one of Britain's very first women traffic wardens – Mrs Meta Davis – retired, she told reporters that the highlight of her long career was actually booking Paul McCartney. It happened several months before the Sergeant Pepper project when Paul's car had overstayed its time on a meter in a St John's Wood side street, around the corner from the Abbey Road recording studios in London.

'I can't remember his car, but the fine was for ten shillings,' Meta Davis told newspapermen. 'We got talking because he saw my name on the ticket and he joked about it. He said it would make a good jingle.'

She added: 'We chatted for a few minutes and then he drove off. I never thought any more about it, until the song came out.'

MAGICAL MYSTERY TOUR
Written in collaboration with John Lennon. The song was recorded *without* words, apart from the opening phrase of 'Roll up, roll up for the Magical Mystery Tour . . .' The words were added later, when John and Paul simply shouted out anything that came into their heads that was associated with mystery tours, or coach trips. Words like 'reservation' . . . 'invitation' . . . 'satisfaction guaranteed', which were used for their rhyming qualities *not* as a story-line to the song. It was inspired by Paul's childhood, memories of mystery tour rides on charabancs.

YOUR MOTHER SHOULD KNOW
Written in the music hall vein, and conjuring up pictures of white tie, top hat and tails. Inspired by Fred Astaire and song-and-dance-men in general. Another musical tribute to Jim McCartney. Featured in 'Magical Mystery Tour'.

FLYING
Instrumental. Written in collaboration with John Lennon, George Harrison and Ringo Starr. Compiled out of a studio jam session. Featured in 'Magical Mystery Tour'.

FOOL ON THE HILL
McCartney whimsy once more, a fairy-tale song with loneliness as its theme. Paul uses an oompah-oompah middle-eight section, a feature he often repeats in other songs, including 'Martha My Dear' and 'Mother Nature's Son'. Indeed, 'Mother Nature's Son' seems an ideal extension to 'Fool On The Hill'. Featured in 'Magical Mystery Tour'.

LADY MADONNA
Influenced by – and originally written for – Fats Domino. Another whimsical song, again with loneliness as its theme. An out-and-out rock 'n' roller.
HEY JUDE
Written by Paul when driving to see Cynthia Lennon after she had broken up with John. The original opening phrase was 'Hey Jules . . .' after their son, Julian. Paul thought Jude was a better name because it was more 'country and western'.
BACK IN THE USSR
Originally called 'I'm Backing The USSR' and inspired by The Beach Boys' 'Surfin' USA'.
OB-LA-DI OB-LA-DA
Early attempts at reggae. Paul borrowed the expression from a Jamaican friend of his, Jimmy Scott, who ran his own band – Jimmy Scott And The Ob-La-Di Ob-La-Da Band. Fantasy story song.
WILD HONEY PIE
Whimsical mumblings. Mainly instrumental, written in India when The Beatles were on their meditation trip. Paul was going to scrap the whole song until Jane Asher said she liked it and he should put it down on record. On the recorded track, McCartney played all the instruments.
MARTHA MY DEAR
Vaudeville-type song in the 'thirties mould. Written for his old English sheepdog called Martha. Shades of Noël Coward on the lyrical phraseology.
BLACKBIRD
Loneliness is the main theme again. Several people have hinted that the song is a sympathetic gesture towards the then emerging Black Power movement. Others have said it stands for the alienation black immigrants felt by their rejection in a foreign country by the local population.
WHY DON'T WE DO IT IN THE ROAD
Twelve-bar musical construction with the title words sung over and over again. John Lennon's favourite Paul McCartney song.
I WILL
Whimsical love song, inspired by Jane Asher.
ROCKY RACCOON
Written in collaboration with John Lennon and Donovan. Originally called 'Rocky Sassoon'. Written in India during their sessions with the Maharishi. Cowboy-styled country rock flavoured song.
BIRTHDAY
Written in collaboration with John, in India, to celebrate Patti Harrison's birthday. An up-to-date version of 'Happy Birthday To You'. Built around a guitar riff, using a 12-bar blues phrase.

MOTHER NATURE'S SON
Written in India. Country-life song, let-me-get-out-into-the-fresh-air. Whimsical song in the style of 'Fool On The Hill', with an oompah oompah middle.
HELTER SKELTER
A forerunner to heavy metal, and inspired by The Who. Paul wrote the song after reading a music paper article in which The Who were reported as having recorded the loudest, most raucous piece of rock 'n' roll music ever. Not to be outdone, McCartney sat down and wrote the song that would make The Beatles record the loudest, most raucous piece of rock 'n' roll music ever. After the Charles Manson affair, when commenting on the song, Lennon called it 'a song about a fairground slide'.
ALL TOGETHER NOW
Skiffle meets vaudeville. Written as a send up of skiffle groups and how they used to implore their audiences to join in with the songs. 'Come on, all together now'.
HONEY PIE
A tribute to the Hollywood movies. Inspired by Jim McCartney and written in the style of the flappers from the 1920s. A shy salute to the Temperance Seven, and a gentle send-up of Noël Coward.
GET BACK
Written in the studio and influenced by Chuck Berry, though inspired by the type of material Creedence Clearwater Revival were doing at the time. A great example of country rock.
MAXWELL'S SILVER HAMMER
A whimsical, fairy-tale song, featuring another of McCartney's story-book characters, this time a psychopathic medical student. Typical Paul McCartney story song, written in the form of a play. He said: 'This epitomises the downfalls in life. Just when everything is going smoothly, "bang bang" down comes Maxwell's silver hammer and ruins everything.'
OH! DARLING
Influenced by the early rock 'n' roll material Paul Anka wrote. 12-bar blues musical construction. A few years later, Paul re-wrote it as 'Let Me Roll It'.
YOU NEVER GIVE ME YOUR MONEY
Written as a reaction to the financial difficulties at Apple and all the boardroom intrigue. It was a song about the break-up of The Beatles.
SHE CAME IN THROUGH THE BATHROOM WINDOW
Inspired by the early tours of America when fans would do anything to try and get into the group's hotel rooms or dressing rooms. One fan scaled a hotel drain pipe in an effort to reach The Beatles, and clambered into Paul's bathroom window, much to his surprise.
GOLDEN SLUMBERS
Written at his father's house in Heswell, and inspired by an old

music book his step-sister, Ruth, showed him. He came across the traditional 'Golden Slumbers' written in the 16th century by Thomas Dekker, and decided to put his own musical interpretation to the words, and wrote another lyric of his own.
CARRY THAT WEIGHT
A song written about the responsibility of keeping The Beatles together after Brian Epstein died.
THE END
A short musical phrase to top and tail the opera-style linked songs of 'Golden Slumbers' and 'Carry That Weight' on the 'Abbey Road' album. 'And in the end, the love you take is equal to the love you make' . . . the last lyric, in the last song, on the last Beatles album.
HER MAJESTY
Paul McCartney's re-write of the National Anthem, to finish off the 'Abbey Road' album. A country and western chug-along song.
LET IT BE
Written as an anthem to his mother, Mary McCartney. A song of loneliness. A cry for help. A classic ballad.
TWO OF US
Originally called 'On Our Way Home' and written as a reaction to Yoko Ono's arrival on the scene, to show the great bond that existed between Paul and Linda.
I'VE GOT A FEELING
Written in collaboration with John Lennon. Two songs combined together as one. Paul wrote 'I've Got A Feeling'; John chipped in with 'Everybody Had A . . .'
ONE AFTER 909
Written in collaboration with John Lennon, in 1958. One of the very first songs they wrote together. Written about a train.
THE LONG AND WINDING ROAD
A song of loneliness and disappointment . . . 'it's a long road we all have to travel through life.' A song that has its roots in a warm and loving family background. Reprised on 'Give My Regards To Broad Street'.
DIG IT
Written in collaboration with John Lennon, George Harrison and Ringo Starr and compiled from a jam session in the studio.

* * *

Songs written by Paul McCartney during The Beatles' days, recorded, yet never released.

IF YOU GOT TROUBLES
THINKING OF LINKING
ALWAYS AND ONLY
ANNIE
HEATHER
I LOST MY LITTLE GIRL

* * *

Paul McCartney songs, written since 1957, which have been recorded by other artists.

I'LL BE ON MY WAY – Billy J. Kramer

TIP OF MY TONGUE – Tommy Quickly

LOVE OF THE LOVED – Cilla Black

I'LL KEEP YOU SATISFIED – Billy J. Kramer

WORLD WITHOUT LOVE – Peter And Gordon

ONE AND ONE IS TWO – Mike Shannon And The Strangers

NOBODY I KNOW – Peter And Gordon

LIKE DREAMERS DO – The Applejacks

FROM A WINDOW – Billy J. Kramer

IT'S FOR YOU – Cilla Black

THAT MEANS A LOT – P.J. Proby

WOMAN – Peter And Gordon . . . written under the pseudonym of Bernard Webb

CATCALL – Chris Barber's Jazz Band

STEP INSIDE LOVE – Cilla Black

THINGUMYBOB – Black Dyke Mills Brass Band

GOODBYE – Mary Hopkin

COME AND GET IT – Badfinger

PENINA – Jotta Herre/Carlos Mendes

I DON'T WANT TO SEE YOU AGAIN – Peter and Gordon

TEN YEARS AFTER ON STRAWBERRY JAM – Scaffold . . . written with Mike McGear

4th OF JULY – John Christie . . . written with Mike McGear

MINE FOR ME – Rod Stewart

LET'S LOVE – Peggy Lee

ON THE WINGS OF A NIGHTINGALE – Everly Brothers

SIX O'CLOCK – Ringo Starr

SEA BREEZES/SWEET BABY – Mike McGear . . . written with Mike McGear

LEAVE IT – Mike McGear

WHAT DO YOU REALLY KNOW – Mike McGear

NORTON – Mike McGear . . . written with Mike McGear

HAVE YOU GOT PROBLEMS – Mike McGear . . . written with Mike McGear

THE CASKET – Mike McGear . . . written with Mike McGear

RAINBOW LADY – Mike McGear . . . written with Mike McGear

SIMPLY LOVE – Mike McGear . . . written with Mike McGear

GIVIN' GREASE A RIDE – Mike McGear . . . written with Mike McGear

THE MAN WHO FOUND GOD ON THE MOON – Mike McGear . . . written with Mike McGear

BRIDGE OVER THE RIVER SUITE – Country Hams . . . written with Linda McCartney

DANCE THE DO – Mike McGear . . . written with Mike McGear

PURE GOLD – Ringo Starr

GIDDY – Roger Daltrey

SEND ME YOUR HEART – Denny Laine . . . written with Denny Laine

PRIVATE PROPERTY AND ATTENTION – Ringo Starr

LOVE IN THE OPEN AIR – George Martin

THEME FROM THE FAMILY WAY – George Martin

APPENDIX II

The Songs of Paul McCartney (2)

These songs were written by Paul McCartney, or in collaboration with others, and recorded either as solo projects or with Wings, from 1969 onwards.

THE LOVELY LINDA
A love song to his wife, Linda, a trailer for a full song, although never fully developed.
THAT WOULD BE SOMETHING
Paul called this song 'a throwaway'. A bluesy guitar riff, with inane lyrics, that goes nowhere.
VALENTINE DAY
Instrumental based on a guitar riff.
EVERY NIGHT
Written on holiday in Greece. Well constructed love song. Phoebe Snow did an excellent cover version in 1979.
HOT AS SUN
Written in 1958 and developed over the next twelve years. Instrumental.
GLASSES
Taken from an uncompleted song called 'Suicide'. Paul described the number as 'wine glasses played at random and overdubbed.'
JUNK
Written in India during The Beatles' meditation days. It was originally called 'Jubilee' and was written for 'The Beatles' (White Album) LP, and later recorded to appear on 'Abbey Road'. McCartney whimsy.
MAN WE WAS LONELY
Rockabilly, influenced by Carl Perkins.
OO YOU
Bluesy song sung over guitar riff construction. Under-developed song.

MOMMA MISS AMERICA
Two songs combined together to make one.
TEDDY BOY
One of McCartney's 'character' songs introducing the listener '. . . to a boy named Ed'. Song about the relationship of a boy with his mother. Written in India and scheduled for the 'Let It Be' album.
SINGALONG JUNK
Instrumental version of 'Junk'.
MAYBE I'M AMAZED
Classic ballad in McCartney mould of 'Hey Jude'. A love song to Linda.
KREEN-AKRORE
Instrumental inspired by a television film about the South American Kreen-Akrore tribe. Written as a tribute to them . . . complete with sound effects of the jungle when recorded.
ANOTHER DAY
Same subject matter as 'For No One' – based on a lonely career girl who is looking for love.
OH WOMAN OH WHY
Screamer! A re-written version of 'Why Don't We Do It In The Road'.
TOO MANY PEOPLE
A bitchy reference to John Lennon and the Apple situation, through the lyric, 'too many people preaching', to which Paul later owned up.
3 LEGS
12-bar blues, rockabilly in the style of Carl Perkins or Gene Vincent. Similar in style to Buddy Holly material.
RAM ON
Ukulele Music Hall opener. Whimsical song.
DEAR BOY
Written in collaboration with Linda McCartney. Jazzy feel to the song. John Lennon thought some of the lyrics in the song made bitchy reference to him. McCartney denied it.
UNCLE ALBERT/ADMIRAL HALSEY
Written in collaboration with Linda McCartney. Appears to be two songs put together to form one. Distinct change of style and tempo as one song merges into the next. Very whimsical, with McCartney singing part of the lyric in a Noël Coward voice on record.
SMILE AWAY
12-bar rock 'n' roller, with uninspired lyrics, about smelly feet!
HEART OF THE COUNTRY
Written in collaboration with Linda McCartney. Influenced by Carl Perkins. Rockabilly, with McCartney out on the farm extolling the virtues of country life.

MONKBERRY MOON DELIGHT
Written in collaboration with Linda McCartney. Honky-tonk styled-song, based around a guitar riff.
EAT AT HOME
Written in collaboration with Linda McCartney. Influenced by Buddy Holly, but the song contains shades of early British rock 'n' roll as presented by Adam Faith or Shane Fenton. The guitar intro borrows much from 'Daytripper'.
LONG HAIRED LADY
Written in collaboration with Linda McCartney. Shades of 'Baby You're A Rich Man'. Paul back to his Music Hall roots again, although the song goes nowhere.
BACK SEAT OF MY CAR
Well-constructed song featuring McCartney whimsy once more. Nice changes of pace and tempo throughout the song with an ending that borrows much from the style of 'Hey Jude'.
MUMBO
Written in collaboration with Linda McCartney. Instrumental and incessant screaming combined.
BIP BOP
Written in collaboration with Linda McCartney. Inspired by Mary McCartney, Paul's daughter, in Gene Vincent style. 12-bar blues song with inane lyrics.
WILD LIFE
Written in collaboration with Linda McCartney. Paul's contribution to ecology and animal conservation. A dirge of a song, which loosely resembles James Brown's 'It's A Man's World'.
SOME PEOPLE NEVER KNOW
Written in collaboration with Linda McCartney.
I AM YOUR SINGER
Written in collaboration with Linda McCartney.
TOMORROW
Written in collaboration with Linda McCartney. A song with a great hook, but very much undeveloped as a production. With a little more thought and care, it could have been brilliant.
DEAR FRIENDS
Written in collaboration with Linda McCartney. Another song that never reaches its full potential; has all the ingredients of a classic.
GIVE IRELAND BACK TO THE IRISH
Written in collaboration with Linda McCartney. Written as a political statement in reaction to the Bloody Sunday massacres in Northern Ireland in 1972.
MARY HAD A LITTLE LAMB
Written in collaboration with Linda McCartney. A new musical version of the traditional nursery rhyme. Paul admitted to writing

the song because his daughter Mary liked hearing her name sung over and over again.
LITTLE WOMAN LOVE
Written in collaboration with Linda McCartney.
HI, HI, HI
Written in collaboration with Linda McCartney. 'It's basically a straight rock 'n' rolling thing, written on three rock 'n' roll chords,' said Paul.
C MOON
Written in collaboration with Linda McCartney. Influenced by the reggae rhythm and tempo, and said to be inspired by Sam The Sham's 'Woolly Bully'.
MY LOVE
Classic McCartney ballad celebrating love. Written to, and inspired by, Linda.
THE MESS
Powerful stomper, written for a live audience.
BIG RED BARN
GET ON THE RIGHT THING
Written in the style of boogie-woogie and hot gospel, but lightweight.
LITTLE LAMB DRAGONFLY
Could have been put together from two separate songs, with a nice key change in the middle of the verse. Inspired by the death of one of Paul's sheep on the Scottish farm. A touch of 'You Never Give Me Your Money'.
SINGLE PIGEON
A song of rejected love.
WHEN THE NIGHT
Soul-filled, influenced by Ben E. King and 'Stand By Me'.
LOUP (1st INDIAN ON THE MOON)
Instrumental with chants! Influenced by Pink Floyd in parts.
HOLD ME TIGHT
Unusual chord sequence and unexpected formation of the melody line are the song's strength, although it is reminiscent in parts, of 'Don't Make My Baby Blue'.
LAZY DYNAMITE
Inane lyrics with words used for sounds and effects rather than meaning.
HANDS OF LOVE
Country rock meets Music Hall.
POWER CUT
Reggae-styled rhythm, but lacks any kind of development.
ONE MORE KISS
Polished rockabilly, and influenced by Carl Perkins.

LIVE AND LET DIE
Written as the theme to the James Bond movie of the same name. The song is written in three sections. A ballad for openers, leading into an exciting instrumental middle that is punctuated by a reggae-type sequence which leads back into the instrumental. Paul admitted the number was contrived in parts for the film soundtrack.
I LIE AROUND
Typical piece of McCartney whimsy.
HELEN WHEELS
Inspired by the McCartney's Land Rover, called Helen Wheels. The song is a story about a journey down to London from the Scottish farm.
COUNTRY DREAMER
A gentle, country-styled song, showing exactly where Paul's head was at when he wrote it.
JET
Inspired by the name of one of the McCartneys' Labrador puppies. Great rocker, built around a guitar riff. Whimsical words are written for effect more than any meaning.
BAND ON THE RUN
Inspired by a remark made by George Harrison during a lengthy Apple board meeting – 'if we ever get out of here', which Paul picked up. The song is the title track from an album that was loosely based on a prison break-out theme. Written in three distinct sections – a slow beginning, starting off pessimistically, building through a bluesy second piece, to charge optimistically into a rocking end sequence.
BLUEBIRD
Whimsical and gentle love song, written with a latin-flavoured calypso rhythm.
MRS VANDERBILT
A rocking number, filled with good humour and jollity. The opening lyric was taken from a humorous poem written by British comedian Charlie Chester and featured regularly on radio broadcasts during the 1940s and 1950s, which Paul paraphrased. The 'down in the jungle' line was used extensively in the 1950s as the basis of new jokey poems and limericks by comedians and school children which were as popular then as 'Knock Knock' jokes today.
LET ME ROLL IT
Based on a 12-bar blues theme in the mould of Gene Vincent, although very much a tribute to John Lennon and the Plastic Ono Band.
MAMUNIA
Obscure title, featuring more McCartney whimsy. Paul borrows a musical sequence from 'Rocky Raccoon' to add to the song.

NO WORDS
Written for the harmony effect and based on a guitar riff. It's very reminiscent of early Beatles material, and there is a subtle hint of 'You Never Give Me Your Money', and a musical phrase from 'Nowhere Man'.
PICASSO'S LAST WORDS (DRINK TO ME)
A story song, but a true story and not part of Paul's imagination. Very enlightening, and written in several styles and tempos, but with a very 1940s middle section, leading into an out-and-out drinking song. The song was inspired by actor Dustin Hoffman. The McCartneys were on holiday in Jamaica where they met Dustin Hoffman during the filming of 'Papillon'. Over dinner one evening, Hoffman asked McCartney if he could write a song to order. When McCartney said he could, the actor challenged him to write one, using the last words Picasso said before he died – 'Drink to me, drink to my health, you know I can't drink anymore.' Paul grabbed his guitar . . . and obliged, there and then, which completely amazed the American who ran shouting – 'Look, he's doing it!'
NINETEEN HUNDRED AND EIGHTY FIVE
A rocker in the style of 'Lady Madonna'. The dateline has no significance apart from the fact that it gave a meaning to a rhyme.
ZOO GANG
Written specifically for the television series of the same name.
JUNIOR'S FARM
Written in Nashville, Tennessee, and inspired by the environment Paul found himself in. He was staying on Junior Putnam's farm at the time, and the song evokes shades of barn dances and calico shirts. The lyrics once again are used for effect and rhyme, more than meaning. Oliver Hardy is featured in one verse.
SALLY G
Another song written in Nashville, and inspired after visiting Printer's Alley in the Tennessee city, where he met Waylon Jennings, and spent the evening talking about Buddy Holly.
VENUS AND MARS
Gentle song, which is rumoured to be about Paul and Linda, although McCartney denied it saying the song was really about a friend of his whose girlfriend was into astrology. Inspired by an Asimov novel.
ROCK SHOW
1970s rock 'n' roll at its best. Written specifically as an opening number for Wings' stage act. Paul said: 'I really wanted it to be sweaty.' The lyrics mention several famous concert venues like Holland's Concertgebau, London's Rainbow, the Hollywood Bowl and Madison Square as part of the rhyme, and draws reference to Jimmy Page, the guitarist with Led Zeppelin.

LOVE IN SONG
Haunting ballad in the style of 'Mother Nature's Son'. Its strength is in its magnificent hook-line . . . 'Happiness in the homeland'.
YOU GAVE ME THE ANSWER
Dedicated to Fred Astaire and very much in his style. Similar in style to 'Your Mother Should Know', and very much in the vaudeville vein.
MAGNETO AND TITANIUM MAN
Inspired by reading the super-heroes in *Marvel* comics – 'I love the whole comic book thing,' said Paul.
LETTING GO
Underrated rocker with its roots in soul music, inspired by the type of material Chicago played.
SPIRITS OF ANCIENT EGYPT
Atmospheric-bluesy song in the Gene Vincent style, which becomes more subtle on the hook. Paul was inspired to write the song after reading a book on Egypt.
CALL ME BACK AGAIN
Influenced by blues and soul material and ideal fodder for Cliff Bennett. Reminiscent of James Brown.
LISTEN TO WHAT THE MAN SAID
Paul writing at his best; mature pop music. Chug-along rock 'n' roll. Happy-go-lucky love song. Unpretentious.
TREAT HER GENTLY
Not really a song, just an undeveloped musical phrase and hook.
LONELY OLD PEOPLE
A Paul McCartney lament on loneliness . . .
LET 'EM IN
Marching rock 'n' roll, in a funky style. The lyrics were chosen for rhyming pattern more than for significance. Paul mentions Brother John (Lennon), brother Michael (McCartney), his Aunty Jin, Phil and Don (Everly), Martin Luther (King), and his own Uncle Ernie, in the words.
THE NOTE YOU NEVER WROTE
Morose dirge of a song and instantly forgettable.
SHE'S MY BABY
Lightweight Music Hall-styled song, designed as an album filler.
BEWARE MY LOVE
Nicely constructed song, influenced by Tamla Motown, and has shades of The Four Tops' 'Reach Out And I'll Be There'.
SILLY LOVE SONGS
Paul wrote the song as a reaction to the constant criticism that he could only write ballads. The market at that time was flooded with heavier material with Alice Cooper as one of the main protagonists. He conveys a very strong message of 'what's wrong with silly love songs?' 'I was striking a blow for nice sentimental love songs,' he

said. Paul revised the song in the movie 'Give My Regards To Broad Street' and it was featured as one of the film's main production numbers, and given a very futuristic set.

COOK OF THE HOUSE

Written for Linda. It was written in Australia and inspired by their stay in a rented house in Adelaide where after the concerts every night, Paul and Linda would find themselves in the kitchen looking to cook a meal for themselves. A tongue-in-cheek parody, complete with a lyric that in places is just a list of foodstuffs found in a kitchen.

MUST DO SOMETHING ABOUT IT

Very much in the style of The Carpenters. A gentle rocker with 'I-don't-know-what-to-do-with-myself' sentiments. Loneliness is the overriding theme again. The opening line is reminiscent of 'Let's Turn Out The Light And Go To Sleep' with its . . . 'No more money in the bank . . .' -type sequence.

SAN FERRY ANNE

Country rock, but very much in the style of 'Take Five' or 'Cutty Sark' with that overall laid back feel.

WARM AND BEAUTIFUL

McCartney's anthem-come-hymn to love. Very regal, and conjures up great presence, and stature.

SOILY

Heavy metal in the Jimi Hendrix mould, typifies 'Purple Haze', only faster.

MULL OF KINTYRE

Written in collaboration with Denny Laine. Paul started the song in 1976 and was inspired by the beauty and peacefulness of the Scottish country near to the Mull, and his own farm. Written in four-time and very much in the style of 'Amazing Grace'. 'I'd like to hear the football crowd at Hampden Park sing it,' said Paul.

GIRLS SCHOOL

Originally called 'Love School', the song was inspired by a newspaper advert for a pornographic film. A raucous rocker.

LONDON TOWN

Written in collaboration with Denny Laine, and penned in Australia, Mexico and Scotland . . . about London! Interesting chord construction leads into a haunting melody. Loneliness is the main theme.

CAFE ON THE LEFT BANK

Well-written melody line with lyrics to match. Gentle rocker.

I'M CARRYING

Often acclaimed song as being 'stylish', 'delicate', 'atmospheric'. Simple song, very reminiscent of the type of material Clifford T. Ward writes, with poignant lyrics of love.

BACKWARDS TRAVELLER

A rocking phrase that Paul didn't seem to know what to do with, or where to take it. A phrase that hasn't been developed into a full song.

CUFF LINK

Meandering instrumental.

CHILDREN, CHILDREN

Written in collaboration with Denny Laine and inspired by the waterfalls in Paul's garden. Very folksy in flavour.

GIRLFRIEND

Written for Michael Jackson, and composed in Scotland. Chug-along romantic song, which captures Jackson's own gentle style. The song feels like an extension of 'Silly Love Songs' and 'Take It A Way'.

I'VE HAD ENOUGH

Well constructed rocker in 1950s style. 12-bar blues-type chorus.

WITH A LITTLE LUCK

Vintage McCartney. Well constructed pop song which would actually have suited Michael Jackson better than 'Girlfriend'. A song of optimism, with hope-filled lyrics. Polished pop.

FAMOUS GROUPIES

Vaudeville re-visited à la Don Partridge, a British busker who enjoyed chart success in England in the 1960s. A comedy song, with well-observed – and McCartney's most humorous – lyrics to date. Cutting satire.

DELIVER YOUR CHILDREN

Written in collaboration with Denny Laine. Owes a lot to the style of Crosby, Stills, Nash, and Young.

NAME AND ADDRESS

Influenced by Elvis Presley – in fact the recording of this song on the 'London Town' album was a parody on Presley – and the early Sun Records recordings. Borrowed a lot from 'That's Alright Momma'.

DON'T LET IT BRING YOU DOWN

Written in collaboration with Denny Laine. Sophisticated Irish reel music, and similar in style to the type of material credited to The Chieftains.

MOUSE MOOSE AND THE GREY GOOSE

Written in collaboration with Denny Laine, with a nautical flavour. Sea shanties. Emanated from a jam session while the group were recording.

GOODNIGHT TONIGHT

Written specifically for the Disco market. Clever lyrics and a well-constructed song.

DAYTIME, NIGHTTIME SUFFERING

Happy-go-lucky pop song, written to get the most out of harmony.

RECEPTION

Instrumental written as the opener for the 'Back To The Egg' album.

GETTING CLOSER
Gutsy rocker written with harmony in mind. A sophisticated pop song.
WE'RE OPEN TONIGHT
Gentle song built around a whimsical guitar phrase, but the whole entity goes nowhere. A string of musical phrases put together without direction.
SPIN IT ON
One note rocker . . . Paul's concession to punk rock. Shades of 'Helter Skelter' in parts, and the words used simply for effect, not meaning.
OLD SIAM SIR
Heavy, two note rocker, owing a lot to Jimi Hendrix.
ARROW THROUGH ME
Jazzy-come-bluesy song . . . late night cabaret bar material.
ROCKESTRA THEME
'Hi, Hi, Hi' re-visited. Won a Grammy Award in 1979 for Best Instrumental. Based around a descending chord sequence, with certain phrases reminiscent of Booker T.
TO YOU
Messy rock 'n' roller which goes nowhere.
AFTER THE BALL
Very much influenced by gospel music, but in the style of 'Amazing Grace'.
MILLION MILES
An extension of 'After The Ball', written on the gospel theme.
WINTER ROSE
Haunting ballad in waltz time, though not developed to its full potential.
LOVE AWAKE
Gentle love song. Optimistic in its aims, a good melody which is not immediate.
THE BROADCAST
Instrumental phrase used on record to accompany two poems – The Sport Of Kings by Ian Hay, and The Little Man by John Galsworthy. Rumour has it that it is one of David Bowie's favourite tracks.
SO GLAD TO SEE YOU HERE TONIGHT
Rocking number in the style of The Spencer Davis Group and reminiscent of 'Gimme Some Loving'.
BABY'S REQUEST
Originally written for The Mills Brothers. Very much in the style of 1930s/1940s lounge band music of the Big Band era, which would have ideally suited Manhattan Transfer. Captures the mood of the times.
WONDERFUL CHRISTMASTIME
Paul McCartney's contribution to the Christmas festivities. He always wanted to write a definitive Christmas song like 'White

Christmas' or 'Have Yourself A Merry Little Christmas'. The song is too specific in its aims, pointed directly at the disco market. Clever lyrics, though.

LUNCHEON BOX/ODD SOX

Forgettable instrumental.

COMING UP

Brassy and bold rocker with its strength in the hook-line. Optimistic funky rhythm.

TEMPORARY SECRETARY

The melody captures the motion and rhythm of a typewriter with its three note jerky sequence. McCartney returns to an idea first used on 'Paperback Writer' with The Beatles, writing the lyrics as if penning a letter . . . this time to the Alfred Marks Bureau.

ON THE WAY

Blues song, influenced by Alexis Korner.

WATERFALLS

Beautifully put together ballad. Haunting and sensitive. A plaintive plea for love. Its obscure lyrics, however, get home the message of 'I need you', 'I love you'. Very much rooted in family life – Waterfalls is the name of Paul's house. Written initially for the family.

NOBODY KNOWS

12-bar bluesy number reminiscent of the blues singers of the 1920s and '30s. Influenced by Alexis Korner.

FRONT PARLOUR

Instrumental, written in the front room of Paul's farmhouse. Would be excellent as the theme tune to a television series on computers. Conjures up visions of mathematics and computers.

SUMMER'S DAY LONG

Could have been another 'Hey Jude' if it had been developed fully. Paul McCartney's classical piece! Mainly instrumental, but it is an anthem to summer, and captures the mood.

FROZEN JAP

Oriental-phrasing, electronic instrumental.

BOGEY MUSIC

Inspired by 'Fungus The Bogeyman' by Raymond Briggs. A boogie-woogie 12-bar – or bogey-wogey!

DARK ROOM

Eastern-flavoured album filler . . . throwaway.

ONE OF THESE DAYS

Very underrated song. Another ballad full of hope and optimism. Great melody line that grows. Based on a variation of the theme of 'Mother Nature's Son', only much more polished and mature.

CHECK MY MACHINE

Electronic song which meanders.

SECRET FRIEND

A gentle, soothing ballad.

RAINCLOUDS
Written in collaboration with Denny Laine. Singalong happy-go-lucky song.
TUG OF WAR
Gentle, simple song that develops into a classy ballad. Good lyrics.
TAKE IT AWAY
Jazz-funk in the style of Earth Wind and Fire. Nice change of key in the middle. Very stylish.
SOMEBODY WHO CARES
Gentle ballad, with a nice change from verse to hook-line. The whole song sounds disjointed with a melody line that can't quite seem to fit the music. And yet, the whole song works perfectly.
WHAT'S THAT YOU'RE DOING
Written in collaboration with Stevie Wonder, and created out of a recording jam session. Shades of 'Superstition'.
HERE TODAY
A McCartney classic, written as a tribute to John Lennon. Very much in the vein of 'For No One' – quality words and wistful melody.
BALLROOM DANCING
Rock 'n' rolling childhood memories; from a very young boy playing fantasy games, to a teenager going to ballrooms to look for girls. Paul calls upon all his memories of the early Beatles playing ballroom engagements in Liverpool. The song is featured in 'Broad Street' as the movie's big production number.
THE POUND IS SINKING
A song which features several styles of music – from country rock, to vaudeville to rock 'n' roll. Inspired by a newspaper headline, and written tongue-in-cheek. 'To me it's a joke,' says Paul. 'You always see the headline – The Pound Is Sinking . . . no wait a minute, it's rising . . . no, it's sinking again. Wait a minute, the dollar's going up now. It's a money market song. A Fun song.'
WUNDERLUST
Classic ballad, constructed like an anthem. Rich and mature in presence. Inspired by the boat, *Wunderlust*, on which Paul and the family stayed when recording the 'London Town' album in the Virgin Islands. Paul said *Wunderlust*, the boat, stood for 'freedom'. Very dramatic ballad, featured in 'Give My Regards To Broad Street'.
GET IT
Rockabilly song, evoking the true flavour and style of country rock; full of good humour and well-being.
BE WHAT YOU SEE
Half a musical phrase, used as an album filler on 'Tug Of War'.
DRESS ME UP AS A ROBBER
Jazz-funk in the style of Earth Wind And Fire, with the subtle hint of the latin-beat McCartney was very partial to using in The Beatles.

EBONY AND IVORY
McCartney classic, although he was heavily criticized for the twee lyrics of black and white people living in harmony together. A simple song, conveying its simple message, which is captured perfectly through the melody line and hook. Well constructed pop music.
I'LL GIVE YOU A RING
ODE TO A KOALA BEAR
A whimsical song, with shades of 'You Really Got A Hold On Me'. Nicely put together which suggests that it was originally composed exclusively for the McCartney children.
PIPES OF PEACE
An anti-war song and plea for peace by Paul, conveying his sentiments through a very powerful love song. Opening phrases introduce the song, which is something The Beatles liked to do with their songs, using two or three lines at the beginning of a song as an introduction away from the main body of the song. They used it to great effect on 'Here There And Everywhere' and 'If I Fell'. A ploy used by '30s and '40s songwriters.
SAY, SAY, SAY
Written in collaboration with Michael Jackson, in the jazz-funk style.
THE OTHER ME
'I'm sorry, please forgive me', lyrics set against a gentle rocker.
KEEP UNDER COVER
Built around a descending scale construction Paul likes so much. Meaty rocker in the vein of 'Lady Madonna'. A question and answer-type song – 'What good is butter without bread?'
SO BAD
Simplistic love song about the pain of being in love. Inspired by Linda and the children, particularly James McCartney, Paul's son. Unpretentious 'this-is-how-it-feels' ballad, featured in the 'Give My Regards To Broad Street' movie.
THE MAN
Written in collaboration with Michael Jackson, in the style of The Isley Brothers. The song smacks of 'Who's That Lady' and 'Harvest Of The World'. Whimsical song . . . gentle, funky rocker.
SWEETEST LITTLE SHOW
Rockabilly song, similar to 'Getting Better'. Happy-go-lucky number with echoes of Tamla Motown, and seems ideally suited to The Drifters.
AVERAGE PERSON
Music-Hall parody McCartney loves so much. A Beatles fall-back. A fantasy fun song, full of jokes and humour . . . 'average people have ambitions – so what?' Paul at his story-telling best.

HEY HEY
Instrumental with shades of 'Birthday' guitar riff. Funky bass instrumental which probably came out of a studio jam session.
TUG OF PEACE
Latin-flavoured song in counterpoint to 'Tug Of War'. Reminiscent of the style of music Adam Ant was playing, with the incessant reliance on drum beat.
THROUGH OUR LOVE
Gentle ballad that craves the big production. Maturely constructed love song that says nothing more than 'love can triumph over everything if we all believe it can'.
NOT SUCH A BAD BOY
A rock 'n' roller, written specially for 'Give My Regards To Broad Street', and featured in the sequence which shows the group performing 'live' in the rehearsal rooms.
NO VALUES
The inspiration for this song came to Paul in a dream. He was on holiday at the time, and he dreamt he saw The Rolling Stones on stage performing the number. When he woke up, he knew the song completely, every word, every chord in his head, but was convinced The Stones had recorded it. When he checked and found out they hadn't . . . he sat down at the piano and wrote it himself. Another song featured in 'Broad Street'.
NO MORE LONELY NIGHTS
The title theme song from 'Give My Regards To Broad Street', constructed out of a bass riff, and played through a repeating echo device, which Paul built on after playing around with ideas and tempos in the studio. It developed into a love song, with the lyrics telling about the nervousness of love.
WE ALL STAND TOGETHER
Written for the animated cartoon feature 'Rupert Bear And The Frog Song', and built up on a background of oompahs. A fantasy song, and could easily develop into a nursery rhyme 'standard' in years to come. Whimsical McCartney at his best.
SPIES LIKE US
Written for the comedy spy-spoof movie of the same name. Built around a bass riff, reminiscent of 'Lady Madonna' in parts. Good rock 'n' roll, with nice changes of tempo and catchy chorus.
MY CARNIVAL
Written in New Orleans in 1975 and inspired by the Mardi Gras festival and colourful celebrations.

*   *   *

MISCELLANEOUS SONGS

SUICIDE
Written in 1969 and never finished. A section, called 'Glasses' was taken from it and used on the album 'McCartney'.
GOTTA SING, GOTTA DANCE
Written for Twiggy and performed by Paul on his TV special 'James Paul McCartney' in 1963. Song-and-dance number.
KARATE CHAOS
Abstract percussion piece written for the karate film, 'Empty Hand' which featured Wings' drummer of the time, Geoff Britton.
BOIL OIL
Paul McCartney's concession to punk.
HAVEN'T WE MET SOMEWHERE BEFORE?
Written exclusively for the movie 'Heaven Can Wait' and never used on the soundtrack.
THE HONORARY CONSUL
Paul composed the theme music for the soundtrack to the 1983 Michael Caine movie.

* * *

APPENDIX III

Paul McCartney Discography

WITH THE BEATLES

SINGLES

LOVE ME DO/P.S. I LOVE YOU	Parlophone	R4949
PLEASE PLEASE ME/ASK ME WHY	Parlophone	R4983
FROM ME TO YOU/THANK YOU GIRL	Parlophone	R5015
SHE LOVES YOU/I'LL GET YOU	Parlophone	R5055
I WANT TO HOLD YOUR HAND/THIS BOY	Parlophone	R5084
CAN'T BUY ME LOVE/YOU CAN'T DO THAT	Parlophone	R5114
A HARD DAY'S NIGHT/THINGS WE SAID TODAY	Parlophone	R5160
I FEEL FINE/SHE'S A WOMAN	Parlophone	R5200
TICKET TO RIDE/YES IT IS	Parlophone	R5265
HELP/I'M DOWN	Parlophone	R5305
DAY TRIPPER/WE CAN WORK IT OUT	Parlophone	R5389
PAPERBACK WRITER/RAIN	Parlophone	R5452
ELEANOR RIGBY/YELLOW SUBMARINE	Parlophone	R5493
PENNY LANE/STRAWBERRY FIELDS FOREVER	Parlophone	R5570
ALL YOU NEED IS LOVE/BABY YOU'RE A RICH MAN	Parlophone	R5620
HELLO GOODBYE/I AM THE WALRUS	Parlophone	R5655
LADY MADONNA/THE INNER LIGHT	Parlophone	R5675
HEY JUDE/REVOLUTION	Apple	R5722
GET BACK/DON'T LET ME DOWN	Apple	R5777
THE BALLAD OF JOHN AND YOKO/OLD BROWN SHOE	Apple	R5786
SOMETHING/COME TOGETHER	Apple	R5814
LET IT BE/YOU KNOW MY NAME (LOOK UP THE NUMBER)	Apple	R5833
YESTERDAY/I SHOULD HAVE KNOWN BETTER	Apple	R6013

BACK IN THE USSR/TWIST AND SHOUT Parlophone R6016
SERGEANT PEPPER'S LONELY HEARTS CLUB BAND/WITH A LITTLE HELP FROM MY FRIENDS/A DAY IN THE LIFE Parlophone R6022
THE BEATLES MOVIE MEDLEY/I'M HAPPY JUST TO DANCE WITH YOU Parlophone R6055

* * *

EPs

TWIST AND SHOUT Parlophone GEP8882
Twist And Shout; A Taste Of Honey; Do You Want To Know A Secret; There's A Place.
THE BEATLES' HITS Parlophone GEP8880
From Me To You; Thank You Girl; Please Please Me; Love Me Do.
THE BEATLES No. 1 Parlophone GEP8883
I Saw Her Standing There; Misery; Anna; Chains.
ALL MY LOVING Parlophone GEP8891
All My Loving; Ask My Why; Money; P.S. I Love You.
LONG TALL SALLY Parlophone GEP8913
I Call Your Name; Slow Down; Long Tall Sally; Matchbox.
A HARD DAY'S NIGHT No. 1 Parlophone GEP8920
I Should Have Known Better; If I Fell; Tell Me Why; And I Love Her.
A HARD DAY'S NIGHT No. 2 Parlophone GEP8924
Any Time At All; I'll Cry Instead; Things We Said Today; When I Get Home.
BEATLES FOR SALE No. 1 Parlophone GEP8931
No Reply; I'm A Loser; Rock And Roll Music; Eight Days A Week.
BEATLES FOR SALE No. 2 Parlophone GEP8938
I'll Follow The Sun; Baby's In Black; Words Of Love; I Don't Want To Spoil The Party.
THE BEATLES' MILLION SELLERS Parlophone GEP8946
She Loves You; I Want To Hold Your Hand; Can't Buy Me Love; I Feel Fine.
YESTERDAY Parlophone GEP8948
Act Naturally; You Like Me Too Much; Yesterday; It's Only Love.
NOWHERE MAN Parlophone GEP8952
Nowhere Man; Drive My Car; Michelle; You Won't See Me.
MAGICAL MYSTERY TOUR Parlophone SMMT 1*2
Magical Mystery Tour; Your Mother Should Know; I Am The Walrus; The Fool On The Hill; Flying; Blue Jay Way.
THE BEATLES EP COLLECTION Parlophone BEP14
Boxed set of all 13 EPs.

ALBUMS

PLEASE PLEASE ME Parlophone PCS3042
I Saw Her Standing There; Misery; Anna; Chains; Boys; Ask Me Why; Please Please Me; Love Me Do; P.S. I Love You; Baby It's You; Do You Want To Know A Secret; A Taste Of Honey; There's A Place; Twist And Shout.

WITH THE BEATLES Parlophone PCS3045
It Won't Be Long; All I've Got To Do; All My Loving; Don't Bother Me; Little Child; Till There Was You; Please Mr Postman; Roll Over Beethoven; Hold Me Tight; You Really Got A Hold On Me; I Wanna Be Your Man; Devil In Her Heart; Not A Second Time; Money.

A HARD DAY'S NIGHT Parlophone PCS3058
A Hard Day's Night; I Should Have Known Better; If I Fell; I'm Happy Just To Dance With You; And I Love Her; Tell Me Why; Can't Buy Me Love; Any Time At All; I'll Cry Instead; Things We Said Today; When I Get Home; You Can't Do That; I'll Be Back.

BEATLES FOR SALE Parlophone PCS3062
No Reply; I'm A Loser; Baby's In Black; Rock And Roll Music; I'll Follow The Sun; Mr Moonlight; Kansas City; Eight Days A Week; Words Of Love; Honey Don't; Every Little Thing; I Don't Want To Spoil The Party; What You're Doing; Everybody's Trying To Be My Baby.

HELP Parlophone PCS3071
Help; The Night Before; You've Got To Hide Your Love Away; I Need You; Another Girl; You're Gonna Lose That Girl; Ticket To Ride; Act Naturally; It's Only Love; You Like Me Too Much; Tell Me What You See; I've Just Seen A Face; Yesterday; Dizzy Miss Lizzy.

RUBBER SOUL Parlophone PCS3075
Drive My Car; Norwegian Wood; You Won't See Me; Nowhere Man; Think For Yourself; The Word; Michelle; What Goes On; Girl; I'm Looking Through You; In My Life; Wait; If I Needed Someone; Run For Your Life.

REVOLVER Parlophone PCS7009
Taxman; Eleanor Rigby; I'm Only Sleeping; Love You To; Here, There And Everywhere; Yellow Submarine; She Said, She Said; Good Day Sunshine; And Your Bird Can Sing; For No One; Doctor Robert; I Want To Tell You; Got To Get You Into My Life; Tomorrow Never Knows.

SERGEANT PEPPER'S LONELY HEARTS CLUB BAND Parlophone PCS7027
Sergeant Pepper's Lonely Hearts Club Band; With A Little Help From My Friends; Lucy In The Sky With Diamonds; Getting Better; Fixing A Hole; She's Leaving Home; Being For The Benefit Of Mr Kite; Within You, Without You; When I'm Sixy Four; Lovely Rita; Good Morning, Good Morning; A Day In The Life.

THE BEATLES Apple PCS7067*8 (Double)
Back In The USSR; Dear Prudence; Glass Onion; Ob-La-Di Ob-La-Da; Wild Honey Pie; The Continuing Story Of Bungalow Bill; While My Guitar Gently Weeps; Happiness Is A Warm Gun; Martha My Dear; I'm So Tired; Blackbird; Piggies; Rocky Raccoon; Don't Pass Me By; Why Don't We Do It In The Road; I Will; Julia; Birthday; Yer Blues; Mother Nature's Son; Everyboy's Got Something To Hide Except Me And My Monkey; Sexy Sadie; Helter Skelter; Long, Long, Long; Revolution 1; Honey Pie; Savoy Truffle; Cry Baby Cry; Revolution 9; Goodnight.

YELLOW SUBMARINE Apple PCS7070
Yellow Submarine; Only A Northern Song; All Together Now; Hey Bulldog; It's All Too Much; All You Need Is Love; Pepperland; Sea Of Time; Sea Of Holes; Sea Of Monsters; March Of The Meanies; Pepperland Laid Waste; Yellow Submarine In Pepperland.

ABBEY ROAD Apple PCS7088
Come Together; Something; Maxwell's Silver Hammer; Oh! Darling; Octopus's Garden; I Want You – She's So Heavy; Here Comes The Sun; Because; You Never Give Me Your Money; Sun King; Mean Mr Mustard; Polythene Pam; She Came In Through The Bathroom Window; Golden Slumbers; Carry That Weight; The End; Her Majesty.

LET IT BE Apple PCS7096
Two Of Us; Dig A Pony; Across The Universe; I Me Mine; Dig It; Let It Be; Maggie May; I've Got A Feeling; One After 909; The Long And Winding Road; For You Blue; Get Back.

COMPILATIONS

A COLLECTION OF BEATLES OLDIES (BUT GOLDIES)
Parlophone PCS7016
She Loves You; From Me To You; We Can Work It Out; Help; Michelle; Yesterday; I Feel Fine; Yellow Submarine; Can't Buy Me Love; Bad Boy; Day Tripper; A Hard Day's Night; Ticket To Ride; Paperback Writer; Eleanor Rigby; I Want To Hold Your Hand.

THE BEATLES 1962–1966 Apple PCSP717 (Double)
Love Me Do; Please Please Me; From Me To You; She Loves You; I Want To Hold Your Hand; All My Loving; Can't Buy Me Love; A Hard Day's Night; And I Love Her; Eight Days A Week; I Feel Fine; Ticket To Ride; Yesterday; Help; You've Got To Hide Your Love Away; We Can Work It Out; Day Tripper; Drive My Car; Norwegian Wood; Nowhere Man; Michelle; In My Life; Girl; Paperback Writer; Eleanor Rigby; Yellow Submarine.

THE BEATLES 1967–70 Apple PCSP718 (Double)
Strawberry Fields Forever; Penny Lane; Sergeant Pepper's Lonely

Hearts Club Band; With A Little Help From My Friends; Lucy In The Sky With Diamonds; A Day In The Life; All You Need Is Love; I Am The Walrus; Hello Goodbye; The Fool On The Hill; Magical Mystery Tour; Lady Madonna; Hey Jude; Revolution; Back In The USSR; While My Guitar Gently Weeps; Ob-La-Di Ob-La-Da; Get Back; Don't Let Me Down; The Ballad Of John And Yoko; Old Brown Shoe; Here Comes The Sun; Come Together; Something; Octopus's Garden; Let It Be; Across The Universe; The Long And Winding Road.

ROCK 'N' ROLL MUSIC Parlophone PCSP719

Twist And Shout; I Saw Her Standing There; You Can't Do That; I Wanna Be Your Man; I Call Your Name; Boys; Long Tall Sally; Rock And Roll Music; Slow Down; Kansas City; Money; Bad Boy; Matchbox; Roll Over Beethoven; Dizzy Miss Lizzy; Anytime At All; Drive My Car; Everybody's Trying To Be My Baby; The Night Before; I'm Down; Revolution; Back In The USSR; Helter Skelter; Taxman; Got To Get You Into My Life; Hey Bulldog; Birthday; Get Back.

THE BEATLES TAPES Polydor 2683 068

David Wigg interviews The Beatles.

Music Tracks: Because; Come Together; Give Peace A Chance; Here Comes The Sun; Hey Jude; Imagine; Octopus's Garden; Something; Yellow Submarine.

MAGICAL MYSTERY TOUR Parlophone PCTC255

Magical Mystery Tour; The Fool On The Hill; Flying; Blue Jay Way; Your Mother Should Know; I Am The Walrus; Hello Goodbye; Strawberry Fields Forever; Penny Lane; Baby You're A Rich Man; All You Need Is Love.

THE BEATLES AT THE HOLLYWOOD BOWL Parlophone EMTV4

Twist And Shout; She's A Woman; Dizzy Miss Lizzy; Ticket To Ride; Can't Buy Me Love; Things We Said Today; Roll Over Beethoven; Boys; A Hard Day's Night; Help!; All My Loving; She Loves You; Long Tall Sally.

LOVE SONGS Parlophone PCSP721 (Double)

Yesterday; I'll Follow The Sun; I Need You; Girl; In My Life; Words Of Love; Here, There And Everywhere; Something; And I Love Her; If I Fell; I'll Be Back; Tell Me What You See; Yes It Is; Michelle; It's Only Love; You're Gonna Lose That Girl; Every Little Thing; For No One; She's Leaving Home; The Long And Winding Road; This Boy; Norwegian Wood; You've Got To Hide Your Love Away; I Will; P.S. I Love You.

THE BEATLES COLLECTION Parlophone BC13

Boxed set of all 13 original Beatles' albums.

HEY JUDE Parlophone PCS7184

Can't Buy Me Love; I Should Have Known Better; Paperback Writer; Rain; Lady Madonna; Revolution; Hey Jude; Old Brown Shoe; Don't Let Me Down; The Ballad Of John And Yoko.

RARITIES Parlophone PCM1001
Across The Universe; Yes It Is; This Boy; The Inner Light; I'll Get You; Thank You Girl; Komm Gibt Mir Deine Hand; You Know My Name (Look Up The Number); Sie Leibt Dich; Rain; She's A Woman; Matchbox; I Call Your Name; Bad Boy; Slow Down; I'm Down; Long Tall Sally.
THE BEATLES BALLADS Parlophone PCS7214
Yesterday; Norwegian Wood; Do You Want To Know A Secret; For No One; Michelle; Nowhere Man; You're Got To Hide Your Love Away; Across The Universe; All My Loving; Hey Jude; Something; The Fool On The Hill; Till There Was You; The Long And Winding Road; Here Comes The Sun; Blackbird; And I Love Her; She's Leaving Home; Here, There And Everywhere; Let It Be.
REEL MUSIC Parlophone PCS7218
A Hard Day's Night; I Should Have Known Better; Can't Buy Me Love; And I Love Her; Help; You've Got To Hide Your Love Away; Ticket To Ride; Magical Mystey Tour; I Am The Walrus; Yellow Submarine; All You Need Is Love; Let It Be; Get Back; The Long And Winding Road.
20 GREATEST HITS Parlophone PCTC260
Love Me Do; From Me To You; She Loves You; I Want To Hold Your Hand; Can't Buy Me Love; A Hard Day's Night; I Feel Fine; Ticket To Ride; Help!; Day Tripper; We Can Work It Out; Paperback Writer; Yellow Submarine; Eleanor Rigby; All You Need Is Love; Hello Goodbye; Lady Madonna; Hey Jude; Get Back; The Ballad Of John And Yoko.

EARLY BEATLES

THE BEATLES FIRST Polydor Hi-fi 46432
Ain't She Sweet; Cry For A Shadow; Let's Dance; My Bonnie; Take Out Some Insurance On Me Baby; What'd I Say; Sweet Georgia Brown; The Saints; Ruby Baby; Why; Nobody's Child; Ya Ya.
THE COMPLETE SILVER BEATLES AFELP 1047
Three Cool Cats; Crying, Waiting Hoping; Besame Mucho; Searchin'; Sheik Of Araby; Money; To Know Him Is To Love Him; Take Good Care Of My Baby; Memphis; Sure To Fall; Till There Was You; September In The Rain.
THE BEATLES LIVE AT THE STAR CLUB HAMBURG LNL1 (Double)
I Saw Her Standing There; Roll Over Beethoven; Hippy Hippy Shake; Sweet Little Sixteen; Lend Me Your Comb; Your Feet's Too Big; Twist And Shout; Mr Moonlight; A Taste Of Honey; Besame Mucho; Reminiscing; Kansas City; Ain't Nothing Shakin'; To Know Her Is To Love Her; Little Queenie; Falling In Love Again; Ask Me Why; Be-Bop-A-Lula; Hallelujah I Love Her So; Red Sails In The Sunset; Everybody's Trying To Be My Baby; Matchbox; Talkin' Bout You; Shimmy Shake; Long Tall Sally; I Remember You.

POST-BEATLES

SINGLES

ANOTHER DAY/OH WOMAN OH WHY	Apple R5889
THE BACK SEAT OF MY CAR/HEART OF THE COUNTRY	Apple R5914
GIVE IRELAND BACK TO THE IRISH/GIVE IRELAND BACK TO THE IRISH (version)	Apple R5936
MARY HAD A LITTLE LAMB/LITTLE WOMAN LOVE	Apple R5949
HI, HI, HI/C MOON	Apple R5973
MY LOVE/THE MESS	Apple R5985
LIVE AND LET DIE/I LIE AROUND	Apple R5987
HELEN WHEELS/COUNTRY DREAMER	Apple R5993
JET/LET ME ROLL IT	Apple R5996
BAND ON THE RUN/ZOO GANG	Apple R5997
WALKING IN THE PARK WITH ELOISE/BRIDGE OVER THE RIVER SUITE *(as The Country Hams)**	EMI 2220
JUNIOR'S FARM/SALLY-G	Apple R5999
SALLY-G/JUNIOR'S FARM	Apple R5999
LISTEN TO WHAT THE MAN SAID/LOVE IN SONG	Capitol R6006
LETTING GO/YOU GAVE ME THE ANSWER	Capitol R6008
VENUS AND MARS/ROCK SHOW/MAGNETO AND TITANIUM MAN	Capitol R6010
SILLY LOVE SONGS/COOK OF THE HOUSE	Parlophone R6014
LET 'EM IN/BEWARE MY LOVE	Parlophone R6015
MAYBE I'M AMAZED/SOILY	Parlophone R6017
UNCLE ALBERT/ADMIRAL HALSEY/EAT AT HOME *By Percy 'Thrills' Thrillington*†	Regal Zonophone EMI 2594
MULL OF KINTYRE/GIRLS SCHOOL	Capitol R6018
WITH A LITTLE LUCK/BACKWARDS TRAVELLER/CUFF LINK	Parlophone R6019
I'VE HAD ENOUGH/DELIVER YOUR CHILDREN	Parlophone R6020
LONDON TOWN/I'M CARRYING	Parlophone R6021
GOODNIGHT TONIGHT/DAYTIME NIGHT-TIME SUFFERING	Parlophone R6023
OLD SIAM SIR/SPIN IT ON	Parlophone R60260
GETTING CLOSER/BABY'S REQUEST	Parlophone R60270
SEASIDE WOMAN/B SIDE TO SEASIDE *(By Susy And The Red Stripes)*‡	A & M AMS7461
WONDERFUL CHRISTMASTIME/RUDOLPH THE RED NOSED REGGAE	Parlophone R6029

COMING UP/COMING UP (Live At Glasgow)/LUNCH BOX-ODD SOX — Parlophone R6035
WATERFALLS/CHECK MY MACHINE — Parlophone R6037
TEMPORARY SECRETARY/SECRET FRIEND — Parlophone R6039
EBONY AND IVORY/RAINCLOUDS (With Stevie Wonder) — Parlophone R6054
TAKE IT AWAY/I'LL GIVE YOU A RING — Parlophone R60560
TUG OF WAR/GET IT (With Carl Perkins) — Parlophone R60570
THE GIRL IS MINE (With Michael Jackson)/CAN'T GET OUTTA THE RAIN (By Michael Jackson) — EPIC EPC A2729
SAY, SAY, SAY (With Michael Jackson)/ODE TO A KOALA BEAR — Parlophone R60620
PIPES OF PEACE/SO BAD — Parlophone R60640
NO MORE LONELY NIGHTS (ballad)/SILLY LOVE SONGS — Parlophone R6080
WE ALL STAND TOGETHER (By Paul McCartney and The Frog Chorus)/HUMMING VERSION (By Paul McCartney and the Finchley Frogettes) — Parlophone R6086
SPIES LIKE US/MY CARNIVAL — Parlophone R6118

* * *

* THE COUNTRY HAMS are Paul McCartney and Wings, with Chet Atkins and Floyd Cramer
† PERCY 'THRILLS' THRILLINGTON is a Paul McCartney pseudonym
‡ SUSY AND THE RED STRIPES is a Paul, Linda and Wings pseudonym

* * *

THE ALBUMS

McCARTNEY — Apple PCS7102
The Lovely Linda; That Would Be Something; Valentine Day; Every Night; Hot As Sun; Glasses; Junk; Man We Was Lonely; Oo You; Momma Miss America; Teddy Boys; Singalong Junk; Maybe I'm Amazed; Kreen-Akrore. BY PAUL McCARTNEY

RAM — Apple PAS1003
Too Many People; 3 Legs; Ram On; Dear Boy; Uncle Albert/Admiral Halsey; Smile Away; Heart Of The Country; Monkberry Moon Delight; Eat At Home; Long Haired Lady; Ram On; The Back Seat Of My Car. BY PAUL AND LINDA McCARTNEY

WILD LIFE Parlophone PCS7142
Mumbo; Bip Bop; Love Is Strange; Wild Life; Some People Never Know; I Am Your Singer; Tomorrow; Dear Friend. BY WINGS

RED ROSE SPEEDWAY EMI PCTC251
Big Barn Bed; My Love; Get On The Right Thing; One More Kiss; Little Lamb Dragonfly; Single Pigeon; When The Night; Loup (1st Indian On The Moon); Hold Me Tight; Lazy Dynamite; Hands Of Love; Power Cut. BY PAUL McCARTNEY AND WINGS

BAND ON THE RUN Apple PAS10007
Band On The Run; Jet; Bluebird; Mrs Vanderbilt; Let Me Roll It; Mamunia; No Words (For My Love); Picasso's Last Words (Drink To Me); Nineteen Hundred And Eighty Five.
BY PAUL McCARTNEY AND WINGS

VENUS AND MARS Capitol PCTC254
Venus And Mars/Rock Show; Love In Song; You Gave Me The Answer; Magneto And Titanium Man; Letting Go; Venus And Mars (Reprise); Spirits Of Ancient Egypt; Medicine Jar; Call Me Back Again; Listen To What The Man Said; Treat Her Gently/Lonely Old People; Crossroads. BY WINGS

WINGS AT THE SPEED OF SOUND Parlophone PAS10010
Let 'Em In; The Note You Never Wrote; She's My Baby; Beware My Love; Wino Junko; Silly Love Songs; Cook Of The House; Time To Hide; Must Do Something About It; San Ferry Anne; Warm And Beautiful. BY WINGS

WINGS OVER AMERICA Parlophone PCSP720 (Triple)
Venus And Mars/Rock Show; Jet; Let Me Roll It; Spirits Of Ancient Egypt; Medicine Jar; Maybe I'm Amazed; Call Me Back Again; Lady Madonna; The Long And Winding Road; Live And Let Die; Picasso's Last Words (Drink To Me); Richard Cory; Bluebird; I've Just Seen A Face; Blackbird; Yesterday; You Gave Me The Answer; Magneto And Titanium Man; Go Now; My Love; Listen To What The Man Said; Let 'Em In; Time To Hide; Silly Love Songs; Beware My Love; Letting Go; Band On The Run; Hi, Hi, Hi; Soily.
BY WINGS

THRILLINGTON Regal Zonophone EMC3175
Too Many People; 3 Legs; Ram On; Dear Boy; Uncle Albert/Admiral Halsey; Smile Away; Heart Of The Country; Monkberry Moon Delight; Eat At Home; Long Haired Lady; The Back Seat Of My Car.
BY PERCY 'THRILLS' THRILLINGTON

LONDON TOWN Parlophone PAS10012
London Town; Cafe On The Left Bank; I'm Carrying; Backwards Traveller; Cuff Link; Children Children; Girlfriend; I've Had Enough; With A Little Luck; Famous Groupies; Deliver Your Children; Name And Address; Don't Let It Bring You Down; Mouse Moose And The Grey Goose. BY WINGS

WINGS GREATEST Parlophone PCTC256
Another Day; Silly Love Songs; Live And Let Die; Junior's Farm; With A Little Luck; Band On The Run; Uncle Albert/Admiral Halsey; Hi, Hi, Hi; Let 'Em In; My Love; Jet; Mull Of Kintyre. BY WINGS

BACK TO THE EGG Parlophone PCTC257
Reception; Getting Closer; We're Open Tonight; Spin It On; Again, And Again, And Again; Old Siam Sir; Arrow Through Me; Rockestra Theme; To You; After The Ball; Million Miles; Winter Rose; Love Awake; The Broadcast; So Glad To See You Here; Baby's Request. BY WINGS

McCARTNEY II Parlophone PCTC258
Coming Up; Temporary Secretary; On The Way; Waterfalls; Nobody Knows; Front Parlour; Summer's Day Song; Frozen Jap; Bogey Music; Dark Room; One Of These Days.
BY PAUL McCARTNEY

TUG OF WAR Parlophone PCTC259
Tug Of War; Take It Away; Somebody Who Cares; What's That You're Doing (with Stevie Wonder); Here Today; Ballroom Dancing; The Pound Is Sinking; Wunderlust; Get It (with Carl Perkins); Be What You See (Link); Dress Me Up As A Robber; Ebony And Ivory (with Stevie Wonder). BY PAUL McCARTNEY

PIPES OF PEACE Parlophone PCTC1652301
Pipes Of Peace; Say, Say, Say (with Michael Jackson); The Other Me; Keep Under Cover; So Bad; The Man (with Michael Jackson); Sweetest Little Show; Average Person; Hey Hey; Tug Of Peace; Through Our Love. BY PAUL McCARTNEY

GIVE MY REGARDS TO BROAD STREET Parlophone PCTC2
No More Lonely Nights (ballad); Good Day Sunshine; Corridor Music; Yesterday; Here, There And Everywhere; Wunderlust; Ballroom Dancing; Silly Love Songs; Silly Love Songs (reprise); Not Such A Bad Boy; No Values; No More Lonely Nights (ballad reprise); For No One; Eleanor Rigby/Eleanor's Dream; The Long And Winding Road; No More Lonely Nights (playout version).
BY PAUL McCARTNEY

MISCELLANEOUS

THE McCARTNEY INTERVIEW Parlophone CHAT1
Paul McCartney in Interview with Vic Garbarini of Musician: Player and Listener.
McCartney discusses: McCartney II; Negative Criticism of Beatles and Wings; Influences; Venus And Mars/Wild Life; Band On The Run; Musical Direction: Ringo, George, Hey Jude; The White Album, Tension, Helter Skelter; Abbey Road; Musical background: trumpet, guitar, piano, learning bass in Hamburg; Early Beatles

mixes, Motown and Stax influences; The Sgt Pepper Story, The Beach Boys' Pet Sounds; Rubber Soul/Revolver; Fame and success, Paul and John's reactions; Stage fright during The Beatles and Wings; How Wings started; New Wave, Early Beatles; Creating The Beatles' sound, Love Me Do, and early songs; The Beatles' conquest of America; Beatles' haircuts and image; paying dues in Hamburg and Liverpool, early tours; Weathering pressure, the break up; Video of Coming Up, reliving The Beatles image; Playing bass; Lennon–McCartney songwriting, dislike of formulas; Beatles' imitators; I Am The Walrus/The Black Carnation, Sgt Pepper cover; New Wave, Bowie, Ferry, Elvis; Pop music and radio; Getting married, changing perspective, Waterfalls; Give Ireland Back To The Irish, Hi, Hi, Hi, Banned songs, Children's songs, Mary Had A Little Lamb.

THE CONCERTS FOR THE PEOPLE OF KAMPUCHEA
Atlantic K60153

A double album from the London Concerts for The People Of Kampuchea featuring The Who, The Pretenders, Elvis Costello, Rockpile, Rockpile with Robert Plant, Queen, The Clash, Ian Drury and the Blockheads, and The Specials. Paul McCartney And Wings contributed Got To Get You Into My Life; Every Night; Coming Up. Paul McCartney and the Rockestra contributed Lucille; Let It Be; and Rockestra Theme.

* * *

RECOMMENDED

Here is a short list of recommended listening which conveys the tremendous versatility of Paul McCartney's (and John Lennon's) music in a diverse range of musical styles and treatments.

MOTOWN SINGS THE BEATLES — Tamla Motown WL72348
Various Artists

ALL THIS AND WORLD WAR II — Riva RVLP2
Various Artists

JAMES LAST PLAYS THE GREATEST SONGS OF THE BEATLES — Polydor POLD5119
James Last

HARMONICA BEATLEMANIA — Mercury 20974
Billy Lee Riley

LOVE SONGS TO THE BEATLES — Stateside 10171
Mary Wells

KEELY SMITH SINGS THE JOHN LENNON AND PAUL McCARTNEY SONG BOOK — Reprise R6142
Keely Smith

MARCHING WITH THE BEATLES	Columbia Two125
Band Of The Irish Guards	
THE ROYAL PHILHARMONIC ORCHESTRA PLAYS THE BEATLES	SRFL 1001
Royal Philharmonic Orchestra	
SONGS OF THE BEATLES	Atlantic SD16037
Sarah Vaughan	
McGEAR	Warner Brothers BS2825
Mike McGear	
THE FAMILY WAY	Decca SKL4847
George Martin	
OFF THE BEATLE TRACK	Parlophone PCS3057
George Martin	
FRANCOIS GLORIEUX PLAYS THE BEATLES	Vanguard VSD79417
François Glorieux	
CHET ATKINS PICKS ON THE BEATLES	RCA Victor LSP3531
Chet Atkins	
HAPPY BANJOS PLAY THE BEATLES	Capitol 2642
Big Ben Banjo Band	
YESTERDAY	
Elena Duran	
THE BEATLES CONCERTO	
Rostill & Schaffer	
BAROQUE BEATLES BOOK	Electra 7306
Joshua Rifkin	
BEATLE CRACKER SUITE	HMV 7EG8919 (EP)
Arthur Wilkinson and his Orchestra	
BEATLE CONCERTO	HMV 7EG8968 (EP)
Arthur Wilkinson and his Orchestra	
EINE KLEINE BEATLEMUSIK	HMV 7EG8887 (EP)
Fritz Spiegl	
THE LENNON AND McCARTNEY SONG BOOK – WITH A LITTLE HELP FROM THEIR FRIENDS	K-TEL NE 1317/CE 2317
Various Artists	

APPENDIX IV

Bibliography

Since the early 1960s, over 250 books have been written and published specifically about The Beatles – detailing virtually every single aspect of the life and times of John Lennon, Paul McCartney, George Harrison and Ringo Starr, and their achievements . . .

This Bibliography is a small selection of them, together with a series of related – and informative – publications, containing reference to The Beatles . . . and Paul McCartney.

Aldridge, Alan (Ed.) *The Beatles Illustrated Lyrics* Macdonald 1969

Aldridge, Alan (Ed.) *The Beatles Illustrated Lyrics Vol.* 2 BCI Publishing Ltd 1971

Barrow, Tony *P.S. We Love You* Mirror Books 1982

Best, Pete and Doncaster, Patrick *Beatle: The Pete Best Story* Plexus Publishing 1985

Black, Cilla *Step Inside Love* J. M. Dent & Sons 1985

Blake, John *All You Needed Was Love: The Beatles After The Beatles* Hamlyn 1981

Braun, Michael *Love Me Do – The Beatles' Progress* Penguin Books 1964

Brown, Peter and Gaines, Steven *The Love You Make: An Insider's Story Of The Beatles* Macmillan 1983

Campbell, Colin and Murphy, Allan *Things We Said Today* Pierian Press 1980

Carr, Roy and Tyler, Tony *The Beatles: An Illustrated Record* New English Library 1975; New English Library 1978 (revised)

Castleman, Harry and Podrazik, Walter J. *All Together Now* Pierian Press 1976

Castleman, Harry and Podrazik, Walter J. *The Beatles Again* Pierian Press 1977

Coleman, Ray *John Winston Lennon Vol I* 1940–1966 Sidgwick & Jackson 1984

Coleman, Ray *John Ono Lennon Vol. 2 1967–1980* Sidgwick & Jackson 1984
Connolly, Ray *Stardust Memories* Pavilion Books 1983
Cott, Jonathan and Dalton, David *The Beatles Get Back* Apple Publishing 1970
Cowan, Philip *Behind The Beatles Songs* Polytantric Press 1978
Davies, Hunter *The Beatles: The Authorised Biography* Heinemann 1968, 1978, 1985
DiLello, Richard *The Longest Cocktail Party* Charisma Books 1972; Pierian Press 1984
Doney, Malcolm *Lennon & McCartney* Midas Books 1981
Elson, Howard *Early Rockers* Proteus Books 1982
Epstein, Brian *A Cellarful Of Noise* Souvenir Press 1964; New English Library 1981; Pierian Press 1984
Evans, Mike *The Art Of The Beatles* Anthony Blond 1984
Fast, Julius *The Beatles: The Real Story* Putnam & Sons 1968
Frame, Pete *Rock Family Trees* Omnibus Press 1980
Friede, Goldie; Titone, Robin and Weiner, Sue *The Beatles A To Z* Eyre Methuen 1980
Gambaccini, Paul *Paul McCartney In His Own Words* Omnibus Press 1976
Gambaccini, Paul *Masters Of Rock* BBC Publications/Omnibus Press 1982
Gillett, Charlie *The Sound Of The City: The Rise Of Rock And Roll* Outerbridge & Dienstfrey 1970; Souvenir Press 1984 (revised)
Grove, Martin A. *Paul McCartney: Beatle With Wings* Manor Books 1978
Hamilton, Alan *Paul McCartney* Hamish Hamilton 1983
Harrison, George *I, Me, Mine* Genesis Publications 1980; W.H. Allen, 1982; Comet Books 1986
Harry, Bill *Merseybeat: The Beginnings Of The Beatles* Omnibus Press 1977
Harry, Bill *The Beatles Who's Who* Aurum Press 1982
Harry, Bill *The Beatles: Paperback Writers – The History Of The Beatles In Print* Virgin Books 1984
Harry, Bill *The Beatles: Beatlemania – The History Of The Beatles On Film* Virgin Books 1984
Harry, Bill *The Beatles: Beatles For Sale – The Beatles Memorabilia* Virgin Books 1985
Harry, Bill *The Book Of Beatle Lists* Javelin Books 1985
Harvey, Andrew *Give My Regards To Broad Street* MPL Communications Ltd/Pavilion Books 1984
Herbst, Peter *The Rolling Stone Interviews 1967–1980* Rolling Stone/Arthur Barker 1981
Herman, Gary *Rock 'n' Roll Babylon* Plexus Publishing 1982

Hipgnosis; Thorgerson, Storm and Christopherson, Peter (Eds.) *Hands Across The Water: Wings Tour USA* Paper Tiger/Dragon's World 1978
Hoffmann, Dezo *With The Beatles* Omnibus Press 1982
Howlett, Kevin *The Beatles At The Beeb* BBC Publications 1982
Humphrey-Smith, Cecil R.; Heenan, Michael G. and Mount, Jennifer *Up The Beatles Family Tree* Achievements Ltd 1966
Jasper, Tony *Paul McCartney And Wings* Octopus Books 1977
Jewell, Derek *The Popular Voice – A Musical Record Of The Sixties & Seventies* André Deutsch 1980
Leigh, Spencer with Frame, Pete *Let's Go Down The Cavern* Vermilion & Co. 1984
Lennon, Cynthia *A Twist Of Lennon* Star Books 1978, 1986
Martin, George *All You Need Is Ears* Macmillan 1979
McCabe, Peter and Schonfeld, Robert D. *Apple To The Core: The Unmaking Of The Beatles* Pocket Books/Simon & Schuster 1972
McCartney, Linda *Linda's Pictures* Alfred A. Knopf 1976
McCartney, Paul *Paul McCartney Composer/Artist* Pavilion Books 1981
McCartney, Mike *Thank U Very Much* Arthur Barker 1981
McCartney, Linda *Photographs* MPL Communications 1982
Mellors, Wilfred *Twilight Of The Gods: The Beatles In Retrospect* Viking Books 1973
Mendelssohn, John *Paul McCartney: A Biography In Words And Pictures* Sire/Chappell Music 1977
Miles *The Beatles In Their Own Words* Omnibus Press 1978; W.H. Allen 1981
Miles *John Lennon In His Own Words* Omnibus Press 1980; W.H. Allen 1981
Miller, Jim (Ed.) *The Rolling Stone Illustrated History Of Rock And Roll* Random House, New York 1976; Random House, New York 1980 (revised)
Murrells, Joseph *Million Selling Records: An Illustrated Directory* B. T. Batsford Ltd 1984
Norman, Philip *Shout! The True Story Of The Beatles* Elm Tree Books 1981
Norman, Philip *The Road Goes On Forever* Elm Tree Books/Hamish Hamilton 1982
Norman, Philip *The Stones* Elm Tree Books 1984
Ocean, Humphrey *The Ocean View: Paintings And Drawings Of Wings' American Tour April To June 1976* MPL Communications Ltd 1982
Palmer, Tony *All You Need Is Love* Weidenfeld & Nicolson & Chappell 1976
Pareles, Jon and Romanowski, Patricia *The Rolling Stone Encyclopaedia Of Rock And Roll* Michael Joseph Ltd 1983
Pascall, Jeremy *Paul McCartney And Wings* Hamlyn 1977

Peebles, Andy *The Lennon Tapes* BBC Publications 1981
Reinhart, Charles *You Can't Do That: Beatles Bootlegs & Novelty Discs* Pierian Press 1981
Russell, Jeff *The Beatles Album File & Complete Discography* Blandford Press 1982
Schaffner, Nicholas *The Beatles Forever* McGraw-Hill 1978
Schaffner, Nicholas *The Boys From Liverpool: John, Paul, George, Ringo* Methuen 1980
Schulteiss, Tom *The Beatles: A Day In The Life* Pierian Press 1980
Sheff, David *The Playboy Interviews With John Lennon & Yoko Ono* Playboy Press 1982
Shepherd, Billy *The True Story Of The Beatles* Beat Publications 1964
Southall, Brian *Abbey Road* Patrick Stephens Ltd 1982
Spence, Helen *The Beatles Forever* Colour Library International 1981
Stannard, Neville *The Long And Winding Road: A History Of The Beatles On Record* Virgin Books 1982
Stannard, Neville *The Beatles: Working Class Heroes – The History Of The Beatles' Solo Recordings* Virgin Books 1983
Staveacre, Tony *The Songwriters* BBC Publications 1980
Stokes, Geoffrey *The Beatles* Time Books 1981
Taylor, Derek *As Time Goes By* Davis-Poynter Ltd 1973; Pierian Press 1984
Tobler, John *The Beatles* Deans International Publishing 1984
Tobler, John and Grundy, Stuart *The Record Producers* BBC Publications 1982
Tremlett, George *The Paul McCartney Story* Futura Books 1975
Tremlett, George *The John Lennon Story* Futura Books 1975
Various *The Beatles: For The Record* Stafford Pemberton Publishing 1981
Various *The Complete Beatles Lyrics* Omnibus Press 1982
Various *The Compleat Beatles* Delilah/ATV/Bantam 1981
Various *The Story Of Pop* Octopus Books 1974
Vollmer, Jurgen *Rock 'n' Roll Times: The Style And Spirit Of The Early Beatles And Their First Fans* Google Plex Books 1981
Wallgren, Mark *The Beatles On Record* Simon & Schuster 1982
Welch, Chris *Paul McCartney: The Definitive Biography* Proteus Books 1984
Wenner, Jann *Lennon Remembers* Straight Arrow 1971
Williams, Allan and Marshall, William *The Man Who Gave The Beatles Away* Elm Tree Books 1975
Woffinden, Bob *The Beatles Apart* Proteus Books 1981

Acknowledgements

Many people helped me in the compiling of this book to whom I would like to express my sincere thanks and gratitude . . .
To Judy Totton, to Bob and Tricia Reed, to Audrey Barber
To Rosie Hardman, to Mick Bovee, to Carolyn Whitaker
To Francis Rossi, to Chris Barber, to Neil Murray
To Barry Mason, to Elena Duran
To Alvin Stardust and Gene Pitney
Thank you

Howard Elson 1985

Index